Best of BUSY PEOPLE'S Cookbooks

BY DAWN HALL

AWARD WINNING COOKBOOKS

3 BEST

Low Fat Recipes from **3** AWARD-WINNING COOKBOOKS

Best of Busy People's Cookbooks is published by Cookbook Resources in cooperation with Dawn Hall. Ms. Hall's cookbooks focus on the importance of healthy, family lifestyles. Cookbook Resources salutes Dawn Hall and her award-winning cookbooks, *Down Home Cookin'*, *Busy People's Low Fat Cookbook and 2nd Serving Busy People's Low Fat Cookbook.*

1st Printing   July 2001   10,000 copies

ISBN 1-931294-05-4

Edited, Designed, Published and Manufactured in the
United States of America by

cookbook
resources

Cookbook Resources, LLC
541 Doubletree Drive
Highland Village, Texas 75077
972-317-0245
Toll-Free Orders: 866/229-2665
www.cookbookresources.com

Voted by North American Bookdealers Exchange as "1996 Best Book of the YEAR" in the Category of Cooking

Chosen as One of Ohio's BEST of the BEST COOKBOOKS by Quail Ridge Press

"Great for the working family and those on the go."
Lori L. Scovel
Manchester Press

"This cookbook author not only has a winning cookbook, but the story behind her foray into the publishing world is an inspiring one."
Susan Lockhart
Local Flavor-Northern
Wyoming Daily News

"Her dishes were an absolute hit. We are fans of Hall's cookbooks and believe they just may be the best low-fat cookbooks around."
Theresa Campbell
The Herald Bulletin, Anderson, IN

"Dawn Hall could be a poster child for Good Housekeeping or Better Homes and Gardens."
Karen Zielinski
Healthy Living News, Sylvaina, OH

"We truly can enjoy good food that is also low in fat. The recipes in *Down Home Cookin'* are perfect examples of just such recipes."
JoAnna Lund
Food Writer and Author
Healthy Exchanges, Inc.

"This cookbook has been a wonderful tool for people trying to adjust to their new lifestyle after their cardiac event."
Samantha Christies, R.N.
Cardiac Rehab Nurse

FOR INFORMATION ON:

Dawn Hall's other award-winning

low-fat cookbooks

call toll-free (888) 436-9646

"Busy People's
Low-Fat
Cookbook"

"Down Home
Cookin' Without the
Down Home Fat"

"2nd Serving of
Busy People's
Low-Fat
Cookbook"

ABOUT THE AUTHOR

Dawn Hall is also the author of two award-winning low-fat cookbooks. *"Down Home Cookin' Without the Down Home Fat,"* was selected as "1996 Best Book of the Year in the Category of Cooking" by North American Bookdealers Exchange and one of "Ohio's Best of the Best Cookbooks." The original *"Busy People's Low-Fat Cookbook"* received a certificate of merit from Writer's Digest and won "1998 Best Book of the Year in the Category of Cooking" by North American Book Dealers Exchange.

As an accomplished aerobic instructor and facilitator for W.O.W. (Watching Our Weight – low-fat living class) Dawn feels like she was born watching her weight. She is a successful recovering, compulsive over eater and food addict; for which she is very gratefull!! Dawn walks her talk and is living proof "you can have your cake and eat it too" without eating and weeping!

She strongly believes her talent for creating extremely low-fat, mouthwatering foods that are made quickly and effortlessly is a gift from God. Therefore, 10% of the author's profits go to "Solid Rock" an inner-city outreach program for children and teens with hopes of building a strong moral foundation for our future generation.

As a popular inspirational speaker and veteran talk show guest, Dawn has appeared on *"The 700 Club," "CBN," "Woman to Woman," "Good Morning A.M."* along with numerous other T.V. and radio programs nationwide.

To contact the author call, write or fax:

Cozy Homestead Publishing
c/o Dawn Hall
5425 S. Fulton-Lucas Road
Swanton, OH 43558
(419) 826-2665 or Fax (419) 826-2700

CONTENTS

DAWN HALL'S AMAZING STORY

An in-depth, behind the scenes look. . .

As a recovering compulsive overeater and food addict, Dawn Hall thought surely something was wrong with her when she would dream of recipes in her sleep. In 1990 she decided to quit fighting and resisting her dreams of food and instead write her recipes in her dreams down. In the middle of the night, with pen and paper next to the bed she began scribbling down her low-fat ideas.

The next day she tested her cooking ideas. When she created a winner, her family gave her two thumbs up. Any leftovers would be taste tested by her students the following day. Soon her students were encouraging Dawn to write a cookbook.

Having only a high school education and not knowing how to type or use a computer, Dawn Hall would hand write the recipes for her students and calculate the nutritional information for them. She saved her hand written recipes on top of the refrigerator for years, never really thinking she'd ever have her recipes published.

In 1994 her loving husband, Tracy Hall, was diagnosed with an aggressive brain cancer the size of a baseball. Doctors removed one pound of cancer and the surgery left him completely paralyzed on his entire left side. The doctors said he may never walk again.

Tracy had approximately a thumb size of cancer still remaining, which the doctors were not able to surgically remove. Massive doses of radiation did not make Tracy's remaining cancer any smaller. The oncologist told Tracy and Dawn to, "Go home and enjoy Spring, there is nothing else we can do."

Determined not to quit trying, Dawn and Tracy decided to try an experimental treatment out of Houston, Texas by a man named Dr. Stanislaw Burzyinski. The treatment was not covered by their insurance, and cost thousands of dollars monthly.

Dawn decided to self-publish her pile of hand written recipes that she'd written over the years that were on top of the refrigerator. 18,000 copies were sold in 10 weeks! Her first book was *"Down Home Cookin' Without the Down Home Fat."* It won 1996 Best Cookbook Award by North American Book Dealers Exchange and was selected as one of Ohio's Best of the Best Cookbooks by Quail Ridge Press. Enough money had been raised to pay for one year of Tracy's treatment.

Tracy continued on Dr. Burzynski's experimental treatment of antineoplastons with great success, but money was running out. Dawn published her next book, " *Busy People's Low-Fat Cookbook"* with the hope of again raising enough money to allow her husband to continue the experimental treatment of Dr. Burzynski's. The cookbook won 1998 best Cookbook Award by North American Book Dealers and also received a Certificate of Merit By Readers Digest. The Pfizer Company had over 118,000 copies printed for doctors to give their diabetic patients.

As Dawn's life became busier, her recipes became faster and easier to prepare and cook. Now, not only were the profits of her cookbooks paying for her husband's cancer treatments, but she was also trying to help supplement her family's income.

In 2000 her third book, *"2nd Serving of Busy People's Low-Fat Recipes"* was published. Once again Dawn's hopes were to be able to raise enough money to keep her loving husband on the cancer treatments that were saving his life. Although *"2nd Serving of Busy People's Low-Fat Recipes"* was a huge success and was honored to receive the Pinnacle Cookbook Award for books published in 2000 and also an honorable mention by the Benjamin Franklin Awards; the Hall family was experiencing tremendous challenges.

Prior to her third book's release, Tracy was doing very well. One would have never known by looking at Tracy that he was a brain cancer survivor. He was back to work full-time and looking great! Tracy was to the best of the doctor's knowledge "cancer free!" He was a walking, modern day miracle!

Dr. Burzynski left the decision to continue using his antineoplaston treatments as a maintenance drug and safeguard completely up to the Halls. Tracy had made a full recovery using the experimental medication, but it was very costly.

Because of the humongous financial bondage of the expensive experimental treatment, Tracy and Dawn decided to discontinue using Dr. Burzynski's treatment in early 1999. By the fall of 1999 Tracy was diagnosed with two new brain tumors. Tracy went back on the treatment, but this time Dr. Burzynski's experimental medicine did not reduce the tumors. Dr. Burzynski thought Tracy had either built up an immunity to the treatment or that the tumors were not cancerous, but rather radiation build up from radiation treatments Tracy had received five years prior.

In defense of conventional medicine and radiation therapy the doctors never thought Tracy was going to live more than six to eight months originally when he was first diagnosed with brain cancer in 1994; less more be concerned with the possible long term effects of the radiation.

By early February of 2000 Tracy was with Hospice of Northwest Ohio. He was given six weeks to six months to live. On February 9, 2000 Tracy and Dawn went away for a few days to plan Tracy's funeral. On February

13, 2000 they had a house fire. The fire also damaged the publishing business, which was attached to their home.

Tracy, Dawn, and their two daughters Whitney age 12 and Ashley age 11 moved into an assisted living nursing home to live for four months until their home was ready to be moved back into.

By this point, Tracy was swollen up like a huge balloon and had gone from his healthy 180 lbs. to 219 lbs. (caused by all the steroids, etc.) Dawn was shaving him, showering him, and helping him roll over in bed. Tracy also was wheelchair bound. He had three blood clots in his left leg and one blood clot in his right leg. Tracy's writing was barely legible and his speech slurred. Death felt near.

In the meantime, the Hospice doctor and Dr. Burzynski both encouraged Tracy and Dawn to get the opinion of another specialist. The specialist did not think the new tumors were cancer, since the tumors did not respond to Dr. Burzynski's treatment. He thought they were radiation build up from treatments Tracy had received six years prior.

To make a long story short, Tracy was put on blood thinners, which the doctors are hoping will stop the radiation tumors from growing. Shortly afterwards Tracy was released from Hospice. Yes! Tracy is a Hospice Reject! (Have you ever heard of such a thing?)

As of today, April 25, 2001, Tracy is doing very well considering all he is going through. He still has the two radiation tumors, but they are not growing currently. The Halls are hoping it will stay that way and not grow. Tracy is able to walk with a cane and daily overcomes the many challenges he endures from the many side effects of the radiation build up. He is very tired and struggles with a lack of balance and short term memory loss. None the less, Tracy and Dawn remain optimistic and hopeful that Tracy will remain a modern day miracle.

The Hall's house has been restored and the family is back in the comforts of the home Tracy and Dawn built with their very own hands together back in 1991.

"We would never choose to go through all we've been through," Dawn shares, "but we are very thankful for all of the good that has come from our challenges. We have put all of our financial security on the line by self-publishing my three cookbooks in order to raise enough money for the experimental treatment that helped save my husband's life. We did it not only for Tracy, but for all mankind. The research that has been gathered while Tracy was on the experimental treatment may someday help your loved one, your spouse, your neighbor or friend."

Not only did Tracy and Dawn put everything on the line financially in order for Tracy to use this experimental treatment, but the Halls also fought the Food and Drug Administration.

In the late 1990's Dr. Burzynski was indicted on 72 counts of treating terminally patients who lived outside of the state of Texas with his experimental treatment of antineoplaston medicine. The FDA had a law that said it was illegal for anyone to try the experimental treatment unless the patient actually lived in Texas. The court case was NOT about whether the treatment was helpful or not, but rather was Dr. Burzynski treating terminally ill patients outside of the state of Texas. Tracy and Dawn went to Washington, and spoke at a press conference with the hopes that the government would change the laws to allow terminally ill people the freedom to choose for themselves if they wanted to try an experimental treatment. Dawn also spoke at a press conference outside of the courthouse on behalf of Dr. Burzynski's patients. The Hall's primary goal was to allow each terminally ill American the freedom to choose for themselves what treatments they would and would not choose, and not have the USA government making those choices for the people.

In the Houston press conference Dawn Hall said, "Something is seriously wrong with our government when it is legal for (fourteen-year-old) girls to have abortions without their parent's consent, but it is illegal for me to bring my husband over state lines for an experimental treatment that is not toxic and is currently saving his life." This statement made national news and the Halls were seen on numerous national television magazine shows.

Dr. Burzynski was found not guilty on all of the 72 counts. Now all terminally ill patients across America can use Doctor Burzynski's experimental treatment without the fear of going to jail by getting an "Investigate New Drug" (IND) from the government.

For more information about **Dr. Burzynski** call (713) 335-5697.

SOLID ROCK

*10% of Author's profits help
inner city children's outreach "Solid Rock"*

"Fewer things in life have given me greater joy than knowing we are making a positive difference in our inner city by helping support 'Solid Rock Ministries,'" says Dawn Hall.

"Solid Rock Ministries" is an inner city outreach. Our goals are to cross over racial, economic and religious barriers in order to give our inner city children a strong biblical foundation in which to base their lives on. People don't care how much you know until they know how much you care. Solid Rock Ministries is an outreach that shows how much they care by offering free meals on Wednesdays, a free packed lunch to all children on Sunday mornings, free bus transportation, along with clothing, a safe game room, environment, mentoring and counseling.

Many of us don't have a clue the everyday challenges our inner city children grow up with. Gangs, their safety, drugs, alcohol, and violence are often a common occurrence for many of these young people. By reaching and helping these young people we are able to reach the parents. Entire families have turned their lives around for the good because of the positive difference Solid Rock's out reaches.

Together, we can each help make a positive difference. We can be the helping hand these children need in order for them to turn their lives around.

A great way to make the difference in the life of a child is "Child Sponsorship" through Solid Rock. It only cost $24.00 a month and the money is used to help underwrite the cost of the many programs I have mentioned. By sponsoring a child, you will get a photo and information on the child's likes, along with age, birthday, etc. Besides sending the $24.00 for child sponsorship (sent directly to Solid Rock Outreach Ministries) you will also have the wonderful opportunity to make a positive difference in the life of the child you sponsor by sending letters of encouragement to them and remembering their birthday, etc.

I encourage you! If you have ever thought, *I'd like to do more to help make our world a better place,* this is a terrific opportunity to bless yourself by helping and sponsoring a child

For information on child sponsorship please call: **Solid Rock** (419) 244-7020.

MAINTAINING IDEAL BODY WEIGHT

For many of us it's a complicated and complex issue that many people have tried to simplify with comments such as,: "If you don't want to be fat, just don't eat fat". Wouldn't it be nice if it were so simple! Then there are those who say, "If you don't want to be fat, just stop eating when you feel comfortable". That's a fine idea for those who are overweight because they simply keep eating even though they are full. What about those of us who already quit eating when we are comfortable and we happen to have a large appetite than our bodies need? Another way of looking at this is that we don't eat too much, our body is just shorter than it ought to be for the weight we are. It's very frustrating & annoying trying to stop eating once you know you've eaten what is a so called portion when your head, stomach and watering mouth cry out "I'm still hungry!" One way to help calm hunger cries is to drink water before, during and after your meal.

Other ideas to help satisfy a hungry tummy are:

♥ Set your alarm 5 minutes earlier than you need to get up. Think positive, reinforcement thoughts such as "eating healthy is a gift I give myself. I love to eat healthy, etc . . . "

♥ Eat a cup of vegetable soup or a clear broth before your meal.

♥ Eat more salad with fat-free salad dressing or fat-free green vegetables at the end of the meal to help feel satisfied.

♥ Sip on decaffeinated herbal flavored teas. There's something very soothing and relaxing about sipping on flavorful teas. A unique beverage for sipping is placing 8 to 10 tic-tacs per 10 cup pot in the filter holder of your coffee maker instead of coffee. This will create a hot, flavorful beverage that is virtually calorie free. (One calorie per cup.)

♥ Drink a glass of Metamucil (the flavored ones aren't bad.) Not only does it help you feel fuller, but it provides 3 grams of natural fiber per glass full. It is not addictive and is helpful to those with digestive problems. Daily recommendation on box is no more than 3 glasses per day. For those who can't stomach the thought, (thinking you can't bear the taste), the orange flavor is not bad. At night time, before bed when I'm hungry I find drinking a warm glass of Metamusil helpful before I brush my teeth to go to bed. Also, in the morning before eating breakfast I have a glass.

♥ Sometimes we still feel hungry because our "sweet tooth" is not satisfied. With this in mind, try a tic-tac or chewing a piece of gum. If that doesn't work, try a small fat-free cookie, sugar-free jello, Popsicle or a piece of fruit. Sometimes all we need is just a little something to satisfy the sweet tooth.

♥ Ask the advise of your family doctor or holistic medical doctor. Explain your hunger. See if there are some natural herbs, vitamins or minerals that maybe helpful in curbing your appetite. For those who say, "It's all in your head . . . that's why you think you're hungry", a part of their statement is true. Hunger signals are released from the brain. However, being overweight usually is more complicated and complex than simply just that. By going to a holistic medical doctor, the doctor can actually test your blood. Sometimes a deficiency in one area or another can make you feel hungry, tired, etc.

♥ My mother, Wendy Oberhouse has lost over 80 pounds, and my stepfather Donald Oberhouse has lost 70 pounds. They've kept the weight off for years. I am so proud of them. Along with the switch to a low-fat, low calorie lifestyle they use herbs to help curb their large appetites. They both feel the herbs help take "the edge off" so they can maintain their healthier lifestyle. For more information you can talk to them personally at #419-867-9907.

Here are photos of my parents then and now.

♥ Out of sight out of mind theory. Sometimes we think we're hungry because the delicious, mouth-watering foods that are leftover from the meal are staring us in the face from their serving bowls. We think we're hungry, when in all reality, we are not hungry. It tasted good and we'd like more. Keeping this possibility in mind, do not serve any food homestyle except vegetables and salad. (Which can be used as filler, if still hungry after meal is eaten.) All other foods place on dinner plates before serving. Do not put into serving bowls or platter, as this encourages overeating.

♥ Learn the difference between the true feeling of feeling "satisfied" without feeling "full". There is a difference. Let me say up front, that it is not necessarily our fault as Americans that we are fat. Years ago when the media stressed: eat 5-6 meals a day not 3, many of us took the media literally. What they should have said is eat 5-6 healthy "snacks" a day and no longer eat big meals. Many of us think of meals as what Mrs. Cleaver (Beaver's mom) used to serve, complete with meat, potatoes, gravy, vegetable, rolls, butter and of course dessert. Please media – eating 6 full course meals a day is a sure fire way to put on the pounds and fast!

♥ The media also encourages "grazing", which if done correctly is absolutely wonderful at helping keep blood sugar levels good and energy levels strong. However, what we graze on is of the utmost importance. Yes, cows like to graze for the most part of the day, and if we grazed on greens such as green leafy salads most of the day we'd be thinner and healthier.

♥ The problem is, just like ranchers do to fatten their cattle for slaughter by feeding them lots of high calorie, low-fat foods such as corn and oats, a lot of us are grazing on high caloric, fat-free foods or low-fat foods such as light Twinkies and cookies. Beware of "compacted caloric foods"!

♥ Instead of thinking of eating 5-6 meals a day, think of it as eating 5-6 snacks a day. Only on special occasions – like dinner out or a holiday will you eat a full meal. Instead, what I encourage you do is break-up your regular 3 meals a day into 6. Let me explain:

OLD WAY OF EATING
3 low-fat meals a day

NEW WAY OF GRAZING
and eating 6 snacks a day

Breakfast
1 slice toast, orange juice, cereal with skim milk

Breakfast
Cereal with skim milk and toast

Lunch
Turkey sandwich, Baked Lays Potato Crisp, Apple, Herbal Tea and fat-free cookie

Snack
Orange (instead of juice because it's more filling & satisfying to chew)

Dinner
Barbecued Chicken Breast, Tossed Salad with fat-free dressing, roll, baked potato and green beans

Lunch
Turkey sandwich, Baked Lays, apple and tea

Snack
Fat-free cookie

Dinner
Barbecued Chicken Breast, Tossed Salad w/fat-free salad dressing, baked potato and green beans (skip roll)

Snack
100 calorie snack such as fat-free cookies, instead of roll which we skipped at dinner

TOTAL CALORIES AND FATS:

1225 Calories & 8 fats

1225 Calories & 8 fats

As you can see, we simply broke up our meals and used part of our meal as snacks. You never get really full nor do you ever get really hungry.

Eating low fat fights disease

Remember, eating a low-fat lifestyle helps fight countless diseases including heart disease, cancer and diabetes. Why eat a Snickers at 12 grams of fat if a Milky Way Lite will do the trick and satisfy the sweet craving for only 5 grams of fat and almost half the calories? Or how about a bite size Milky Way Lite at 1 gram of fat and 30 calories? Why eat regular French fries at 20 grams of fat and 300 calories when the baked ones are equally delicious and practically no fat and 1/3 of the calories? With todays endless array of wonderful low-fat, lower caloric choices why not make the healthier choice and eat what you're hungry for?

As I stated in my 1st book *"Down Home Cookin' Without the Down Home Fat,"* there are going to be times when we will choose to wander from our healthier lifestyle of low-fat. However, those choices will be special occasions and not the norm. The problem is what used to be a special treat 50 years ago is now in many families the daily norm. A special candy bar from the five and dime store or a hamburger, fries and milk shake at the local diner was a special treat. Nowadays, people think nothing of having an Egg McMuffin loaded down with sausage, cheese and a side of fried hash browns for breakfast; Quarter Pounder with cheese and mayo, fries and a milk shake for lunch; a candy bar for a snack; pizza for dinner and then a bowl of ice cream before going to bed.

That's the problem. It's the norm. In our fast paced, go, go, go world it's eat on the run. Unfortunately it's high fat, high calorie and usually very low on nutrition. Once in a blue moon to splurge on pizza or a real hamburger is fine for a special occasion. Doing it daily is trouble. Sooner or later it'll catch up with you one way or another.

Don't think of low-fat eating as a diet. Think of it as a lifestyle change. What you do to get thinner and healthier is what you need to continue doing after you've reached your goal to maintain.

Focus on Health

I strongly encourage people to get their focus off the scale and on to overall health. Isn't it a shame how so many of us base our self worth, how we feel about ourselves or even how good our day is, on what the scale says we weigh? In all honesty – isn't it ridiculous? I know. I've been there. Throwing my scale out and asking myself these questions daily has made a world of difference in releasing the bondage and preoccupation of my weight. It also got me to focus on the real issues – was I eating healthy, and was I treating myself healthy? Important questions we can ask ourselves daily are, "Am I treating myself healthy? Did I eat healthy? Did I take time to exercise? Am I getting enough rest?"

Helpful ideas for doing the low-fat thing

Purchase an inexpensive complete and up-to-date fat and calorie counting book titled *"FAT BOOK".* The one I use is by Avery Publishing

Group by Karen J. Bellerson. ISBN# 0-89529-483-4. It costs approximately $5.95. This book list over 25,000 food products by name and in many instances by brand. Highlight items in the book you like that have less than 3 grams of fat per 100 calories. You will be surprised by the countless foods you like, have been eating and can continue eating that are low in fat and fall within the American Heart Association's guidelines of 30% or less of your daily calories deriving from fat. This simple rule of thumb: 3 fat grams or less per 100 calories will help you stay within those guidelines.

♥ Write down for your own personal reference what items you highlighted in the FAT BOOK in a handy little writing tablet that you can keep with you in your purse, pocket or car. If you are not already very familiar with your very favorite low-fat foods this will be a quick and handy resource for you.

♥ Keep eating the foods you love, but modify or substitute. Doing the first two ideas listed will be helpful in allowing you to not feel deprived and will allow you to keep eating the foods you love. A perfect example. Let's say you have a sweet tooth. A lot of so called "diet". It is a lifestyle change. By writing your personal list of low-fat sweet favorites you've opened your eyes to your healthier food choices. So now when your sweet tooth is driving you nuts, instead of going crazy you'll know from your list of your favorite low-fat sweets what are your healthier choices.

Example of my list for:

♥ Low-fat Candy: Peppermint Patty, Sugar Babies, Sugar Daddy, liorice, Milk Duds, Milky way Lite, Tootsie Roll, Taffy, 3 Musketeers, Kraft Toffee, Skittles, Starburst Fruit Chews, Kraft Butter Party Mints, Mike & Ike, Gum Drops, Jaw Breakers, Jelly Beans, Junior Mints, Hot Tamales, Life Savers, Tic-Tacs, Breath Saver Mints – Sugar Free, Butterscotch Disc, Candy Corn, Chuckles, Milk Maid Caramels, Jellied Candied, Peppermint Kisses, Red Twist & Red Laces, Sweet Tarts, most hard candies, Dark Chocolate Covered Cherries, Marshmallow eggs and Bit-O-Honey.

♥ Surprised: Hopefully you are "pleasingly surprised!" Isn't it nice to know we can still eat the things we've grown to love and not eat like a rabbit in order to be healthier? Some simple substitutions such as a Milky Way Lite candy bar instead of a Snickers candy bar can save oodles of fat and calories (7 fat grams and 110 calories saved!) Yet, you don't feel deprived. You feel satisfied and you've done your body good. (Or at least better!) However, let us not forget sugar is still fattening if eaten too much. Remember, moderation is the key in not ending up a big fatty.

Parents have told us for years, "Eat your vegetables." Nowadays, if someone does not know vegetables are good for us, they must live under a rock. It's everywhere! I have found it helpful to immediately (after arriving home from the market) to clean, cut and prepare all fresh vegetables and fruits for the week. The saying "out of sight, out of mind" falls true when satisfying our hunger pains also. For most of us, the last thing we feel like doing when we're hungry is peeling a carrot! Please! It's no wonder we probably eat more prepackage junk foods now than ever before. Of course, in our moment of weakness, we grab the prepackaged junk food so beautifully prepared and staring us in the face over the fresh carrot which still lies boring, all dirty, not peeled and unappetizing! I've said all that to say this,

"Cut and clean to be appealing!"

Large ziplock, clear plastic bags are absolutely wonderful for storing visually beautiful and prepared fresh vegetables and fruits. Most vegetables last a good 5 days. Cutting vegetables thicker versus thinner helps them stay fresher longer.

If you don't have a good "one hour" extra per week to prepare these delicious delectables then spend the extra money on already prepared vegetable and fruit snacks. You will pay more (at least double) however, you'll find you are eating a lot more vegetables and fruits. Don't store in drawers of refrigerator where they are out of sight. Instead keep on shelves up front where you will immediately see them.

Keep a wide variety of your favorite fat-free salad dressings on hand and refrigerated in an organized, easily visible spot at all times for using not only as a salad dressing but also as a dip for vegetables and marinade.

Keep fresh, whole fruits (apples, oranges, pears, bananas, etc.) out on the counter for snacks instead of sweets. Fat-free cookies, cakes and treats are usually higher in sugars and lower in actual nutritional value than fruits.

EXERCISE

It's important. Not only physically, but mentally and emotionally. When you take care of yourself, you can't help but feel better about yourself.

When you exercise

♥ Your body releases endorphins which help you feel good and better about yourself.

♥ Energy creates energy – by burning energy when exercising you will feel more energetic afterwards.

♥ You build muscle, which in turn burns more calories throughout the day, than if you had less muscle.

♥ Helps relieve stress.

♥ Helps fight numerous diseases.

Studies show: People who exercise first thing in the morning are more apt to sticking with it, than those who exercise at other times of the day. It seems like it's happened to all of us at one time or another. We have the best intentions of exercising at such and such a time during the day. Before you know it, our day has blown by, we're tired or exhausted and the last thing we feel like doing is exercising.

How Not to be a Quitter and Stick to Exercising

♥ Do something aerobically you enjoy. If you don't enjoy it, no matter how wonderful your intentions are, chances are you won't stick to it.

♥ Find something to preoccupy your mind during your exercise. Video a favorite show you can watch when you want to exercise, visit with a friend while exercising, listen to something of interest, read, or be in a prayerful state of mind.

♥ Plan it into your day as a priority. Again, remember, exercising first thing in the morning increases your chances of sticking with it for the long haul.

WHAT I LIKE TO STOCK IN MY KITCHEN

My motto regarding low-fat foods is, "if it doesn't taste good don't eat it." There are too many delicious choices available for any of us to waste calories on food that doesn't taste good.

The following is a list of products I enjoy using. An asterick (*) in front of the product means the generic brands of these items are less expensive and good.

An easy rule of thumb when reading labels: if it has more than 3 grams of fat per 100 calories, don't buy it, don't use it, and pitch it! The only time I break that rule is for super lean beef such as:

Type of Beef	Serving Size	Fat Grams	Calories	% Fat Calories
London Broil/Flank Steak	3 oz.	6	167	32%
Top Loin (Lean Only)	3 oz.	6	162	33%
Eye of Round (As a steak, roast or have butcher grind for super lean hamburger)	3 oz.	5	150	30%

If you enjoy eating red meat and do not want to refrain, then I encourage you to make the switch to ground eye of round. You'll be doing your heart, health, and waistline a lot of good!

(Note: I am not a big fan of fat-free cheeses or margarines, but in my recipes, they taste good.)

Butter & Margarines

Butter Buds (found in spice or diet section)

Butter-flavored Pan Spray

Non-fat cooking sprays (generic brands are fine)

I Can't Believe It's Not Butter Spray

Ultra Fat-free Promise Margarine

Breads & Grains

*Enriched flour

Flour tortillas fat-free

*Graham crackers

Health Valley fat-free cookies

Breads & Grains continued

Health Valley fat-free granola (I use for my homemade granola bars)

*Italian seasoned bread crumbs

Lite breads with 40 calories and no fat per slice

Nabisco Reduced Fat Ritz Crackers

*Oyster crackers

*Pastas (except egg noodles; pastas from whole durum wheat are best)

Pillsbury Buttermilk Biscuits

Pillsbury Pizza Crust

Quaker Rice Cakes (caramel and strawberry flavored)

Rice (whole grain enriched)
Vegetable bread
*Whole grain and white rice
*Whole wheat flour

Beverages
*Bottled water
*Cider
Country Time Lemonade (sugar free)
Crystal Light (sugar free)
Dole fruit juices (100%)
*Grapefruit juice (100%)
Kool-aid (sugar free)
*Orange juice (100%)
*Prune juice (100%)
Tea (instant or tea bag)
*Tomato juice

Cheese
(To be honest with you, I do not like
    fat-free cheese, but used properly
    in recipes they can taste delicious!)
Border Fat-Free cheese slices-Sharp
    Cheddar flavor
Healthy Choice fat-free cheese
*Italian topping (grated)
Kraft Fat-Free cheeses - all flavors
Kraft "Free" Parmesan cheese
Krogers brand of dairy products
    including frozen
*Parmesan (grated)
Sargenta Fat-Free Ricotta

Condiments
A1 Sauce
*almond extract
Barbecue Sauces (all – I haven't found
    one high in fat)
Braum's fat-free fudge topping
*Cocoa
Coconut extract
*Cornstarch

Condiments continued
Equal
Evaporated skim milk (Lite)
Heinz 57 Sauce
Hershey's Lite Syrup
Hidden Valley Fat-Free Salad
    Dressing
Hidden Valley Reduced Calorie Dry
    Salad Dressing Mix
*Honey
*Karo Syrup
*Ketchup
Kraft Free Mayonnaise and Miracle
    Whip
Kraft Fat-Free Tartar Sauce
Kroger Fat-Free ice cream toppings
Liquid smoke
*Lite soy sauce
Lite teriyaki marinade
*Lite syrups
*Mint extract
Fat-free ice cream topping
*Mustard
NutraSweet
*Pam non-fat cooking spray
Preserves and jellies (low sugar)
Seven Seas "Free" Ranch Salad
    Dressing
Seven Seas "Free" Red Wine Vinegar
    Salad Dressing
Seven Seas "Free" Viva Italian Salad
    Dressing
Smucker's fat-free toppings
*Taco seasoning mix
*Tomato sauce
*Vanilla

Dairy
Buttermilk (non-fat)
*Cottage cheese (non-fat)
*Dry powdered milk (non-fat) (best
    used in recipes)

Dairy continued

Eagle brand Fat-Free condensed sweetened milk

Flavorite Fat-Free yogurts and non-fat cottage cheese

Fleishmann's Fat-Free Buttery Spread (comes in a bottle)

Fleishmann's Fat-Free Cheese Spread (comes in a bottle)

Kroger grocery stores' name brand fat-free cheeses, yogurts, etc.

Pet Fat-Free evaporated canned skimmed milk

Fat-free whipped topping

Skim milk

Sour cream-Fat-Free

Yogurts – Fat-Free (watch labels)

Junk Food

Baked Tostitos, Salsa & Cream Cheese, Cool Ranch, and regular flavors

Dole fruit & juice bars

Fat-free ice cream

Frito Lay Potato Crisps

Frozen fat-free yogurts

*Fudge bars

Health Valley fat-free tarts

Hostess "Lite" twinkies, cupcakes, brownies, and muffins

Jello fat-free pudding and pudding cups

Keebler Elfin Delights

Little Debbie's Lite Oatmeal Pies and Brownies

*Marshmallows

*Marshmallow Crème

Pepperidge Farm Fat-Free Brownies and Blondies (too good!)

Pop Secret Popcorn Bars

*Popsicles - all

*Pretzels

Quaker low-fat granola

Rice cakes (Quaker strawberry, rice, corn & caramel flavored)

Junk Food continued

Smart Pop microwave popcorn

Snack Well's cookies, tarts and breakfast bars

Super Pretzels - soft pretzels

Sweet Escapes Candies (by Hershey's)

*Welch's frozen juice bars

Meats, Fish, Poultry

Beef (eye of round, London broil, flank steak, top lion)

ButterBall Fat-Free sausage, turkey breast and lunchmeats

Canadian bacon (usually very low in fat)

Chicken breast (no skin; dark meat has twice as much fat!)

Crab meat flake or stick (imitation)

Eckrich fat-free meats (hot dogs, lunch meats, smoked sausage, kielbasa)

Fish (the white ones are lower in fats; i.e., flounder, grouper, pike, sole, cod, orange roughy, monk fish, perch, scallops)

Healthy Choice lunch meat, hot dogs and smoked sausage

Hillshire Farms Fat-Free smoked sausage & kielbasa

Hotdogs - Healthy Choice - 1 fat gram; Hormel Light & Lean - 1 fat gram; Oscar Mayer Fat-Free

Shellfish (Lobster, Crab, Shrimp)

*Tuna (packed in water)

Turkey breast (no skin; dark meat has twice as much fat!)

Pre-Packaged Items

*Applesauce

Betty Crocker "Lite" Cake, Brownie, Bread & Muffin mixes

*Bouillon cubes (chicken, beef, and vegetable flavors)

Healthy choice low-fat frozen meals

Hot chili beans

Fat-free, sugar free hot chocolate

Simply potatoes shredded hasbrowns

Fruits and Veggies

*Canned vegetables - no salt added

*Canned fruits in fruit juice only

*Cranberry sauce

Fresh vegetables - all (except for avocado - major fat!!)

*Frozen vegetables and fruits - all - with no sugar added

*Lite fruit cocktail

*Lite pie fillings - cherry, apple, and blueberry

Other Items

*Bac-O's (imitation bacon bits)

Betty Crocker Reduced Fat Sweet Rewards Cake Mix

Campbell's Healthy Request low-fat & fat-free soups

Cool Whip Free

Dream Whip

Eggs (use only the whites)

*Egg Beaters

Gold medal Fudge Brownie Mix

Health Valley Chili and Soups

Healthy Choice soups and sauces (low- and no-fat)

*Instant mashed potatoes

Other Items continued

Jiffy cake mixes

Beans - canned or dry

Martha Whites's Lite mixes (muffins, etc.)

Nabisco's "Royal" Lite cheesecake mixes

Old El Paso fat-free refried beans

*Pancake and buttermilk pancake mix

*Pasta

Pillsbury Lovin's Lites frostings

Progresso "Healthy Calssics" soups

Special K Fat-free Waffles

Sauces

Campbell's Healthy Request low-fat & fat-free sauces

Healthy Choice Spaghetti Sauce

Heinz Homestyle Lite gravies (in a jar)

Hunts "Light" fat-free pasta sauce

Pepperidge Farm Stroganoff Gravy

Prego spaghetti and pizza sauce (Lite ones)

Ragu Lite "Garden Harvest" & "Tomato & Herb"

Ragu Pizza Quick Sauce

Best of BUSY PEOPLE'S Cookbooks

BY DAWN HALL

SPEEDY STARTERS

Low Fat Recipes from 3 AWARD-WINNING COOKBOOKS

"Chili Cheeser Pleaser" Dip

It's hard to believe it's only 1 gram of fat!

1   pound ground
    eye of round (beef)
2   15-ounce cans fat-free
    Chili with black beans
    (I use Health Valley
    spicy vegetarian)

8   ounces fat-free fancy
    shredded cheddar cheese
    (I use Healthy Choice)

♥ Brown hamburger. Add chili and cheddar cheese. Mix well over medium-low heat until cheese is melted. Serve warm with either low-fat tortilla chips, fat-free pretzel chips, or low-fat Bugles.

Yield: 15 servings

Calories: 100
Percent Fat Calories: 11%
Carbohydrate: 8 grams
Protein: 14 grams

Total Fat: 1 gram
Cholesterol: 19 mg
Dietary Fiber: 3 grams
Sodium: 192 mg

Total preparation time: 7 minutes.

Down Home Cookin'

Mexican Confetti Dip

This is a great source of protein. I like to eat this for lunch.

1   12-ounce can whole
    kernel corn, drained
1   15.5-ounce can black
    beans, drained

⅓ cup fat-free Italian salad
   dressing (I use Marzetti)
1 16-ounce jar of your
   favorite chunky salsa

♥ Mix all together. Chill. Presto! You're done! Serve with Baked Tostito Chips.

♥ Other ways to use this recipe:

Warm a flour tortilla in microwave. Fill center with ¼ cup of dip. Fold up as you would a burrito.

Toss ½ cup with 1½ cups of your favorite lettuces for a tasty twist to your salad!

Yield: 6 servings

Calories: 127
Percent Fat Calories: 5%
Carbohydrate: 23 grams
Protein: 5 grams

Total Fat: 1 gram
Cholesterol: 0 mg
Dietary Fiber: 5 grams
Sodium: 685 mg

Total preparation time: 5 minutes.

Down Home Cookin'

Cool & Creamy Spicy Tortilla Dip

*I created this recipe especially for Oprah as a gift
when I was fortunate enough to be in her studio audience.
(By the way, she is even more beautiful in person!)
She was so kind; she even sent me a thank you note!*

16 ounces fat-free sour cream

1 16-ounce jar of your favorite chunky salsa

♥ Mix together and refrigerate. Serve with low-fat tortilla chips or any other of your favorite snacks as a dip (like low-fat Bugles).

♥ For a heartier dip add 8 ounces fancy shredded fat-free cheddar cheese. (I like Healthy Choice.) If you like spicier foods, feel free to add a few drops of Tabasco sauce. I like to use a chunky salsa rather than a regular salsa.

Yield: 30 servings

Calories: 22
Percent Fat Calories: 0%
Carbohydrate: 3 grams
Protein: 1 gram

Total Fat: 0 grams
Cholesterol: 1 mg
Dietary Fiber: 0 grams
Sodium: 82 mg

Total preparation time: 3 minutes.

Down Home Cookin'

No Cooking Mexican Dip

8 ounces fat-free cream cheese
  (I use Healthy Choice)
8 ounces fat-free sour cream
16 ounces your favorite
  thick and chunky salsa
  (Picante or taco sauce
  may be used, if desired)

2 green onions, chopped
1½ cups thinly sliced lettuce
1 medium tomato, diced
8 ounces fat-free Mexican
  shredded cheese or fat-free
  shredded cheddar cheese
  (I use Healthy Choice)
  Low-fat tortilla chips

♥ Beat cream cheese and sour cream together. Spread on cake plate. Layer other ingredients on top of cream mixture in exact order as listed above. Serve with tortilla chips.

Yield: 15 servings

Calories: 66
Percent Fat Calories: 0%
Carbohydrate: 7 grams
Protein: 8 grams

Total Fat: 0 grams
Cholesterol: 5 mg
Dietary Fiber: 0 grams
Sodium: 328 mg

Total preparation time: 15 minutes.

Down Home Cookin'

"Seconds Please" Mexican Dip

It doesn't get any easier (or tastier) than this!
Eat as a meal or appetizer.

1 pound ground eye of round
   (beef)
1 8-ounce package
   no-fat Mexican cheese
   (I use Healthy Choice)

1 16-ounce jar of mild
   thick 'n chunky picante
   or thick chunky salsa
   (I use Old El Paso picante)
1 16-ounce can vegetarian
   refried beans
   (I use Old El Paso)

♥ In large pan brown beef. Do not drain juice. Add cheese, picante, and refried beans. Stir until well mixed and hot. Keep warm in a Crock-Pot. Serve warm with low-fat tortilla chips! MMM! MMM! GOOD!

Yield: 15 servings

Calories: 97
Percent Fat Calories: 15%
Carbohydrate: 7 grams
Protein: 12 grams

Total Fat: 2 grams
Cholesterol: 18 mg
Dietary Fiber: 2 grams
Sodium: 492 mg

Total preparation time: 10 minutes.

Down Home Cookin'

ITALIAN DIP

My husband, who doesn't like to cook, came up with this version himself. Jokingly he told me, "Your creations are becoming contagious! You've even got me doing it now!"

14 ounces Ragu Pizza Sauce (We like garlic and basil flavor)

16 ounces fat-free sour cream

8 ounces fat-free fancy shredded mozzarella cheese (We like Healthy Choice)

♥ Mix together. Serve chilled. Great for baked Tostitos or pretzels.

Yield: 19 servings

Calories: 52
Percent Fat Calories: 0%
Carbohydrate: 7 grams
Protein: 5 grams

Total Fat: 0 grams
Cholesterol: 4 mg
Dietary Fiber: 0 grams
Sodium: 105 mg

Total preparation time: 3 minutes.

Down Home Cookin'

VEGETABLE DIP (FAT-FREE)

¾ cup non-fat cottage cheese

1 package reduced calorie ranch dressing mix (I use Hidden Valley)

1 packet Equal (OR 2 teaspoons sugar)

4 ounces fat-free cream cheese

¾ cup non-fat sour cream

3 tablespoons water

♥ Beat cottage cheese on high for 1-2 minutes (until smooth and creamy). Add everything else. Beat on medium until well blended.

Yield: 8 servings

Calories: 64
Percent Fat Calories: 0%
Carbohydrate: 8 grams
Protein: 7 grams

Total Fat: 0 grams
Cholesterol: 5 mg
Dietary Fiber: 0 grams
Sodium: 570 mg

Total preparation time: 7 minutes.

Down Home Cookin'

Chicken Onion Dip

A friend of mine (Mable) introduced me to a high-fat version of this recipe. I modified it to low-fat. It's now a family favorite!

2 (8-ounce) package fat-free Healthy Choice cream cheese - softened

1 (10-ounce) can premium chunk chicken in water (Swanson) - do not drain

²/₃ cup chopped sweet onion (½ medium onion) (I like Vidalia onions)

1 teaspoon mustard

♥ Put all ingredients in medium bowl. Mix well with fork until well blended.

♥ Keep chilled until ready to serve.

Yield: 15 (3-tablespoon) servings

Calories: 50
Cholesterol: 10 mg

Total Fat: 0.3 grams (23% fat)
Sodium: 225 mg

Total preparation time: 5-6 minutes.

Busy People's Low-Fat Cookbook

Menu Ideas: Dip - With fat-free crackers as a spread

Dip - Serve with Baked Tostitos tortilla chips

*Salad - On a bed of leafy greens as a salad
(top with croutons)*

*Appetizer - Cut cherry tomatoes in half. Take out inside
of tomatoes. Stuff with chicken onion dip.
Sprinkle with paprika for a prettier color.*

*Sandwich - Spread on toast.
Top with slice of tomato and lettuce.*

*Warm Dip - Microwave on high for a few minutes, until hot,
and bubbly. Stir. Serve with crackers or Baked Tostitos
Tortilla Chips as a warm appetizer.*

BAGEL CHIPS

*This wonderful and easy snack was sent
in by Carolyn Henderson of Howell, Michigan. Wait until
you try this one. You will want to make more than one!*

1 onion or garlic bagel
Non-fat butter-flavored
   cooking spray

1 teaspoon Italian seasoning
¼ teaspoon garlic salt

♥ Preheat oven to 350 degrees.

♥ Spray a cookie sheet with non-fat cooking spray.

♥ With a serrated knife, slice bagel vertically into thin slices.

♥ Arrange on cookie sheet and spray lightly with butter-flavored
cooking spray.

♥ Sprinkle with Italian seasoning and garlic salt.

♥ Bake at 350 degrees for 12 minutes or until crispy.

Yield: 2 servings

Calories: 153
Percent Fat Calories: 5%
Carbohydrate: 30 grams
Protein: 6 grams

Total Fat: 1 gram
Cholesterol: 0 mg
Dietary Fiber: 1 gram
Sodium: 520 mg

Total time: 16 minutes.

2nd *Serving Busy People's Low Fat Cookbook*

*Menu Ideas: Goes good with
Greek Pasta Salad (page 115) or any fresh,
tossed garden salad.*

RANCH STACKS

A versatile appetizer that is satisfying enough to substitute in place of a sandwich for packed lunches.

1 (8-ounce) package fat-free cream cheese - softened
1 cup fat-free sour cream
1 (1-ounce) package Hidden Valley Ranch dip mix - dry

½ cup finely chopped celery
¼ cup finely chopped green onion
9 fat-free flour tortillas

♥ With a mixer on medium speed, beat cream cheese, sour cream and dry Hidden Valley Ranch dip mix together until well mixed.

♥ With a spoon, stir in celery and green onions.

♥ Divide mixture among six individual flour tortillas.

♥ Put one tortilla spread with mixture on top of another tortilla spread with mixture.

♥ Place a third tortilla (which has not been spread with mixture) on top.

♥ You will have 3 tortilla stacks, each 3 layers high.

♥ Press stacks firmly down with hands to secure together.

♥ Cut each stack into 6 pieces.

Yield: 18 (1-wedge) servings

Calories: 87
Percent Fat Calories: 0%
Carbohydrate: 17 grams
Protein: 4 grams

Total Fat: 0 grams
Cholesterol: 2 mg
Dietary Fiber: 1 gram
Sodium: 429 mg

Total time: 20 minutes or less.

2nd Serving Busy People's Low Fat Cookbook

Menu Ideas: Appetizers or lunch.

Deviled Eggs –
(no-fat, no cholesterol)

Sharon Swick, from Delta, Ohio sent me this one.

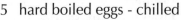

5 hard boiled eggs - chilled	½ teaspoon Grey Poupon mustard
1 cup Egg Beaters	½ teaspoon vinegar
3 tablespoons fat-free Miracle Whip	½ teaspoon salt - optional
¼ teaspoon horseradish	Black pepper and paprika - optional

♥ (If you prefer a sweeter taste, use less mustard and add 1 to 2 tablespoons sweet relish).

♥ Cut boiled eggs in half and discard yolks. Set aside.

♥ Spray a skillet with non-fat cooking spray. Add Egg Beaters and cook and stir over medium heat until done. Cool.

♥ Combine cooled Egg Beaters and all remaining ingredients except paprika in a food processor until smooth.

♥ Fill mixture into egg halves and sprinkle with paprika.

Yield: 10 servings

Calories: 25
Cholesterol: 0 mg

Total Fat: 0 grams (0% fat)
Sodium: 109 mg

Preparation time: 10 minutes.

Total time: 20 minutes.

Busy People's Low-Fat Cookbook

Menu Ideas: Serve as an appetizer and
also great for picnics.

HAM & CHEESE BALL

4 ounces Healthy Choice ham or turkey ham, very thinly chopped, divided
2 8-ounce containers fat-free cream cheese
4 green onions, chopped
1 4-ounce can mushroom pieces, chopped and drained
1 tablespoon mustard

♥ Set ½ of the chopped ham aside. Mix all remaining ingredients together well. Roll into a ball. Press remaining ham onto ball, covering entire surface. Chill. Serve with fat-free crackers. (I like SnackWell's brand.)

Yield: 12 servings

Calories: 49
Percent Fat Calories: 6%
Carbohydrate: 4 grams
Protein: 7 grams
Total Fat: trace
Cholesterol: 7 mg
Dietary Fiber: 0 grams
Sodium: 320 mg

Total preparation time: 10 minutes.

Down Home Cookin'

CHIPPED BEEF CHEESE BALL

3 8-ounce packages
   fat-free cream cheese
½ teaspoon liquid smoke
2 2.5-ounce packages
   chipped beef, chopped
   (I use Carl Buddig beef)

1 small onion, chopped
   (approximately ½ cup)

♥ Mix all ingredients well with blender. With hands, shape into a ball. Garnish with fresh parsley if desired. Serve with fat-free crackers.

***For a quick chipped beef cheese spread put into food processor for about 1½ to 2 minutes. Pour into bowl and garnish with crackers.

Yield: 16 servings

Calories: 52
Percent Fat Calories: 10%
Carbohydrate: 4 grams
Protein: 8 grams

Total Fat: 1 gram
Cholesterol: 10 mg
Dietary Fiber: 0 grams
Sodium: 332 mg

Total preparation time: 15 minutes.

Down Home Cookin'

SOUTH OF THE BORDER CHEESE SPREAD

8 ounces fat-free cream cheese, softened

16 ounces fat-free sour cream

1 16-ounce jar of your favorite salsa

16 ounces fat-free shredded cheddar or taco cheese

♥ With blender, mix ingredients thoroughly. Serve chilled with crackers (I like SnackWell's fat-free brand) or low-fat tortilla chips.

Yield: 28 servings

Calories: 55
Percent Fat Calories: 0%
Carbohydrate: 5 grams
Protein: 7 grams

Total Fat: 0 grams
Cholesterol: 5 mg
Dietary Fiber: 0 grams
Sodium: 235 mg

Total preparation time: 5 minutes.

Down Home Cookin'

FRUIT-FLAVORED
CREAM CHEESE SPREADS

Great for bagels or crackers! The high fat in those expensive so-called "lite" flavored cheese spreads got my creativity going! I'm so pleased with these! They all taste absolutely delicious and not 1 gram of fat!

2 8-ounce packages
   Healthy Choice fat-free
   cream cheese

½ cup your favorite jam
   (If it's not sweet enough,
   add 1 or 2 envelopes
   NutraSweet)

♥ Here are my favorite types of jam to use in this recipe:

| strawberry | blackberry | blueberry |
| apricot | peach | raspberry |

Yield: 20 servings

Calories: 42
Percent Fat Calories: 0%
Carbohydrate: 7 grams
Protein: 3 grams

Total Fat: 0 grams
Cholesterol: 2 mg
Dietary Fiber: 0 grams
Sodium: 110 mg

Total preparation time: 4 minutes.

Down Home Cookin'

CHICKEN AND ONION CHEESE SPREAD

This multiple use spread is scrumptious no matter how it's used.

1 (10-ounce) can premium chunk white chicken in water - do not drain - (I used Swanson brand)
2 (8-ounce) packages Healthy Choice fat-free cream cheese - softened

½ cup fat-free sour cream
1 envelope dry onion soup mix - (I use Lipton Brand. There are 2 envelopes in a box.)
¼ cup green or red pepper - chopped - optional

♥ Mix all ingredients with a hand mixer on low speed for about 1 to 2 minutes or until well mixed. (Also add the water that is in the can with the chicken.)

♥ Serve with crackers. (Or menu idea listed below.)

Yield: 30 (2-tablespoon) servings

Calories: 30
Cholesterol: 5 mg

Total Fat: 0.2 grams (7% fat)
Sodium: 198 mg

Total preparation time: 6 minutes or less.

Busy People's Low-Fat Cookbook

Menu Ideas: Use as a vegetable dip or stuff in celery sticks. Spread on soft flour tortillas, top with lettuce and tomatoes and roll up. Or spread on one piece of toast for an open faced sandwich. (If desired top with a fresh green pepper ring.)

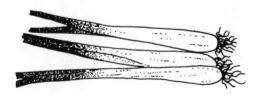

HAM AND CHEESE SPREAD

For years I've had to stay away from the deli's ham and cheese spread. It was one of my favorite high fat foods that I did miss. But no more! Mine is absolutely, positively delicious! On a scale of 1 to 10, with 10 being the best, I think mine's a 12!

¼ cup Kraft Free Miracle Whip	¾ pound extra lean ham (2 ounces of ham = 2 grams of fat)
3 tablespoons Kraft fat-free Thousand Island Salad Dressing	
1 tablespoon mustard	1 cup Healthy Choice fat-free fancy shredded cheddar cheese

♥ In a small bowl, using a fork, mix the first three ingredients together until creamy and well mixed. Set aside.

♥ Cut ham into tiny ¼-inch or smaller pieces and put into a blender or food processor. With setting on grind, press the "pulse" button for a few seconds to turn appliance on and off quickly. You may need to use a spatula to rearrange pieces that are not getting ground. Continue turning on for 3 to 5 second intervals until all ham pieces are ground.

♥ Add ground ham and cheddar cheese to cream mixture. Stir until well mixed. Serve as is or cover and keep chilled until ready to use. You may keep refrigerated and use up to 5 days.

Yield: 6 (¼-cup) servings

Calories: 125	Total Fat: 2.9 grams (23% fat)
Cholesterol: 28 mg	Sodium: 1146 mg

Total preparation time: 10 minutes or less (most of the time derived from cutting and grinding ham.)

Busy People's Low-Fat Cookbook

Menu Ideas: As an appetizer use as a filling to stuff cherry tomatoes or serve with fat-free crackers. It's also great on fat-free bread as a sandwich with lettuce.

SHRIMP SPREAD

Definitely for extra special occasions. More special than just shrimp over cocktail sauce and cream cheese. As pretty as it is yummy!

1½ cups shredded fat-free mozzarella cheese (I use Kraft) - divided
1 (8-ounce) package fat-free cream cheese
1 (8-ounce) container fat-free sour cream

½ cup plus 1 tablespoon chopped fresh chives - divided
1 (8-ounce) jar cocktail sauce
1 pound cooked cocktail shrimp (40/50 count) - remove tails
½ cup finely chopped tomato

♥ Mix 1 cup of the mozzarella cheese with the cream cheese, sour cream and ½ cup fresh chives until smooth.

♥ Spread on a cake plate.

♥ Cover with cocktail sauce.

♥ Top with remaining ½ cup mozzarella cheese, shrimp, remaining 1 tablespoon chives and tomatoes.

Yield: 16 (3-ounce) servings

Calories: 90
Percent Fat Calories: 5%
Carbohydrate: 8 grams
Protein: 13 grams

Total Fat: trace
Cholesterol: 59 mg
Dietary Fiber: 0 grams
Sodium: 420 mg

Menu Ideas: Serve with crackers.

Seafood Spread: Make exactly the same as the Shrimp Spread recipe but use 8 ounces cooked crab and 8 ounces cooked shrimp.

Yield: 16 (3-ounce) servings

Calories: 95
Percent Fat Calories: 12%
Carbohydrate: 8 grams
Protein: 12 grams

Total Fat: 1 gram
Cholesterol: 44 mg
Dietary Fiber: 0 grams
Sodium: 465 mg

Total time: 20 minutes or less.

2nd Serving Busy People's Low Fat Cookbook

CRUNCHY VEGETABLE SPREAD

Absolutely delicious and so versatile!

1 (8-ounce) package fat-free cream cheese
1 (8-ounce) container fat-free sour cream
1 (0.59-ounce) package Hidden Valley Ranch dip mix - dry
1 cup chopped celery
1 medium-size red bell pepper - chopped
1 medium-size cucumber - seeded and chopped
¼ cup fresh or frozen chopped onion

♥ With a mixer beat together cream cheese, sour cream and Hidden Valley Ranch dip mix until well blended and creamy.

♥ With a spoon, stir in vegetables until well blended.

Yield: 10 (¼-cup) servings

Calories: 60
Percent Fat Calories: 0%
Carbohydrate: 9 grams
Protein: 5 grams

Total Fat: 0 grams
Cholesterol: 4 mg
Dietary Fiber: 1 gram
Sodium: 334 mg

Total time: 10 minutes.

2nd Serving Busy People's Low Fat Cookbook

Menu Ideas: Absolutely delicious on Bagel Chips (page 33), toast, pita sandwiches or as a dip.

SHERBET BREEZE

A refreshing refreshment for those lazy summer days.

1 cup frozen sherbet - your favorite flavor	1 cup Diet Sprite - chilled 7 ice cubes

♥ Put all ingredients in a blender on high for 45 seconds or until ice cubes are crushed.

Yield: 2 drinks

Calories: 138
Cholesterol: 5 mg

Total Fat: 2 grams (12% fat)
Sodium: 49 mg

Preparation time: 5 minutes or less.

Busy People's Low-Fat Cookbook

Menu Ideas: As a snack, or cool "pick-me-up" after a long hot day.

FRUITY FREEZE DRINK

An invigorating drink for summer festivities.

1 cup Fat-Free frozen yogurt - your favorite flavor	1 cup Diet Sprite - chilled 7 ice cubes

♥ Put all ingredients in a blender on high for 45 seconds or until ice cubes are crushed.

Yield: 2 drinks

Calories: 97
Cholesterol: 2 mg

Total Fat: 0 grams (0% fat)
Sodium: 67 mg

Preparation time: 5 minutes or less.

Busy People's Low-Fat Cookbook

Menu Ideas: Refreshing on hot summer days, after a good workout or for a snack. Multiplied, this recipe is also great for bridal or baby showers.

BERRY FRUIT FREEZE DRINK

Cool and refreshing for those hot summer days!

2 cups Diet Sprite
(or Diet 7-Up)
10 ice cubes

½ cup blackberries
(or blueberries)
1 cup raspberry sherbet

♥ Put all ingredients in a blender on high speed for 10 to 15 seconds. Turn off. Repeat.

♥ Pour into glasses.

♥ Serve immediately.

Yield: 4 (1-cup) servings

Calories: 79
Cholesterol: 3 mg

Total Fat: 1.1 grams (12% fat)
Sodium: 26 mg

Preparation time: 5 minutes or less.

Busy People's Low-Fat Cookbook

Menu Ideas: Great for picnics, cookouts or a snack on a sizzling, scorcher day!

SPICED TEA

This is wonderful to drink warm or chilled over ice.
A terrific drink for all seasons!

1   gallon hot water
8   tea bags
2   tablespoons cinnamon
    red hots

½   cup brown sugar
2   teaspoons ground
    cinnamon
½   teaspoon ground allspice

♥ Put everything into a large kettle. (Or a soup pot).

♥ Stir until seasonings are dissolved.

♥ Bring to a boil.

♥ Turn off heat. Stir again.

♥ Remove tea bags. Ready to drink as is or served over ice.

Yield: 16 (1-cup) servings

Calories: 34
Cholesterol: 0 mg

Total Fat: a grams (0% fat)
Sodium: 3 mg

Total time: 5 minutes or less.

Busy People's Low-Fat Cookbook

Menu Ideas: Anytime, anyplace!
You can't go wrong with this drink!

BANANA BERRY SLUSHY

1   banana
1   cup black raspberries or
    blackberries
½ cup NutraSweet Spoonful
    (OR ½ cup sugar)

3   cups ice
2   cups water
1   envelope black cherry
    unsweetened Kool-Aid

♥ Put everything in blender on high — mix for 30-45 seconds.
Serve immediately. °

° With Sugar – Calories: 117 – Total Fat: 1 grams
Percent Fat Calories: 3% – Cholesterol: 0 mg
Carbohydrate: 29 grams – Dietary Fiber:1 gram
Protein: 1 gram – Sodium: 25 mg

Yield: 5 servings

Calories: 47
Percent Fat Calories: 9%
Carbohydrate: 9 grams
Protein: 1 gram

Total Fat: 1 gram
Cholesterol: 0 mg
Dietary Fiber: 2 grams
Sodium: 24 mg

Total preparation time: 5 minutes.

Down Home Cookin'

CHERRY SLUSHIES

12 Bing cherries, seeds removed
4 cups ice
½ teaspoon cherry-flavored sugar-free Kool-Aid

2½ cups cold water
½ cup sugar or 7-8 packets Equal

♥ Put everything in blender on "mix" or "ice crush" setting. Leave on for 30-45 seconds. Pour into glasses.°

° With Sugar – Calories: 90 – Total Fat: 0 grams
Percent Fat Calories: 0% – Cholesterol: 0 mg
Carbohydrate: 23 grams – Dietary Fiber: 0 grams
Protein: 0 grams – Sodium: 2 mg

Yield: 5 servings

Calories: 18
Percent Fat Calories: 0%
Carbohydrate: 3 grams
Protein: 2 grams

Total Fat: 0 grams
Cholesterol: 0 mg
Dietary Fiber: 0 grams
Sodium: 2 mg

Total preparation time: 15 minutes.

Down Home Cookin'

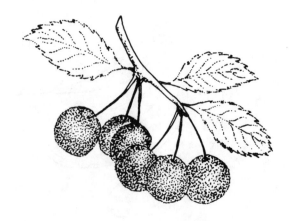

WARM WHATCHA' MACALLIT

1 gallon cider
2 liters diet ginger ale

½ cup red hots (little red cinnamon candies)
Cinnamon sticks (optional)

♥ Mix all ingredients in large saucepan and stir over medium heat until warm (approximately 7-10 minutes). Serve warm with cinnamon stick.

Yield: 24 servings

Calories: 98
Percent Fat Calories: 0%
Carbohydrate: 24 grams
Protein: 0 grams

Total Fat: 0 grams
Cholesterol: 0 mg
Dietary Fiber: 0 grams
Sodium: 18 mg

Total preparation time: 15-18 minutes.

Down Home Cookin'

ORANGE SLUSHY

4½ cups ice
½ teaspoon orange sugar-free Kool-Aid
2½ cups cold water

7 packets Equal (or ⅓ cup sugar)
1 11-ounce can Mandarin oranges with lite syrup

♥ Put all ingredients in blender and blend for 30-45 seconds. Pour into glasses and serve.°

° With Sugar – Calories: 92 – Total Fat: 0 grams
Percent Fat Calories: 0% – Cholesterol: 0 mg
Carbohydrate: 23 grams – Dietary Fiber: 0 grams
Protein: 0 grams – Sodium: 4 mg

Yield: 5 servings

Calories: 46
Percent Fat Calories: 0%
Carbohydrate: 10 grams
Protein: 2 grams

Total Fat: 0 grams
Cholesterol: 0 mg
Dietary Fiber: 0 grams
Sodium: 4 mg

Total preparation time: 5 minutes.

Down Home Cookin'

Fruit Punch

2   2-quart cherry sugar-free
    Kool-Aid
1   2-liter diet cherry Seven-Up

2   12-ounce cans of frozen
    orange juice, prepared

♥ Mix and serve chilled. For a lower calorie punch, use only 1 can (12-ounce) orange juice. I like it just as well as 2 cans, and it's not as fattening.

♥ If using a punch bowl, slice 1 orange and float slices on top of punch.°

° With 1 can juice: – Calories: 17 – Total Fat: 0 grams
Percent Fat Calories: 0% – Cholesterol: 0 mg
Carbohydrate: 4 grams – Dietary Fiber: 0 grams
Protein: 0 grams – Sodium: 4 mg

Yield: 36 servings

Calories: 32
Percent Fat Calories: 0%
Carbohydrate: 8 grams
Protein: 1 gram

Total Fat: 0 grams
Cholesterol: 0 mg
Dietary Fiber: 0 grams
Sodium: 5 mg

Total preparation time: 5 minutes.

Down Home Cookin'

CHRISTMAS PUNCH

The deep redness of this full-bodied punch
gives this special holiday drink its name.

1   gallon apple juice
1   (2-liter) bottle Diet
    Mountain Dew

½   cup cinnamon red hots
⅓   cup lemon juice (bottled
    from concentrate is fine)

♥ In a large pot, bring apple juice, Mountain Dew, and red hots to a boil. Reduce heat. Keep stirring until all red hots are dissolved.

♥ Add lemon juice. Stir well.

♥ Serve warm or chilled.

Yield: 24 (1-cup) servings

Calories: 99
Cholesterol: 0 mg

Total Fat: 0.2 grams (2% fat)
Sodium: 13 mg

Total preparation time: 10 minutes or less.

Busy People's Low-Fat Cookbook

Menu Ideas: Serve with your favorite Christmas meal!
It's also delicious served at showers,
birthday parties and graduations.

Hawaiian Slushy Drink

1 15-ounce can pineapple, in juice (not syrup)
2 bananas
⅓ cup NutraSweet Spoonful (or ⅓ cup sugar)

2 cups ice (depending on how icy you like it)
1 teaspoon of piña-pineapple sugar-free Kool-Aid

♥ Put everything in a blender. Fill blender to top with water. Mix on high for 30-45 seconds, until slushy. °

° With Sugar – Calories: 126 – Total Fat: 0 grams
Percent Fat Calories: 0% – Cholesterol: 0 mg
Carbohydrate: 31 grams – Dietary Fiber: 2 grams
Protein: 1 gram – Sodium: 1 mg

Yield: 6 servings

Calories: 87
Percent Fat Calories: 0%
Carbohydrate: 20 grams
Protein: 1 gram

Total Fat: 0 grams
Cholesterol: 0 mg
Dietary Fiber: 2 grams
Sodium: 1 mg

Total preparation time: 5-7 minutes.

Down Home Cookin'

MINT TEA

If you like Snapple mint tea, you'll love this,
and it'll save you loads of money!

2 quarts hot water	2 drops mint extract
8 tea bags (your favorite brand)	Sugar to taste (optional)

♥ Put tea bags in hot water. Let stand overnight. Remove tea bags. Put 2 drops of mint extract into tea. Serve in tall glasses with ice.

Yield: 8 servings

Calories: 0	Total Fat: 0 grams
Percent Fat Calories: 0%	Cholesterol: 0 mg
Carbohydrate: 0 grams	Dietary Fiber: 0 grams
Protein: 0 grams	Sodium: 0 mg

Total preparation time: 5 minutes.

Down Home Cookin'

POOR BOY'S CAPPUCCINO

Craving a cappuccino, but not owning an expensive cappuccino machine and not wanting to pay the high price of the cappuccino mixes, I created this. It's pretty good! If you like BP gas station's cappuccino, you'll like this. Not a true cappuccino, but mighty tasty!

1 cup water
½ teaspoon instant coffee
2 tablespoons powdered fat-free hot cocoa mix

1 tablespoon of your favorite flavor nondairy fat-free creamer (Coffee Mate)

♥ Microwave water for 1 minute or until piping hot.

♥ Stir in remaining ingredients until dissolved and well mixed.

Yield: 1 (1-cup) serving

Calories: 126
Percent Fat Calories: 0%
Carbohydrate: 23 grams
Protein: 6 grams

Total Fat: 0 grams
Cholesterol: 0 mg
Dietary Fiber: 2 grams
Sodium: 432 mg

Total time: 2 minutes.

2nd Serving Busy People's Low Fat Cookbook

Menu Ideas: Anytime and anywhere.

Back To Basics

So many of my students don't have a clue how to convert many of their old "high fat" favorites to delicious "low-fat" favorites. Everyone is absolutely correct when they complain many fat-free products don't taste good. However, there are many that do!

This section is chock full of "Back to Basic" recipes you might have thought you could no longer enjoy while following a low-fat lifestyle! Hopefully, you'll be pleasingly surprised—even amazed— at how delicious these simple basic foods can still be even while low-fat!

Scrambled Eggs

Every bit as good as the high fat ones
you remember your parents making as a child.

4 egg whites plus 2 drops yellow food coloring (or ½ cup Egg Beaters)	1 teaspoon dry Molly McButter (or Butter Buds Sprinkles) dash of lite salt
1 tablespoon skim milk	dash of pepper

♥ Spray a non-stick skillet with non-fat cooking spray.

♥ With a fork, briskly beat all ingredients together until well blended. Pour into prepared pan and cook over medium heat, stirring constantly with a spatula until fully cooked.

Yield: 1 serving

Calories: 78   Total Fat: 0 grams (0 % fat)
Cholesterol: 0 mg   Sodium: 247 mg

Total preparation and cooking time: 5 minutes or less.

Busy People's Low-Fat Cookbook

CHERRY BREAKFAST SANDWICH

A meal in itself! Looks like a sandwich, but eat it with a fork.

2   Special K fat-free waffles
½   cup lite cherry pie
     filling (warm in the
     microwave, if desired)

1   tablespoon "lite"
     blueberry syrup

♥ Toast waffles until golden brown. Spread cherry pie filling on top of one waffle. Put second waffle on top of cherries. Drizzle syrup over top of second waffle, allowing syrup to run over the edges. Serve immediately.

Yield: 1 serving

Calories: 251
Percent Fat Calories: 0%
Carbohydrate: 59 grams
Protein: 7 grams

Total Fat: 0 grams
Cholesterol: 0 mg
Dietary Fiber: 2 grams
Sodium: 287 mg

Preparation time: 10 minutes.

Down Home Cookin'

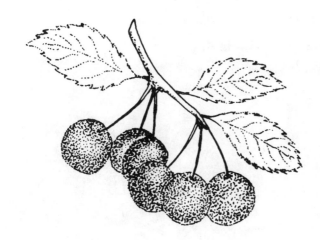

BAKED FRENCH TOAST

*What's great about this recipe is it can be prepared in advance
and kept in the refrigerator, if desired, before baking.*

12 slices raisin bread
1 cup skim milk
8 egg whites
¼ cup packed brown sugar

1 teaspoon vanilla
Powdered sugar (optional)
Syrup (optional)

♥ Preheat oven to 325 degrees. Spray a jelly roll pan (a cookie
sheet with ½-inch sides) with a non-fat cooking spray. Lay 12
slices of raisin bread in three rows of four (sides of bread will be
touching). If bread is slightly stale or dry, that's fine. Beat milk,
egg whites, brown sugar, and vanilla with mixer on high for 1½
to 2 minutes. Pour mixture over slices of bread. Once bread is
covered, turn each slice over to guarantee all bread is wet. Bake
for 27 to 30 minutes. Serve immediately. Sprinkle powdered sugar
lightly on top or syrup if desired.

Yield: 6 servings

Calories: 216
Percent Fat Calories: 10%
Carbohydrate: 39 grams
Protein: 10 grams

Total Fat: 2 grams
Cholesterol: 1 mg
Dietary Fiber: 2 grams
Sodium: 301 mg

Preparation time: 35 minutes.

Down Home Cookin'

ORANGE FRENCH TOAST

A zesty twist to an old time favorite.

2 (4-ounce) containers Egg
   Beaters (or 8 egg whites
   with a couple drops of
   yellow food coloring)
⅔ cup orange juice
8 slices fat-free bread
   (Aunt Millie's)

4 teaspoons powdered
   sugar—optional
¼ cup lite maple syrup
I Can't Believe It's Not
   Butter spray

♥ Spray a nonstick skillet or griddle with non-fat cooking spray and preheat to medium-high heat.

♥ With a fork, briskly beat Egg Beaters (or egg whites with yellow food coloring) with orange juice until well mixed.

♥ Dip bread slices, one at a time, into egg mixture.

♥ Arrange dipped bread slices on prepared skillet (or griddle) making sure edges of bread do not touch. Cook until bottoms are golden brown. Turn over and continue cooking until golden brown.

♥ Serve hot with 1 teaspoon powdered sugar, if desired, 1 tablespoon light maple syrup and up to 10 sprays of I Can't Believe It's Not Butter spray per serving.

Yield: 4 (2-slice) servings

Calories: 215
Percent Fat Calories: 0%
Carbohydrate: 42 grams
Protein: 11 grams

Total Fat: 0 grams
Cholesterol: 0 mg
Dietary Fiber: 2 grams
Sodium: 468 mg

Total time: 7 minutes.

2nd Serving Busy People's Low Fat Cookbook

Menu Ideas:
Fruit cup or orange slices.
Coffee or herbal tea.

OMELETS

A hearty breakfast that is good for the heart!

4 egg whites plus 2 drops yellow food coloring (or ½ cup Egg Beaters)
½ teaspoon dry Butter Buds Sprinkles (or Molly McButter Sprinkles)

1 tablespoon skim milk
dash of lite salt
dash of pepper
1 slice fat-free cheese - your favorite flavor (I use Kraft or Kroger brand)

♥ With a fork, beat all ingredients (except cheese) until well blended but not frothy or foamy.

♥ Spray a 6- to 8-inch non-stick skillet with non-fat cooking spray. Add egg mixture and cook over medium heat.

♥ As eggs set, run a spatula along the outside edge of where the eggs touch the skillet, lifting the eggs just enough to let the uncooked egg mixture flow underneath. When eggs are set but still shiny, remove from heat.

♥ Place cheese slice on half of the omelet. Fold the other half of the omelet over. (Onto the first half with the cheese on it.) Cover for one minute to allow the heat of the omelet to melt cheese.

Yield: 1 omelet

Calories: 90
Cholesterol: 0 mg

Total Fat: 0 grams (0% fat)
Sodium: 392 mg

Preparation time: 2 minutes or less.

Cooking time: 3 minutes or less.

Total time: 5 minutes or less.

Busy People's Low-Fat Cookbook

Menu Ideas: Fat-free toast and fresh fruit cup.

(Omelets continued on next page)

(Omelets continued)

Ham & Cheese Omelet:

Microwave 1 ounce of fat-free ham lunchmeat, chopped, for 10 seconds (or until warm). Place cooked ham pieces over cheese before folding in half.

Yield: 1 omelet

Calories: 111   Total Fat: 0 grams (0% fat)
Cholesterol: 9 mg   Sodium: 706 mg

FRENCH TOAST

A sweet tooth breakfast favorite.

1   cup Egg Beaters (or 8 egg   ⅔ cup skim milk
    whites with a couple drops   8   slices fat-free bread (I use
    of yellow food coloring)   Aunt Millie)

♥ Spray a non-stick skillet or griddle with non-fat cooking spray and preheat to medium-high heat.

♥ With a fork, briskly beat Egg Beaters (or egg whites with yellow food coloring) with skim milk until well mixed.

♥ Dip bread slices (one at a time) into egg mixture.

♥ Arrange dipped bread slices on prepared griddle (or skillet) making sure edges of bread do not touch. Cook until bottom is golden brown. Turn over and continue cooking until golden brown. Serve hot (2 slices per serving) with 1 teaspoon powdered sugar, 1 tablespoon light maple syrup, and up to 10 sprays of "I Can't Believe It's Not Butter" Spray.

Yield: 4 servings

Calories: 185   Total Fat: 0 grams (0% fat)
Cholesterol: 1 mg   Sodium: 444 mg

Preparation time: 7 minutes or less.

Busy People's Low-Fat Cookbook

FRENCH TOAST STICKS

*My children like the high fat version of these at
fast food restaurants. So I created my own just as yummy
and fun to eat, but a whole lot healthier.*

12 slices thick-sliced Texas
toast bread (any thick-
sliced white bread)
2/3 cup skim milk

2 (4-ounce) containers Egg
Beaters (or 8 egg whites
with a couple of drops
yellow food coloring)

♥ Preheat a nonstick griddle to 400 degrees or nonstick skillet to high heat. Spray with non-fat cooking spray.

♥ Cut each slice of bread into 3 strips. Set aside.

♥ In a mixing bowl, mix Egg Beaters and skim milk together until well blended.

♥ Lightly dip the bread sticks (one at a time) into egg mixture.

♥ Cook on hot griddle until bottoms are toasty brown. Turn a quarter turn until all 4 sides of the French toast stick are cooked.

♥ Serve with lite maple syrup on the side for dipping.

This finger food is easy to clean-up after.

Yield: 12 (3-piece) servings

Calories: 134
Percent Fat Calories: 11%
Carbohydrate: 23 grams
Protein: 6 grams

Total Fat: 2 grams
Cholesterol: 1 mg
Dietary Fiber: 1 gram
Sodium: 280 mg

Preparation time: 15 minutes or less.

2nd Serving Busy People's Low Fat Cookbook

Menu Ideas: Orange juice or a fruit cup.

Cinnamon French Toast Sticks: Make exactly the same as French Toast Sticks but also add 1 teaspoon ground cinnamon to the egg mixture. Stir until well mixed.

Note: Same nutritional information as French Toast Sticks.

BREAKFAST ON A STICK

These can be baked ahead of time and frozen. Then just pop one into the microwave and heat for 30 to 60 seconds for a healthy breakfast on the run.

7 popsicle sticks
1 (14-ounce) package fat-free smoked sausage (Butterball)
1 cup reduced-fat Bisquick baking mix

1 tablespoon sugar
⅓ cup skim milk
2 egg whites
½ teaspoon vanilla

♥ Preheat oven to 450 degrees.

♥ Spray a cookie sheet with non-fat cooking spray.

♥ Cut sausage into 7 (2-ounce) pieces.

♥ Insert one popsicle stick into each sausage. Set aside.

♥ Mix together Bisquick, sugar, milk, egg whites and vanilla until dough is well blended.

♥ With hands (sprayed with non-fat cooking spray) completely coat each sausage with dough.

♥ Bake on prepared cookie sheets for 8 to 10 minutes or until golden brown.

Yield: 7 servings

Calories: 140
Percent Fat Calories: 7%
Carbohydrate: 20 grams
Protein: 11 grams

Total Fat: 1 gram
Cholesterol: 25 mg
Dietary Fiber: 0 grams
Sodium: 886 mg

Preparation time: 14 minutes.

2nd Serving Busy People's Low Fat Cookbook

Menu Ideas: Orange juice or a fruit cup.

BREAKFAST PIZZA

A great way to start the day!

1 (10-ounce) can prepared pizza crust (Pillsbury - found in the dairy section)

1 cup finely chopped fully-cooked lean ham

2 cups shredded fat-free Swiss or mozzarella cheese (Kraft)

½ cup Egg Beaters

1 (12-ounce) container fat-free sour cream

½ cup chopped fresh or frozen onion

♥ Preheat oven to 425 degrees.

♥ Spray an 11 × 17-inch jelly-roll pan with non-fat cooking spray.

♥ With hands, spread dough to edge of pan. Arrange ham and cheese over crust. In a medium bowl, beat Egg Beaters, sour cream and onions together with a spoon until well blended.

♥ Pour over pizza.

♥ Bake 17 to 20 minutes or until pizza crust is golden brown.

Yield: 8 entrée servings

Calories: 201
Percent Fat Calories: 9%
Carbohydrate: 25 grams
Protein: 18 grams

Total Fat: 2 grams
Cholesterol: 16 mg
Dietary Fiber: 1 gram
Sodium: 701 mg

Total time: 27 to 30 minutes or less.

2nd Serving Busy People's Low Fat Cookbook

Menu Ideas: Serve with fresh fruit salad or alone with a glass of juice.

CITRUS PANCAKES

A tasty twist to an old time favorite.

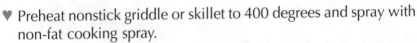

2 egg whites
1¼ cups orange juice
2 cups reduced-fat
  Bisquick baking mix

36 sprays I Can't Believe
  It's Not Butter
1 tablespoon plus 1 teaspoon
  powdered sugar

♥ Preheat nonstick griddle or skillet to 400 degrees and spray with non-fat cooking spray.

♥ In a medium bowl, beat egg whites and orange juice together until well blended.

♥ Stir in Bisquick mix. Batter may be lumpy.

♥ Pour ¼ cup batter onto prepared griddle (or skillet).

♥ Cook until top of pancake is covered with bubbles and edges look dry.

♥ Turn pancake over and cook other side just until lightly browned.

♥ Serve with 9 sprays of I Can't Believe It's Not Butter and 1 teaspoon powdered sugar per serving.

Yield: 4 (3-pancake) servings

Calories: 280
Percent Fat Calories: 13%
Carbohydrate: 53 grams
Protein: 7 grams

Total Fat: 4 grams
Cholesterol: 0 mg
Dietary Fiber: 1 gram
Sodium: 725 mg

Total time: 15 minutes or less.

2nd Serving Busy People's Low Fat Cookbook

Menu Ideas: Scrambled eggs (made with Egg Beaters) and skim milk.

BREAKFAST SCRAMBLE

Don't limit this great entrée to only breakfast . . . it's hearty enough for dinner! Great for brunch, too!

2 tablespoons fat-free, reduced-sodium chicken broth
1 pound frozen fat-free hash browns
8 ounces extra lean honey smoked ham (from the deli)

½ cup frozen chopped onion (or ½ medium onion - chopped)
1 cup Egg Beaters
1 tablespoon fresh chives - chopped
1 cup shredded fat-free cheddar cheese (Kraft)

♥ Spray a nonstick 12-inch skillet with non-fat cooking spray.

♥ Combine chicken broth, hash browns, ham and onion in skillet.

♥ Cover and cook over medium heat for 10 minutes or until potatoes are tender, stirring frequently.

♥ Add Egg Beaters and chives. Cook, stirring frequently, until eggs are fully cooked.

♥ Remove from heat and gently stir in cheese.

Yield: 4 servings

Calories: 246
Percent Fat Calories: 13%
Carbohydrate: 24 grams
Protein: 28 grams

Total Fat: 4 grams
Cholesterol: 32 mg
Dietary Fiber: 2 grams
Sodium: 1173 mg

Preparation time: 20 minutes or less.

2nd Serving Busy People's Low Fat Cookbook

Menu Ideas: Orange juice or fresh fruit cup, and ½ of an English Muffin with jam.

(Breakfast Scramble continued on next page)

(Breakfast Scramble continued)

Southwestern Breakfast Scramble: Follow Breakfast Scramble recipe exactly, except omit the chives and onions. Once completely cooked, heat one cup of your favorite salsa in the microwave for one minute (or until fully heated). Pour ¼ cup salsa over each serving.

Yield: 4 servings

Calories: 258
Percent Fat Calories: 13%
Carbohydrate: 25 grams
Protein: 28 grams

Total Fat: 4 grams
Cholesterol: 32 mg
Dietary Fiber: 2 grams
Sodium: 1452 mg

Italian Breakfast Scramble: Follow Breakfast Scramble recipe exactly except omit chives. Once completely cooked, heat one cup of your favorite fat-free spaghetti sauce in the microwave for one minute (or until fully heated). Pour ¼ cup spaghetti sauce over each serving. (I use Ragu Light pasta sauce.)

Yield: 4 servings

Calories: 267
Percent Fat Calories: 12%
Carbohydrate: 29 grams
Protein: 29 grams

Total Fat: 4 grams
Cholesterol: 32 mg
Dietary Fiber: 3 grams
Sodium: 1368 mg

Breakfast Parfait

This is one of my all time favorites! Good anytime of the day!

1 (8-ounce) container fat-free yogurt - any flavor (I like strawberry)

1 small banana - cut into thin slices
½ cup 98% fat-free granola (I use Health Valley)

♥ Spoon half of the yogurt into the bottom of two pretty parfait glasses. (If you don't have parfait glasses, any wide mouthed glass will be fine as long as it holds 10 ounces.)

♥ Top with half the banana slices.

♥ Sprinkle half the granola on top of bananas.

♥ Repeat layers with remaining yogurt, banana slices and granola.

♥ If you like, save a little yogurt to top off each dessert.

Yield: 2 (1¼-cup) servings

Calories: 197
Percent Fat Calories: 0%
Carbohydrate: 43 grams
Protein: 7 grams

Total Fat: 0 grams
Cholesterol: 3 mg
Dietary Fiber: 3 grams
Sodium: 104 mg

Total time: 5 minutes.

2nd Serving Busy People's Low Fat Cookbook

Menu Ideas: A meal in itself.

Breakfast Burrito

Move over McDonalds! I've created my own breakfast burrito that's fast and easy to prepare. It's delicious and a lot lower in fat and calories than yours. (These can be made in advance, refrigerated, and rewarmed in the microwave when needed.)

½ pound Healthy Choice
   kielbasa - diced into tiny
   pieces
8 egg whites
¼ cup chunky salsa

½ cup fat-free fancy shredded
   cheddar cheese (I use
   Healthy Choice)
10 fat-free soft flour tortillas
   (I use Buena Vida)

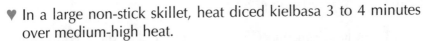

♥ In a large non-stick skillet, heat diced kielbasa 3 to 4 minutes over medium-high heat.

♥ Beat egg whites and chunky salsa together. Cook egg-salsa mixture with kielbasa as you would scrambled eggs, stirring every 30 seconds. When eggs are completely cooked, yet still slightly damp, stir in cheddar cheese. Cook about 30 seconds more to melt cheese.

♥ Microwave tortillas 10 to 30 seconds or until soft and warm.

♥ Fill the middle of each tortilla with the prepared egg mixture. Fold as you would a burrito. Presto! You're done!

Yield: 10 servings

Calories: 163
Cholesterol: 9 mg

Total Fat: 0.6 grams (3% fat)
Sodium: 649 mg

Total time: 10 minutes or less.

Busy People's Low-Fat Cookbook

Menu Ideas: Orange, coffee or tea.

CINNAMON ROLLS (MINI SIZE)

These cinnamon rolls aren't too sweet, they're just right!

1 (10-ounce) can Pillsbury Pizza Crust (found in refrigerator section - just unroll)
2 tablespoons 70% Low-Fat Promise margarine (3 grams fat per tablespoon, not the Fat-Free Ultra Promise)

⅓ cup sugar
2 teaspoons ground cinnamon
1 tablespoon low-fat vanilla frosting (I use Betty Crocker)

♥ Preheat oven to 375 degrees.

♥ Spray a jelly roll pan (17 × 11-inch cookie sheet with 1-inch edge) with non-fat cooking spray.

♥ Roll dough out in jelly roll pan. Press dough out with hands until dough touches edges of pan.

♥ Microwave margarine until melted.

♥ Drizzle melted margarine over dough. With fingertips spread melted margarine over dough evenly.

♥ Mix sugar and cinnamon together and sprinkle ⅔ of the sugar-cinnamon mixture over melted margarine.

♥ Roll up dough, (jelly roll style) beginning from the longest side.

♥ With fingers, pinch the seam of the dough to seal.

♥ Cut into 12 pieces. This is easy to do with a scissors.

♥ Spray 12 mini muffin tins with non-fat cooking spray. (Regular size muffin tins work fine also).

♥ Place one mini roll into each muffin tin.

♥ Sprinkle remaining sugar-cinnamon mixture evenly on tops.

♥ Bake at 375 degrees for 15 minutes.

(Cinnamon Rolls (mini size) continued on next page)

(Cinnamon Rolls (mini size) continued)

♥ Microwave frosting for a few seconds and immediately drizzle frosting lightly on top of cinnamon rolls.

♥ Let cool one to two minutes before eating.

Yield: 12 servings

Calories: 99
Cholesterol: 0 mg

Total Fat: 2.8 grams (25% fat)
Sodium: 148 mg

Preparation time: 10 minutes or less.

Baking time: 15 minutes or less.

Total time: 25 minutes or less.

Busy People's Low-Fat Cookbook

Menu ideas: Brunch, breakfast buffets, showers, or special holidays.

BREAKFAST SANDWICH

2 egg whites
1 Aunt Millie's Lite fat-free
  Potato Hamburger Bun

1 ounce Canadian bacon
1 slice fat-free cheddar
  cheese (I use Kraft Free)
  Pepper to taste, if desired

♥ Spray griddle and a biscuit cutter with non-fat cooking spray. Beat egg whites. Put biscuit cutter onto griddle. Pour eggs into biscuit cutter. Spray insides of hamburger buns with non-fat cooking spray and brown the buns on griddle. Warm bacon slices on griddle. Cut cheese slice in half and lay on top of bacon slices being warmed on the griddle. Once everything is cooked, lay bacon slices with cheese on bottom part of the browned hamburger bun. Lay cooked egg on top of bacon and cheese. Sprinkle with pepper, if desired. Put top of hamburger bun on bottom, and presto! Breakfast!! (Some people like mustard on this sandwich.)

Yield: 1 serving

Calories: 220
Percent Fat Calories: 8%
Carbohydrate: 24 grams
Protein: 25 grams

Total Fat: 2 grams
Cholesterol: 19 mg
Dietary Fiber: 1 gram
Sodium: 927 mg

Preparation time: 25 minutes.

Down Home Cookin'

STICKY BREAKFAST BAGELS

8 ounces fat-free margarine
 (I use Ultra Promise)
½ teaspoon vanilla

1 cup brown sugar
2 teaspoons cinnamon
1 dozen bagels, cut in half

♥ Put margarine, vanilla, brown sugar, and cinnamon into blender and blend on medium speed for 1 minute. Take bagel halves and dip top with spread just prepared. If needed, spread with knife. Broil for 4 to 5 minutes, or until bubbly and brown. Serve warm.

Yield: 12 servings

Calories: 272
Percent Fat Calories: 4%
Carbohydrate: 56 grams
Protein: 8 grams

Total Fat: 1 gram
Cholesterol: 0 mg
Dietary Fiber: 2 grams
Sodium: 508 mg

Preparation time: 8-10 minutes.

Down Home Cookin'

BROCCOLI, HAM & CHEESE FRITTATA

This hearty frittata is good for breakfast, lunch or dinner!

¼ cup finely chopped red onion (or ¼ cup frozen chopped onion)
½ pound turkey ham, chopped
¾ (12 to 16-ounce) bag frozen broccoli
9 egg whites

2 drops yellow food coloring
½ cup fat-free fancy shredded cheddar cheese (I use Healthy Choice)
Dash of Lawry's seasoned salt - optional

♥ Preheat oven to 350 degrees.

♥ Spray a large skillet with non-fat cooking spray. (A teflon non-stick skillet works best but is not necessary).

♥ Cook onion and ham 2 to 3 minutes over medium heat. Microwave broccoli 3 minutes. Beat egg whites and yellow food coloring about 100 strokes. Put broccoli into pan with ham and onion. Pour eggs over mixture in pan. Cook on low heat for 3 minutes.

♥ Sprinkle with cheese. Spray non-fat cooking spray over cheese. (It helps the cheese to not get tough or chewy and makes it melt better.)

♥ Bake at 350 degrees about 5 to 8 minutes or until eggs are fully cooked. Sprinkle with Lawry's seasoned salt if desired. Serve hot. Cut frittata into thirds.

Yield: 3 servings

Calories: 193
Cholesterol: 57 mg

Total Fat: 3.4 grams (16% fat)
Sodium: 1168 mg

Preparation time: 6 minutes.

Cooking time: 14 minutes or less.

Total time: 20 minutes or less.

Busy People's Low-Fat Cookbook

Menu Ideas: Great for breakfast, brunch or lunch. Serve with fat-free toast, jam and fresh melon.

MAN-HANDLER BREAKFAST BAKE

This is an excellent "whip it up fast" entree that is perfect for a hearty breakfast or brunch, without numerous pans and skillets!

3 (8-ounce) cartons Egg Beaters (I use Kroger Break-Free)
1 (8-ounce) package Kroger Healthy Indulgence fat-free shredded pizza cheese (a blend of non-fat mozzarella and non-fat cheddar cheese)
½ pound Canadian bacon, thinly sliced and cut into bite-size pieces (Oscar Mayer 93% Fat-Free)
1 (7.5-ounce) can Pillsbury buttermilk biscuits (10 biscuits per roll)

♥ Preheat oven to 350 degrees.

♥ Spray a 9 × 13-inch pan with non-fat cooking spray.

♥ In a bowl, mix Egg Beaters, cheese and Canadian bacon. Set aside.

♥ Arrange biscuits on bottom of prepared pan.

♥ Pour egg mixture over biscuits. (You may need to press the biscuits down so they are covered with the egg, cheese and Canadian bacon mixture.)

♥ Bake at 350 degrees for 30 minutes or until knife inserted In center comes out clean. Serve hot.

♥ If desired, sprinkle sparingly with lite salt.

Yield: 6 large servings

Calories: 243
Cholesterol: 24 mg
Total Fat: 2.5 grams (10% fat)
Sodium: 1310 mg

Preparation time: 5 minutes or less.

Baking time: 30 minutes.

Total time: 35 minutes or less.

Busy People's Low-Fat Cookbook

Menu Ideas: Fruit cup, skim milk, coffee or tea.

MUSHROOM AND ONION FRITTATA

Terrific for breakfast, brunch, lunch or dinner!
Taste like a thin, crustless quiche.

1 cup chopped onion (for faster preparation, I use frozen chopped onion)

8 ounces fresh mushrooms - sliced (for faster preparation I buy the pre-cut from the produce section)

2 teaspoons minced garlic (I use the kind in a jar)

½ teaspoon dried basil - crushed

2 tablespoons Butter Buds Sprinkles -dry

1 cup Egg Beaters

1 tablespoon Kraft Free grated Parmesan cheese topping

♥ Preheat oven to 450 degrees.

♥ Spray nonstick 12-inch skillet with non-fat cooking spray.

♥ Over high heat cook onion, mushrooms, garlic and basil until fully cooked, about 3 to 4 minutes. Stir frequently.

♥ Once fully cooked, stir in Butter Buds.

♥ Pour Egg Beaters over cooked mixture. Cook for one minute.

♥ Put entire pan into oven. Bake, uncovered, for 4 to 5 minutes or until fully set. Sprinkle with Kraft free non-fat grated topping.

♥ Invert frittata onto a large serving plate. (A cake plate works well).

Yield: 4 servings

Calories: 75
Percent Fat Calories: 0%
Carbohydrate: 12 grams
Protein: 8 grams

Total Fat: 0 grams
Cholesterol: 0 mg
Dietary Fiber: 1 gram
Sodium: 312 mg

Preparation time: 10 minutes or less.

2nd Serving Busy People's Low Fat Cookbook

Menu Ideas: Fresh sliced tomatoes and English muffins.

HONEY BUTTER

Delightfully tasty! A great spread for toasted bagels or toasted raisin bread.

1 (8-ounce) container fat-free Ultra Promise margarine

¼ cup honey
¼ cup powdered sugar

♥ Beat all ingredients together until fluffy and well blended.

Yield: 21 (1-tablespoon) servings

Calories: 22
Percent Fat Calories: 0%
Carbohydrate: 5 grams
Protein: 0 grams

Total Fat: 0 grams
Cholesterol: 0 mg
Dietary Fiber: 0 grams
Sodium: 70 mg

Preparation time: 5 minutes or less.

2nd Serving Busy People's Low Fat Cookbook

Menu Ideas: Great on toast or used as a glaze over cooked carrots or peas.

CINNAMON DROPS

Move over traditional fatty cinnamon rolls,
Cinnamon Drops are here!

½ cup sugar
2 tablespoons ground cinnamon
2 (7.5-ounce) cans Pillsbury buttermilk biscuits (10 per roll - found in refrigerator section)

¼ cup Fleischmann's Fat-Free Buttery Spread
2 tablespoons low-fat frosting (Betty Crocker Creamy Deluxe) - optional

♥ Preheat oven to 350 degrees.

♥ Spray a 9 × 13-inch pan with non-fat cooking spray.

♥ Mix sugar and cinnamon together in a cereal bowl. Set aside.

♥ Cut each biscuit into quarters.

♥ Put a little dab of buttery spread on each biscuit piece. Coat with cinnamon-sugar mixture.

♥ Set coated dough pieces in prepared pan with pieces touching each other. Some overlapping will occur. If there is any leftover cinnamon-sugar, sprinkle it over dough in pan.

♥ Bake at 350 degrees for 15 minutes.

♥ Optional - Microwave frosting a few seconds, just long enough to melt frosting into a glaze. Drizzle glaze over cinnamon drops. Let cool a couple of minutes before eating.

Yield: 7 breakfast entree servings

Calories: 236
Cholesterol: 0 mg

Total Fat: 2.8 grams (10% fat)
Sodium: 525 mg

16 side dish servings

Calories: 103
Cholesterol: 0 mg

Total Fat: 1.2 grams (10% fat)
Sodium: 230 mg

Total time: 20 minutes or less.

Busy People's Low-Fat Cookbook

CHEESE FILLED SOFT BREAD STICKS

*This recipe turns ordinary biscuits
into extraordinary baked goods.*

1 (7.5-ounce) can Pillsbury
buttermilk biscuits
2 slices sharp cheddar
Kraft Free singles - each
slice cut into 5 strips

¼ cup shredded Parmesan
cheese (I use Kraft) -
chopped into tiny pieces
Garlic salt - optional

♥ Preheat oven to 425 degrees.

♥ Spray a cookie sheet with non-fat cooking spray.

♥ Make each bread **individually** as follows:

Roll biscuit into a 3½-inch to 4-inch length by 1-inch width.

Lay one cheese strip down the center of biscuit. Wrap biscuit around cheese slice. Pinch dough at seam to seal seam closed.

Press top of bread stick into Parmesan cheese.

♥ Place bread sticks on prepared cookie sheet, Parmesan cheese side up. If desired, sprinkle lightly with garlic salt.

♥ Bake at 425 degrees for 7 minutes or until tops are light golden brown.

Yield: 10 bread sticks

Calories: 69
Percent Fat Calories: 20%
Carbohydrate: 10 grams
Protein: 3 grams

Total Fat: 2 grams
Cholesterol: 2 mg
Dietary Fiber: 0 grams
Sodium: 270 mg

Total time: 15 minutes or less.

2nd Serving Busy People's Low Fat Cookbook

Menu Ideas: Any Italian meal.

GARLIC TOAST

Perfect for fast and easy meals that aren't fancy.

1 slice fat-free wheat, white, potato or sourdough bread (Aunt Millie or Wonder)

5 sprays "I Can't Believe It's Not Butter" spray
Garlic salt
Dried parsley - optional

♥ Toast slice of bread to desired darkness in toaster.

♥ Spray one side of toast with 5 sprays of "I Can't Believe It's Not Butter".

♥ Sprinkle lightly with garlic salt, then with dried parsley if desired.

Yield: 1 serving

Calories: 71
Cholesterol: 0 mg

Total Fat: 0 grams (0% fat)
Sodium: 161 mg

Preparation time: 3 minutes or less.

Busy People's Low-Fat Cookbook

Menu Ideas: Great with any Italian entrée.

PINWHEEL DINNER ROLLS

As visually pretty as they are delicious!

1 (10 ounce) can Pillsbury pizza crust dough
52 sprays "I Can't Believe It's Not Butter" spray

1 teaspoon garlic salt
1 tablespoon dried parsley - crushed

♥ Preheat oven to 425 degrees.

♥ Spray a cookie sheet with non-fat cooking spray.

♥ Unroll dough and press out to ¼-inch thickness onto cookie sheet.

♥ Spray 40 sprays of "I Can't Believe It's Not Butter" evenly over dough.

♥ Sprinkle garlic salt and parsley evenly on top.

♥ Roll dough up (jelly roll style) starting from the long side of the dough.

♥ Pinch seam of dough once completely rolled to seal.

♥ Cut into 12 pieces, making 12 pinwheels.

♥ Set each pinwheel so that you can see the pinwheel on top of the prepared cookie sheet.

♥ Bake at 425 degrees for 8-10 minutes or until golden brown.

♥ Spray tops of each roll with one spray of "I Can't Believe It's Not Butter" before serving.

Yield: 12 rolls

Calories: 54
Cholesterol: 0 mg

Total Fat: 0.7 grams (12% fat)
Sodium: 271 mg

Preparation time: 5 minutes or less.

Cooking time: 10 minutes or less.

Total time: 15 minutes or less.

Busy People's Low-Fat Cookbook

Menu Ideas: Serve with your favorite main entrée.

CHEESE BISCUITS

*I got this recipe idea from a favorite seafood restaurant.
Betcha' don't have the slightest idea what restaurant
that could be, do you? These are not half as fattening,
but don't let that fool you . . . these babies are delicious!*

2 cups skim milk	2 teaspoons garlic salt
1 (8-ounce) package Healthy Choice fat-free fancy shredded cheddar cheese	5 cups reduced-fat Bisquick baking mix
2 tablespoons dry Butter Buds Sprinkles	48 sprays "I Can't Believe It's Not Butter" spray

♥ Preheat oven to 350 degrees.

♥ Spray 2 cookie sheets with non-fat cooking spray. Set aside.

♥ In a large mixing bowl, pour milk over cheese and let sit for 3 minutes.

♥ Add Butter Buds and garlic salt to milk, stirring until they are dissolved.

♥ Stir in Bisquick. Dough will become very stiff. At the end of stirring you may find it easier to finish mixing with your hands. Keep mixing until there is no Bisquick on bottom or sides of bowl.

♥ Drop by rounded tablespoonfuls onto prepared cookie sheets. (This is easiest to do with two spoons. Using a measuring tablespoon get a rounded tablespoon of dough. Push dough off spoon with second spoon.)

♥ Bake at 350 degrees for 15 to 17 minutes or until tops are golden brown. Spray each biscuit with 2 sprays of "I Can't Believe It's Not Butter" before serving.

Yield: 24 (1-biscuit) servings

Calories: 117	Total Fat: 1.6 grams (13% fat)
Cholesterol: 1 mg	Sodium: 531 mg

Preparation time: 5 minutes.

Baking time: 15-17 minutes.

Total time: 22 minutes or less.

Busy People's Low-Fat Cookbook

TOMATO BISCUITS

No ho-hum biscuit when you pop this baby in your mouth!

1 (7½-ounce) can Pillsbury buttermilk biscuits
⅓ cup Kraft Free non-fat grated topping

½ medium ripe tomato - cut into ¼-inch quartered slices (10 pieces total)
¼ cup grated Parmesan cheese
Garlic salt - optional

♥ Preheat oven to 425 degrees.

♥ Line cookie sheet with aluminum foil.

♥ Spray foil with non-fat cooking spray. Set aside.

♥ Cut tomato into 3 (¼-inch thick) slices. Cut each slice into pie-shaped quarters. Set aside. (There will be 2 quartered slices remaining, discard these.)

♥ Press each biscuit individually into the Kraft non-fat grated topping and place on prepared cookie sheet.

♥ Arrange 1 quartered tomato slice on each biscuit.

♥ Sprinkle grated Parmesan cheese evenly over all tomato biscuits.

♥ Sprinkle lightly with garlic salt if desired.

♥ Bake at 425 degrees for 10 to 13 minutes or until golden brown.

♥ Serve immediately.

Yield: 10 biscuits

Calories: 72
Cholesterol: 5 mg

Total Fat: 1.6 grams (19% fat)
Sodium: 236 mg

Preparation time: 10 minutes.

Baking time: 10 minutes.

Total time: 20 minutes or less.

Busy People's Low-Fat Cookbook

Menu Ideas: These would taste great with Spicy, Thick Vegetarian Chili, or any Italian entrée.

BACON BISCUITS

The light, smoky flavor of these yummy biscuits are good for breakfast, brunch or dinner.

2 cups reduced-fat Bisquick baking mix
½ cup skim milk
¼ cup applesauce
2 egg whites

1 cup finely shredded fat-free cheddar cheese (I use Kraft)
1 (3-ounce) jar real bacon bits (I use Hormel)

♥ Preheat oven to 375 degrees.

♥ Spray a cookie sheet with non-fat cooking spray.

♥ Mix all ingredients together until well blended.

♥ Drop by rounded tablespoonfuls onto prepared cookie sheet.

♥ Bake for 10 to 12 minutes or until golden brown.

Yield: 24 biscuits

Calories: 62
Percent Fat Calories: 19%
Carbohydrate: 8 grams
Protein: 4 grams

Total Fat: 1 gram
Cholesterol: 3 mg
Dietary Fiber: 0 grams
Sodium: 273 mg

Total time: 17 minutes or less.

2nd Serving Busy People's Low Fat Cookbook

Menu Ideas: Tastes good with any entrée.

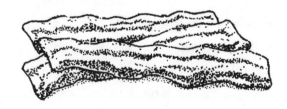

MUSHROOM PINWHEEL BISCUITS

These are extra special, for extra special meals.

1 (10-ounce) can prepared pizza dough (Pillsbury)

½ cup finely shredded Parmesan cheese

¾ cup finely chopped fresh mushrooms

1 tablespoon dried parsley

♥ Preheat oven to 425 degrees.

♥ Spray an 11 × 17-inch cookie sheet with non-fat cooking spray.

♥ Roll pizza dough out and press dough with hands to edges of prepared cookie sheet.

♥ Sprinkle cheese, mushrooms and parsley over dough.

♥ Roll up jelly-roll style (starting on the long side). Pinch dough at edge to seal seam.

♥ With a very sharp knife carefully cut into 12 slices.

♥ Carefully place pinwheels on prepared cookie sheet with each biscuit laying flat on its side, so you can see the pinwheel on top. Arrange pinwheels as you would when baking a dozen cookies, so that sides do not touch.

♥ Bake at 425 degrees for 8 minutes or until tops are golden brown.

Yield: 12 biscuits

Calories: 74
Percent Fat Calories: 24%
Carbohydrate: 10 grams
Protein: 4 grams

Total Fat: 2 grams
Cholesterol: 3 mg
Dietary Fiber: 0 grams
Sodium: 198 mg

Preparation time: 15 minutes.

2nd Serving Busy People's Low Fat Cookbook

Menu Idea: Any special meal.

PARMESAN BISCUITS

Excellent!

2 tablespoons Butter Bud Sprinkles - dry (found in spice or diet section of grocery store)
¼ cup finely shredded Parmesan cheese

½ teaspoon Italian seasoning (found in spice section)
Non-fat cooking spray
1 (7.5-ounce) can Pillsbury buttermilk biscuits

♥ Preheat oven to 425 degrees.

♥ Spray a cookie sheet with non-fat cooking spray.

♥ Mix Butter Buds, cheese and Italian seasoning together in a 1-gallon zip-lock bag.

♥ Spray both sides of biscuits lightly with non-fat cooking spray.

♥ Put biscuits in bag and shake gently until biscuits are coated with mixture.

♥ Place on prepared cookie sheet.

♥ Sprinkle remaining crumb mixture on top of biscuits.

♥ Bake on the top shelf of oven at 425 degrees for 8 minutes or until golden brown.

Yield: 10 biscuits

Calories: 66
Percent Fat Calories: 20%
Carbohydrate: 11 grams
Protein: 3 grams

Total Fat: 2 grams
Cholesterol: 2 mg
Dietary Fiber: 0 grams
Sodium: 284 mg

Total time: 13 minutes or less.

2nd Serving Busy People's Low Fat Cookbook

Menu Ideas: Any dinner, especially Italian foods, such as lasagna or spaghetti.

Best of
BUSY PEOPLE'S
Cookbooks

BY DAWN
HALL

SUPER
EASY SOUPS,
SALADS AND
SANDWICHES

Low Fat Recipes
from 3 AWARD-WINNING
COOKBOOKS

Tomato Bisque (Soup)

1 (26-ounce) can condensed tomato soup (Campbell's)
13 ounces water
(½ of soup can)

1 (14.5-ounce) can no-salt-added diced tomatoes (or 3 plum tomatoes, skinned and chopped)
1 cup fat-free half & half (I use Land O Lakes)

♥ Put all ingredients in a big soup pan. Bring to a low boil, stirring constantly until well blended.

♥ Serve hot.

Yield: 7 (1-cup) servings

Calories: 102
Percent Fat Calories: 0%
Carbohydrate: 22 grams
Protein: 5 grams

Total Fat: 0 grams
Cholesterol: 0 mg
Dietary Fiber: 2 grams
Sodium: 660 mg

Total time: 5 minutes or less.

2nd Serving Busy People's Low Fat Cook Book

Menu Ideas: Grilled cheese (low-fat of course).

UNSTUFFED
GREEN PEPPER SOUP

If you like stuffed green peppers, you'll like this!

½ pound ground beef eye of round

3 cups Health Valley fat-free, no-salt-added beef broth (or made with bouillon)

2 cups low-sodium V8 juice (or three 5.5-ounce cans)

2 (14.5-ounce) cans no-salt-added stewed tomatoes

1 cup frozen or fresh chopped green peppers

1 cup frozen or fresh chopped onion

1 cup instant rice

Stovetop Method:

♥ Bring everything, except rice, to a boil over high heat in a large, nonstick soup pan.

♥ Let boil 2 minutes, stirring occasionally.

♥ Turn off heat. Stir in rice. Cover and let sit for 5 minutes.

♥ Serve hot.

♥ If desired, season with ground black pepper to taste.

Crockpot Method:

♥ Put all ingredients, except rice, in a large crockpot.

♥ Stir until well mixed. Cover.

♥ Cook on low for 8 to 10 hours or on high for 4 to 5 hours.

♥ Before serving, stir in rice. Cover and let sit 5 minutes.

♥ Serve hot.

Yield: 8 (1-cup) servings

Calories: 144
Percent Fat Calories: 8%
Carbohydrate: 21 grams
Protein: 11 grams

Total Fat: 1 gram
Cholesterol: 15 mg
Dietary Fiber: 3 grams
Sodium: 92 mg

Total time: 15 minutes.

2nd Serving Busy People's Low Fat Cook Book

Menu Ideas: Sourdough or French bread.

MINESTRONE SOUP

Hearty and healthy! Just the way we like it!

1 (46-ounce) can tomato juice
1 pound beef eye of round - cut into tiny pieces
1 (14-ounce) jar of your favorite pizza sauce (I use Ragu' Family Style)

3 (15.25-ounce) cans mixed vegetables - do not drain
1 (15-ounce) can red kidney beans - do not drain
2 (14.5-ounce) cans no-salt-added stewed tomatoes - do not drain
2 cups dry elbow macaroni

♥ In a large, nonstick soup pan, bring all ingredients, except macaroni, to a full boil over high heat.

♥ Stir in elbow macaroni. Return to a boil. Cook, uncovered, stirring frequently for 8 minutes.

Yield: 18 (1-cup servings)

Calories: 157
Percent Fat Calories: 10%
Carbohydrate: 25 grams
Protein: 11 grams

Total Fat: 2 grams
Cholesterol: 14 mg
Dietary Fiber: 6 grams
Sodium: 617 mg

Total time: 30 minutes or less.

2nd Serving Busy People's Low Fat Cook Book

Menu Ideas: Garlic Bread or Garlic Toast

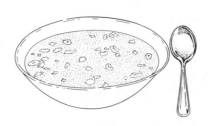

WORLD'S EASIEST VEGETABLE SOUP

Nothin' like a hot bowl of soup on a cold wintry day.

1 (46-ounce) can V8 vegetable juice
4 cups Health Valley fat-free, no-salt-added beef broth (or made from beef bouillon)
4 (15.25-ounce) cans mixed vegetables - drained
1 teaspoon salad seasoning spices (I use Durkee - found in seasoning aisle)

Stovetop Method:

♥ Bring all ingredients to a boil over high heat in a large, nonstick soup pan.

♥ If desired mash soup in pot for a few minutes by hand with a potato masher to make soup a little thicker. Serve hot.

Crockpot Method:

♥ Mix all ingredients in a 6-quart or larger crockpot.

♥ Cook on low for 4 hours or on high for 2 hours.

Yield: 16 (1-cup) servings

Calories: 60	Total Fat: 0 grams
Percent Fat Calories: 0%	Cholesterol: 0 mg
Carbohydrate: 11 grams	Dietary Fiber: 3 grams
Protein: 4 grams	Sodium: 375 mg

Total time: 15 minutes or less.

Total time: 25 minutes or less, including 10 minutes to cut meat.

Beef Vegetable Soup: Make exactly as World's Easiest Vegetable Soup and add 2 pounds of eye of round, cut into tiny bite-size pieces, with other ingredients at beginning of recipe. (No need to pre-cook. The meat will cook while boiling).

2nd Serving Busy People's Low Fat Cook Book

CREAM OF POTATO SOUP

Satisfying and filling.
Excellent for a cold winter's day!

¼ cup all-purpose flour
1 pint fat-free half & half
   (I use Land O Lakes)
2 cups skim milk
1 pound fat-free hash
   browns
½ cup frozen or fresh
   chopped onion

1 (3-ounce) jar real bacon
   bits (I use Hormel)
   (or ¼ pound chopped
   smoked ham)
½ teaspoon dried dill weed
1 tablespoon Butter Buds
   Sprinkles - dry

♥ In a large, nonstick Dutch oven or soup pot, with a whisk, briskly stir flour into half & half and skim milk.

♥ Once flour is completely dissolved, add remaining ingredients and cook over medium-high heat, stirring frequently.

♥ Once boiling, continue to cook and stir at a full boil for 3 to 5 minutes, or until potatoes are tender. Remove from heat.

♥ If desired, season with lite salt and pepper.

Yield: 5 (1-cup) servings

With bacon bits:

Calories: 263
Percent Fat Calories: 13%
Carbohydrate: 42 grams
Protein: 19 grams

Total Fat: 4 grams
Cholesterol: 14 mg
Dietary Fiber: 2 grams
Sodium: 784 mg

With ham:

Calories: 240
Percent Fat Calories: 7%
Carbohydrate: 41 grams
Protein: 18 grams

Total Fat: 2 grams
Cholesterol: 14 mg
Dietary Fiber: 2 grams
Sodium: 540 mg

Total time: 15 minutes or less.

2nd Serving Busy People's Low Fat Cook Book

Menu Ideas: Tossed salad or fresh vegetable tray and fat-free saltine crackers.

DELUXE BEAN SOUP

This savory, thick, hearty soup is a winner.

2 (48-ounce) jars Randall's deluxe beans
8 cups Health Valley fat-free, no-salt-added beef broth (or made from bouillon)
1 cup frozen chopped onions
2 (14-ounce) packages fat-free smoked sausage - cut into ¼-inch pieces - (I use Butterball)
1 (10¾-ounce) can condensed tomato soup
1 teaspoon dried dill

♥ Put beans, beef broth and onions into a large soup pan. Mix well.

♥ Remove 4 cups of beans and broth at a time and puree in a blender until a total of 12 cups has been pureed. Return puree to soup pan.

♥ Turn heat on high. Add smoked sausage, tomato soup and dill. Bring to a boil.

♥ Serve hot.

Yield: 21 (1-cup) servings

Calories: 173
Percent Fat Calories: 3%
Carbohydrate: 27 grams
Protein: 15 grams

Total Fat: 1 gram
Cholesterol: 16 mg
Dietary Fiber: 11 grams
Sodium: 1016 mg

Total time: 20 minutes.

2nd Serving Busy People's Low Fat Cook Book

Menu Ideas: Spice Apples

Unstuffed Cabbage Soup

If you like stuffed cabbage rolls, you'll like this!

1 pound ground beef eye of round

6 cups Health Valley fat-free, no-salt-added beef broth (or made with bouillon)

4 cups low-sodium V8 vegetable juice

2 (14.5-ounce) cans no-salt-added stewed tomatoes

2 cups frozen or fresh chopped onion

1 (1-pound) bag cole slaw mix (or 10 cups shredded fresh green cabbage)

2 cups instant rice

Stovetop Method:

♥ Bring everything, except rice, to a boil over high heat in a large, nonstick soup pan.

♥ Let boil 5 minutes, stirring occasionally.

♥ Turn off heat and stir in rice.

♥ Cover and let sit for 5 minutes.

♥ Serve hot.

♥ If desired, season with ground black pepper to taste.

Crockpot Method:

♥ Put all ingredients, except rice, in a large crockpot. Stir well. Cover.

♥ Cook on low for 8 to 10 hours or on high for 4 to 5 hours.

♥ Before serving, stir in rice. Cover and let sit 5 minutes.

♥ Serve hot.

Yield: 16 (1-cup) servings

Calories: 131
Percent Fat Calories: 9%
Carbohydrate: 18 grams
Protein: 11 grams

Total Fat: 1 gram
Cholesterol: 15 mg
Dietary Fiber: 2 grams
Sodium: 91 mg

Total time: (Stovetop): 13 minutes or less (including sitting time). (Crockpot): 4 to 5 hours on high or 8 to 10 hours on low.

2nd Serving Busy People's Low Fat Cook Book

Menu Ideas: Serve with French bread and Oreo Mousse

HAM AND YAM SOUP

This reminds me of Split Pea Soup,
but with it's own unique, savory flavor.

8 cups fat-free, reduced-sodium chicken broth (or made from bouillon)

3 medium yams - cut into tiny ¼-inch pieces (about 2 pounds)

¼ cup Butter Buds Sprinkles - dry

1 pound extra lean honey smoked ham - cut into tiny pieces

1¼ cups instant potatoes (I use Betty Crocker Potato Buds) - dry

2 tablespoons packed brown sugar

♥ In a large, nonstick soup pan (or Dutch oven) bring chicken broth, yams, Butter Bud Sprinkles and ham to a full boil. Let boil 3 to 4 minutes, or until yams are tender.

♥ Take 3 cups of the ham and yams from the broth and put into a blender. Add 1 cup of broth to the blender. Cover. Turn the blender on high until pureed. Stir puree back into the pot.

♥ Stir in instant potatoes and sugar until potatoes are dissolved.

♥ Serve hot.

Yield: 10 (1-cup) servings

Calories: 304
Percent Fat Calories: 8%
Carbohydrate: 53 grams
Protein: 17 grams

Total Fat: 3 grams
Cholesterol: 25 mg
Dietary Fiber: 5 grams
Sodium: 1132 mg

Total time: 15 minutes.

Menu Ideas: Pinwheel Dinner Rolls
and Peaches and Cream Gelatin Salad.

CREAM OF BROCCOLI AND MUSHROOM SOUP

This thick, rich soup will stick to your bones,
but not your hips, thighs or arteries.

8 ounces fresh mushrooms, sliced

2 (1-pound) bags frozen broccoli stems and pieces

3 (10.75-ounce) cans Campbell's 98% fat-free cream of broccoli soup

½ teaspoon dried thyme, crushed

3 bay leaves

1 pint fat-free half & half

4 ounces extra lean, smoked ham - cut into tiny pieces

♥ Put all ingredients into a crockpot. Mix well. Cover.

♥ Cook on low for 8 to 9 hours or on high for 3½ to 4 hours.

♥ Remove bay leaves before eating.

Yield: 12 (1-cup) servings

Calories: 114
Percent Fat Calories: 19%
Carbohydrate: 17 grams
Protein: 9 grams

Total Fat: 3 grams
Cholesterol: 11 mg
Dietary Fiber: 3 grams
Sodium: 698 mg

Total time: 5 minutes.

2nd Serving Busy People's Low Fat Cook Book

Menu Ideas: Pinwheel Dinner Rolls and
Bacon-Lettuce and Tomato Salad

STEAK & POTATO CATTLEMEN'S SOUP

A terrific way to use leftover steak and potatoes!
(Or an eye of round roast and potatoes.)

2½ cups (1 pound) leftover lean cooked eye of round steak - cut into bite-size chunks
2½ cups (2 large potatoes) leftover fully cooked potatoes (with skins on) - cut into bite-size chunks
4 ounces fresh sliced mushrooms

½ cup your favorite barbecue sauce (I use Bullseye)
½ cup chopped onions (frozen onions work well)
1 (1.25-ounce) envelope dry onion soup mix
4 cups water

♥ **Crockpot method:** Spray a crockpot with non-fat cooking spray. Mix all ingredients together until well mixed. Cover. Cook on low for 4 hours.

♥ **Stovetop method:** Spray a Dutch oven (large saucepan) with non-fat cooking spray. Mix all ingredients over medium-low heat for 5 to 10 minutes or until fully heated.

♥ **Microwave method:** Spray microwavable covered dish with non-fat cooking spray. Mix all ingredients well. Cover. Cook on high power in carousel microwave for 8 minutes. Stir. If needed, cook an additional 2 to 3 minutes.

Yield: 6 servings

Calories: 235
Cholesterol: 53 mg

Total Fat: 4.4 grams (17% fat)
Sodium: 752 mg

Preparation time: 15 minutes or less.

Cooking time: As little as 5 minutes.

Total time: As little as 20 minutes or less.

Busy People's Low-Fat Cook Book

Menu Ideas: This hearty soup is a meal in itself.
Serve with sourdough bread and a tossed salad.

TACO VEGETABLE SOUP

My family thinks this flavorful, zesty soup is delicious served with crushed Baked Tostitos Tortilla Chips sprinkled on top of each serving.

1 pound lean ground turkey breast
1 (2-pound) package frozen Freshlike vegetables for soup
1 (1½-ounce) package taco seasoning mix (your favorite brand)

1 (49½-ounce) can Swanson chicken broth - visible fat removed
1 (16-ounce) jar your favorite salsa

♥ Put all ingredients in a large soup pan. Bring to a boil. Reduce heat to low. Cover. Let simmer for 13 minutes.

♥ If desired, served with crushed Baked Tostitos Tortilla Chips sprinkled on top of each serving.

♥ If you like a spicier soup, add a few drops of Tabasco sauce.

Yield: 12 (1-cup) servings

Calories: 115
Cholesterol: 26 mg

Total Fat: 0.4 grams (3% fat)
Sodium: 1063 mg

Preparation time: 5 minutes or less.

Cooking time: 13 minutes or less.

Total time: 18 minutes or less.

Busy People's Low-Fat Cook Book

Menu Ideas: Mexican Chicken Salad and Southwestern Corn Muffins.

FRENCH ONION SOUP

*Onion lovers rejoice! A low-fat version of
a very popular soup!*

2 quarts water
2 tablespoons sugar
¼ cup flour
2 packets dry Butter Buds
(or 2 tablespoons Butter Bud
Sprinkles)
*6 cups onions - sliced very
thinly (about 3 medium
onions)

8 beef bouillon cubes
2 teaspoons pure sherry
extract (found next to vanilla
flavoring in baking section)
½ cup Kraft Free non-fat grated
topping (Parmesan cheese)
- optional

♥ In a crockpot using a whisk, briskly stir together water, sugar, flour and Butter Buds until flour is dissolved. Add onions and bouillon cubes. Cover. Cook on low for 9 to 10 hours.

♥ After 9 to 10 hours cooking on low, add sherry extract and non-fat grated topping.

♥ Put soup into individual bowls. Sprinkle with fat-free croutons or cubed rye bread.

♥ If desired top each serving with 1 teaspoon fat-free Parmesan cheese. With spoon gently press the cheese into the soup. Let set for about 30 seconds to melt the cheese.

♥ *The fastest way to cut onions without crying is with a food processor.

Yield: 8 servings

Calories: 73
Cholesterol: 0 mg

Total Fat: 0.3 grams (4% fat)
Sodium: 882 mg

Preparation time: 20 minutes or less.

Cooking time: 9 hours.

Total time: 9 hours plus 20 minutes.

Busy People's Low-Fat Cook Book

CHICKEN ASPARAGUS SOUP

12 cups chicken broth
6 chicken breasts (skinless, boneless, with fat removed)
1 teaspoon Cajun seasoning
3 bay leaves
1 4.5-ounce package Staff Cheddar Broccoli Rice & Sauce mix
1 15-ounce can asparagus, cut into pieces
1 teaspoon parsley
Salt to taste (optional)

 ♥ Bring chicken broth to a rapid boil. Add all ingredients, and bring to a rapid boil again. Reduce heat to a low boil. Boil 10 minutes. Remove breasts and chop into bite-sized pieces. Put cut-up breast pieces back into soup. Serve warm. Remove bay leaves before eating.

Yield: 20 servings

Calories: 84
Percent Fat Calories: 22%
Carbohydrate: 6 grams
Protein: 10 grams

Total Fat: 2 grams
Cholesterol: 20 mg
Dietary Fiber: 0 grams
Sodium: 782 mg

Preparation time: 30 minutes.

Down Home Cookin'

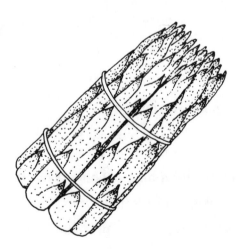

SEAFOOD CHOWDER

An elaborate chowder that is definitely for a special meal!

1 pint fat-free half & half (Land O Lakes)

1 (6-ounce) package frozen small shrimp

2 (6.5-ounce) cans minced clams - do not drain

1 (8-ounce) package imitation scallops (Louis Kemp Seafood Co.)

1 (8-ounce) package imitation crab (Louis Kemp Seafood Co.)

3 (10¾-ounce) cans 98% fat-free Campbell's New England clam chowder

1 pound fat-free frozen hash browns

Stovetop Method:

♥ Put everything into a large, nonstick Dutch oven or soup pot.

♥ Cook on medium-high heat, stirring constantly. (So that the bottom won't burn.)

♥ Once boiling, cook and stir an additional 3 to 4 minutes or until potatoes are tender.

♥ If desired, add pepper to taste before serving.

Crockpot Method:

♥ Mix all ingredients in a crockpot until well mixed. Cover. Cook on low for 8 to 9 hours or on high for 4 hours.

♥ If desired, add pepper to taste before serving.

Yield: 10 (1-cup) servings

Calories: 215
Percent Fat Calories: 10%
Carbohydrate: 31 grams
Protein: 19 grams

Total Fat: 2 grams
Cholesterol: 59 mg
Dietary Fiber: 1 gram
Sodium: 1321 mg

Total time: (Stovetop) 20 minutes or less. (Crockpot) 8 to 9 hours on low or 4 hours on high.

2nd Serving Busy People's Low Fat Cook Book

Menu Ideas: Tossed salad, fresh vegetables with fat-free dip and fat-free oyster crackers.

TACO CHOWDER

*Great served on a cold day! It'll warm you
from head to toe! A flavorful blend of chili and tacos.*

1   pound ground turkey breast
1   (1.25-ounce) packet taco seasoning
1   (28-ounce) can no-salt-added diced tomatoes - do not drain
2   (16-ounce) cans fat-free refried beans (I use Old El Paso)
1   (14.5-ounce) can Health Valley fat-free, no-salt-added beef broth
1   (15-ounce) can light red kidney beans - do not drain
1   (15.25-ounce) can whole kernel golden sweet corn - do not drain

♥ Spray a nonstick soup pan with non-fat cooking spray. Cook meat and taco seasoning over medium heat until fully cooked.

♥ Add diced tomatoes, refried beans, beef broth, kidney beans and corn.

♥ Bring to a boil over high heat. Once it comes to a boil, it's ready to serve.

♥ Serving Ideas: If desired, lightly sprinkle with fat-free cheddar cheese or crushed baked tortilla chips.

Yield: 13 (1-cup servings)

Calories: 172
Percent Fat Calories: 4%
Carbohydrate: 26 grams
Protein: 16 grams

Total Fat: 1 gram
Cholesterol: 24 mg
Dietary Fiber: 7 grams
Sodium: 562 mg

Total time: 15 minutes or less.

2nd Serving Busy People's Low Fat Cook Book

Menu Ideas: Great served with cornbread on the side, or with half of a grilled cheese sandwich.

CLAM CHOWDER

*There's NO WAY anyone would ever know
this is low fat if you didn't tell them! It's super
thick, rich and creamy.*

3 (10.75-ounce) cans
Campbell's 98% fat-free
cream of celery soup
2 (6.5-ounce) cans chopped
clams - do not drain

1 (1-pound) bag frozen fat-
free shredded hash brown
potatoes
½ cup frozen chopped onion
1 pint fat-free half & half

♥ Spray a crockpot with non-fat cooking spray.

♥ Put all ingredients in crockpot. Stir until well mixed.

♥ Cover.

♥ Cook on low for 8 to 9 hours.

Yield: 11 (1-cup) servings

Calories: 130
Percent Fat Calories: 15%
Carbohydrate: 21 grams
Protein: 8 grams

Total Fat: 2 grams
Cholesterol: 15 mg
Dietary Fiber: 1 gram
Sodium: 782 mg

Preparation time: 10 minutes.

2nd Serving Busy People's Low Fat Cook Book

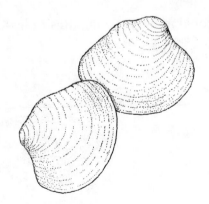

SPICY THICK VEGETARIAN CHILI

This thick, hearty, stick to your bones
(but not your thighs!)
chili is power packed with protein and fiber.

2 (15-ounce) cans Mexican
   style hot chili beans
1 (16-ounce) can vegetarian
   refried beans
   (I use Old El Paso)

1 (15-ounce) can black beans
   (I use Progresso ready to
   serve brand)
2 cups chunky salsa
   (I use Chi-Chi's)
1 (6-ounce) can tomato paste

♥ Stir all ingredients together in a 3-quart or larger non-stick saucepan over medium heat until thoroughly heated and well mixed. Presto! You're done! Now enjoy!

Yield: 9 (1-cup) servings

Calories: 178
Cholesterol: 0 mg

Total Fat: 1.7 grams (8% fat)
Sodium: 1137 mg

Additional ideas: - optional

- for spicier chili add Tabasco Sauce

- for an eye appealing garnish sprinkle bowl of chili with Healthy Choice fancy shredded cheddar cheese

- for a chili not as thick add water or tomato juice -1 cup at a time until desired consistency.

Total preparation and cooking time: 10 minutes or less.

Busy People's Low-Fat Cook Book

CHUNKY CROCKPOT CHILI

*Made with chunks of beef! The meat in
this hearty chili is tenderized as it cooks.*

1 pound beef for stew meat
(eye of round cut into
½-inch chunks)
1 (15-ounce) can Mexican-
style hot chili beans
1 (14½-ounce) can no-salt-
added diced tomatoes

1 (16-ounce) jar your
favorite thick and chunky
salsa (remember the hotter
the salsa the hotter your
chili is going to be)
1 tablespoon sugar

♥ Stir all ingredients together in a crockpot until well mixed.

♥ Cover.

♥ Cook on low for 8 to 10 hours or on high for 4 to 5 hours.

♥ If desired, sprinkle with non-fat shredded cheddar cheese. Let sit
for 1 minute to allow cheese to melt.

Yield: 7 (1-cup) servings

Calories: 167
Percent Fat Calories: 19%
Carbohydrate: 16 grams
Protein: 18 grams

Total Fat: 3 grams
Cholesterol: 35 mg
Dietary Fiber: 3 grams
Sodium: 590 mg

Preparation time: 10 minutes or less.

2nd Serving Busy People's Low Fat Cook Book

BEANIE BABY STEW

This is a breeze to put together and a crowd pleaser every time!

1 (24-ounce) jar Randall's Deluxe Great Northern Beans

2 (10-ounce) cans Swanson white chicken chunks in water

1 (49½-ounce) can Swanson chicken broth - all visible fat removed

1 (12-ounce) bag frozen chopped onions

1 (7-ounce) can d iced green chilies (I used Ortega)

1 (1 pound) bag frozen diced potatoes

½ cup cornstarch

♥ Put all ingredients except cornstarch into a crockpot. Cover. Cook on high for 4 hours or low for 8 to 9 hours.

♥ With a ladle or strainer, remove as much of the cooked ingredients as possible and put into a large bowl. With a potato masher, smash cooked food for about 1 minute. (This will make the broth thicker.)

♥ Combine cornstarch with ½ cup cold water. Stir briskly until cornstarch is completely dissolved.

♥ Stir dissolved cornstarch and water into broth in the crockpot. Stir until well mixed.

♥ Return smashed vegetables to crockpot.

♥ Stir. Turn crockpot to high. Cover and cook for another 20 to 30 minutes. Stew will be a thick and creamy consistency when done.

♥ If desired sprinkle each serving bowl of chowder lightly with fat-free mozzarella cheese just before eating.

Yield: 14 (1-cup) servings

Calories: 185
Cholesterol: 25 mg

Total Fat: 3.7 grams (18% fat)
Sodium: 514 mg

Preparation time: 5 minutes or less.

Cooking time: Varies depending on method of cooking - high or low temperature.

Busy People's Low-Fat Cook Book

Menu Idea: Tossed salad or cornbread.

TABBOULEH TOSSED SALAD

1 (1-pound) bag cut-up
 salad greens (or 1
 medium head of
 iceberg lettuce cut
 into bite-size pieces)
½ (7-ounce) container
 tabbouleh (3½ ounces used)

⅓ cup fat-free Red Wine
 Vinaigrette Salad Dressing
 (I use Wish-Bone)
½ cup fat-free garlic
 croutons

♥ Toss everything together except for croutons.

♥ Chill before serving. When ready to eat, top salad with croutons.
 (Croutons will become soggy if tossed with dressing too long
 before eating.)

Yield: 4 servings

Calories: 128
Percent Fat Calories: 6%
Carbohydrate: 26 grams
Protein: 5 grams

Total Fat: 1 gram
Cholesterol: 0 mg
Dietary Fiber: 4 grams
Sodium: 324 mg

Total time: 5 minutes or less.

2nd Serving Busy People's Low Fat Cook Book

PEAS, CHEESE AND BACON SALAD

Tasty for any picnic, potluck or buffet.

¼ cup T. Marzetti's fat-free Cole Slaw Salad Dressing

¼ cup Kraft Free non-fat mayonnaise

2 teaspoons sugar (or 2 teaspoons Equal Spoonful)

1 (1-pound) bag frozen green peas

½ cup fat-free shredded cheddar cheese (I use Kraft)

¼ cup real bacon bits (I use Hormel)

♥ In a medium serving bowl, mix salad dressing, mayonnaise and sugar (or Equal Spoonful) together briskly until well mixed. Stir in peas, cheese and bacon.

♥ Serve chilled.

Note: If peas have frozen ice crystals on them, put peas in a strainer and run under cold water until ice is dissolved.

Yield: 7 (½-cup) servings

With Sugar:
Calories: 100
Percent Fat Calories: 9%
Carbohydrate: 15 grams
Protein: 8 grams

Total Fat: 1 gram
Cholesterol: 8 mg
Dietary Fiber: 3 grams
Sodium: 435 mg

With Equal:
Calories: 95
Percent Fat Calories: 9%
Carbohydrate: 14 grams
Protein: 8 grams

Total Fat: 1 gram
Cholesterol: 8 mg
Dietary Fiber: 3 grams
Sodium: 435 mg

Total time: 5 minutes or less.

2nd Serving Busy People's Low Fat Cook Book

Menu Ideas: Will accompany any summer meal.

REUBEN SALAD

If you like Reuben sandwiches you'll like this!

5 cups chopped iceberg lettuce (or 1 [10-ounce] bag cut-up lettuce)
1 (14-ounce) can sauerkraut - rinsed and squeezed dry with hands
2 slices fat-free Swiss cheese - cut into pieces (I use Kraft)

1 (2.5-ounce) package lean, thin sliced corned beef (found next to chipped beef in refrigerator section)
½ cup fat-free Thousand Island salad dressing
½ cup rye croutons (fat-free are available)

♥ Toss all ingredients together with dressing.

♥ Serve immediately.

Note: Do not toss with dressing until its time to eat. Otherwise salad will get soggy.

Yield: 5 (1-cup) servings

Calories: 87
Percent Fat Calories: 13%
Carbohydrate: 14 grams
Protein: 5 grams

Total Fat: 1 gram
Cholesterol: 10 mg
Dietary Fiber: 3 grams
Sodium: 957 mg

Total time: 10 minutes.

2nd Serving Busy People's Low Fat Cook Book

Menu Ideas: Grilled chicken or fish entrées.

GREEK SALAD

¼ teaspoon dried oregano - crushed

1 (14.5-ounce) can no-salt-added diced tomatoes drained (or 18 cherry tomatoes)

1 cup fat-free Red Wine Vinegar Salad Dressing (I use Kraft)

12 small, pitted black olives - cut into thin slices

2 (10-ounce) bags cut lettuce (I use Dole - European Brand, or if you'd like, you can cut up a combination totaling 14 cups of iceberg lettuce and curly endive)

½ cup chopped onion (approximately one small onion)

¼ cup finely crumbled feta cheese (approximately 1½ ounces)

♥ In a small bowl, mix together dried oregano, diced tomatoes and salad dressing until well mixed. Set aside and keep refrigerated until ready to eat.

♥ In a large serving bowl, toss lettuce and chopped onion together. Keep chilled until ready to serve.

♥ Just before serving, toss salad with salad dressing mixture until well coated.

♥ Top with olives and sprinkle with finely crumbled feta cheese.

♥ Serve chilled.

Note: Do not toss with salad dressing until ready to serve, as this will make your salad soggy.

Yield: 7 (2-cup) servings

Calories: 60
Percent Fat Calories: 29%
Carbohydrate: 9 grams
Protein: 2 grams

Total Fat: 2 grams
Cholesterol: 5 mg
Dietary Fiber: 2 grams
Sodium: 577 mg

Total time: 10 minutes or less.

2nd Serving Busy People's Low Fat Cook Book

Sassy Slaw

My secret ingredients turn regular cole slaw into an extra special salad which always gets rave reviews!

1 (16-ounce) package ready-to-use classic cole slaw (I use Dole - found in the produce section near cut-up lettuce) or 4½ cups shredded fresh green cabbage and ½ cup shredded carrots)

1 (20-ounce) can crushed pineapple in pineapple juice - 1 cup pineapple juice drained and discarded
¾ cup Marzettis' fat-free slaw dressing
½ teaspoon ground cinnamon

♥ Combine all ingredients in a medium bowl until well mixed.

♥ Keep chilled until ready to use.

Yield: 10 (½-cup) servings

Calories: 58
Cholesterol: 9 mg

Total Fat: 0 grams (0% fat)
Sodium: 242 mg

Total preparation time: 5 minutes or less

Busy People's Low-Fat Cook Book

Menu Ideas: A delicious side vegetable for any cookout or barbecue. Great with chicken, pork, fish or beef entrées.

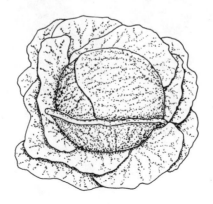

CHICKEN CAESAR SALAD

This is by far my family's favorite salad!!!

2   heads Romaine lettuce,
    cleaned and torn into bite-
    sized pieces
1   cup fat-free Caesar Dressing
    (I like Hidden Valley's)

4   skinless chicken breasts
½   cup finely shredded
    Parmesan cheese
Pepper (optional)
Fat-free croutons (optional)

 ♥ In large bowl, toss lettuce with Caesar dressing. Cook chicken breasts on grill. Slice into thin strips. Divide salad onto 4 plates. Top with chicken strips. Garnish with shredded Parmesan cheese, fat-free croutons and ground pepper. Best when salad is chilled and chicken is hot off the grill. This salad is also excellent without the chicken.

Yield: 8-10 Servings

Calories: 117
Percent Fat Calories: 23%
Carbohydrate: 4 grams
Protein: 18 grams

Total Fat:: 3 grams
Cholesterol: 38 mg
Dietary Fiber: 2 grams
Sodium: 552 mg

Down Home Cookin'

SLAW SALAD

*A tangy and tart salad that
makes a wonderful alternative for cole slaw.*

½ cup Marzetti's fat-free
Cole Slaw Salad Dressing
¼ cup sweetened dried
cranberries (I use Ocean
Spray)

1 (1-pound) bag gourmet
lettuce mixture (iceberg,
romaine, escarole, endive,
radicchio)
1 medium Gala apple (or
Red Delicious) - chopped

♥ Mix all ingredients together.

♥ Serve chilled.

Yield: 5 (1½-cup) servings

Calories: 89
Percent Fat Calories: 0%
Carbohydrate: 21 grams
Protein: 2 grams

Total Fat: 0 grams
Cholesterol: 12 mg
Dietary Fiber: 3 grams
Sodium: 335 mg

Total time: 10 minutes or less.

2nd Serving Busy People's Low Fat Cook Book

Menu Ideas: Goes good with (Oven) Fried Catfish.

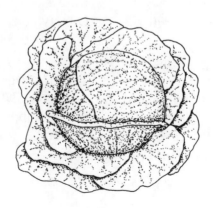

Spinach Orange Salad

1 (10-ounce) package
  fresh spinach - stems
  removed if desired
1 (11-ounce) can
  mandarin oranges
¼ cup real bacon bits
  (I use Hormel - about ⅓ jar)

½ cup fat-free sour cream
  (I use Breakstone)
2 tablespoons sugar
  (or Equal Spoonful)
½ cup fat-free croutons
¼ medium-sized red onion -
  cut into ⅛-inch rings
  and separated

♥ Put spinach in a large bowl. Set aside.

♥ Drain the juice from the mandarin oranges into another bowl. Set oranges in can aside.

♥ With a whisk, briskly mix the drained mandarin juice, bacon bits, fat-free sour cream and sugar until well blended.

♥ Toss spinach with dressing. Garnish salad with orange segments, croutons and onions.

Note: Do not toss salad or croutons in dressing until ready to serve, or salad will become soggy.

Yield: 8 (1-cup) side salads or 4 (2-cups) entrée salads

With Sugar: (8 servings)
Calories: 69
Percent Fat Calories: 10%
Carbohydrate: 12 grams
Protein: 4 grams
Total Fat: 1 gram
Cholesterol: 4 mg
Dietary Fiber: 1 gram
Sodium: 165 mg

With Equal Spoonful: (8 servings)
Calories: 58
Percent Fat Calories: 12%
Carbohydrate: 9 grams
Protein: 4 grams
Total Fat: 1 gram
Cholesterol: 4 mg
Dietary Fiber: 1 gram
Sodium: 165 mg

Total time: 10 minutes or less.

2nd Serving Busy People's Low Fat Cook Book

Menu Ideas: As an entrée serve with Bagel Chips. As a side salad it is delicious with any lean grilled meat.

GREEK PASTA SALAD

You would not believe how good this tastes!

16 ounces of your favorite pasta - cooked (for faster preparation, cook extra pasta sometime the week before. Store cooked pasta in cold water and refrigerate. All you have to do is drain water and the pasta is all set.)

1½ cups fat-free Red Wine Vinegar Salad Dressing (I use Kraft)

1 (7-ounce) package tabbouleh (I use Oasis brand, which has 6 grams of fat per 7 ounces)

1 ounce feta cheese - finely crumbled

1 large tomato - cut into ½-inch chunks

12 medium, pitted black olives slice each into thirds

1 large cucumber - cut into tiny pieces

♥ Mix all ingredients together. Keep chilled until ready to serve.

Yield: 14 (½-cup) servings

Calories: 200
Percent Fat Calories: 8%
Carbohydrate: 39 grams
Protein: 6 grams

Total Fat: 2 grams
Cholesterol: 2 mg
Dietary Fiber: 2 grams
Sodium: 404 mg

Total time: 20 minutes or less (derived mostly from cutting).

2nd Serving Busy People's Low Fat Cook Book

Menu Ideas: Cookouts, salad bars and picnics.

HOT POTATO SALAD

If you like German Potato Salad, you'll like this. It is not sweet. Good for picnics, cookouts, potlucks, etc.

4   large potatoes with skins on (about 2 pounds)
1   tablespoon minced garlic (I use the kind in a jar)
¾   cup fat-free Red Wine Vinegar Salad Dressing
¼   cup fresh chopped chives
1   cup shredded fat-free cheddar cheese (I use Kraft)
1   (3-ounce) jar real bacon bits

♥ Poke holes into potatoes with a fork. Microwave potatoes for about 10 minutes or until fully cooked.

♥ Cut potatoes into bite-size chunks, leaving skins on. Put in freezer for 2 to 3 minutes to cool.

♥ In the meantime, mix garlic, salad dressing and chives together until well blended in large serving bowl.

♥ Gently stir potatoes, cheese and bacon bits into dressing. Serve as is or microwave 3 to 4 minutes.

Yield: 14 (½-cup) servings

Calories: 91
Percent Fat Calories: 12%
Carbohydrate: 14 grams
Protein: 6 grams
Total Fat: 1 gram
Cholesterol: 6 mg
Dietary Fiber: 1 gram
Sodium: 433 mg

Total time: 25 minutes.

2nd Serving Busy People's Low Fat Cook Book

Menu Ideas: Good side dish with any lean meat.

SOUTHWESTERN THREE BEAN SALAD

The zip in this salad will add zest to any meal.

1 (19-ounce) can Progresso black bean soup - drained
½ cup Kraft red wine vinegar fat-free salad dressing
1 (15.5-ounce) can light red kidney beans - drained

1 (16-ounce) jar your favorite thick and chunky salsa (I use Tostitos)
1 (15.5-ounce) can Navy beans - drained

♥ Mix all ingredients together. If you like spicy food, add a few drops of Tabasco sauce.

Yield: 12 (½-cup) servings

Calories: 91
Cholesterol: 0 mg

Total Fat: 0.4 grams (4% fat)
Sodium: 575 mg

Preparation time: 5 minutes or less. The time consuming and hardest part of this recipe is opening the cans! Pretty nice - huh?

Busy People's Low-Fat Cook Book

Menu Ideas: A great side salad for a Mexican meal. Also a terrific dip with fat-free Baked Tostitos Chips.

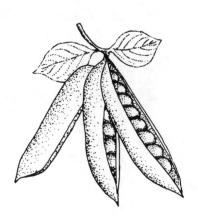

Seafood Salad

1 (8-ounce) package imitation lobster meat (I use Louis Kemp Lobster Delights)

1 (8-ounce) package imitation scallop meat (I use Louis Kemp Scallop Delights)

1 (8-ounce) package imitation king crab meat (I use Louis Kemp Crab Delights)

1 pound cooked shrimp - peeled, deveined and tails removed

2 cups cucumbers - chopped with skin on and seeds removed (about 1 medium cucumber)

1 (8-ounce) bottle Kraft Thousand Island fat-free salad dressing (about 1 cup)

♥ Mix all ingredients. Keep chilled until ready to serve.

♥ *To remove seeds, cut cucumber in half lengthwise. With a spoon, scrape down the center to remove seeds.

Yield: 7 (1-cup) servings

Calories: 209
Cholesterol: 146 mg

Total Fat: 2.0 grams (9% fat)
Sodium: 1241 mg

Total preparation time: 8 minutes or less.

Menu Ideas: Stuff into a pita half or put a half-cup on top of a bed of fresh green assorted lettuce for individual salads.

Cut a honeydew melon in half. Clean and put seafood salad in center, or cut off top of a fresh tomato. Take seeds out of center of tomato and stuff with seafood salad.

Serve on toasted fat-free or regular white bread with lettuce . . . or roll in a soft flour tortilla or serve a dab on crackers.

(Seafood Salad continued on next page)

(Seafood Salad continued)

Seafood Pasta Salad: Make exactly as directed above and toss with 1 pound tricolor bow tie pasta that has been cooked in boiling water for 11 minutes, rinsed with cold water and drained. Add another 8-ounce bottle Kraft Thousand Island fat-free salad dressing.

Yield: 15 (1-cup) servings

Calories: 229   Total Fat: 1.4 grams (6% fat)
Cholesterol: 68 mg   Sodium: 711 mg

Preparation time: 8 minutes or less.

Cooking time: Bow tie Pasta - cook 11 minutes.

Total time: 20 minutes or less.

Busy People's Low-Fat Cook Book

ZESTY SUMMER COTTAGE SALAD

1   (24-ounce) container low-fat   ½ cup fat-free sour cream
    cottage cheese (I use Flavorite 1 packet dry Butter Buds
    brand -1 gram fat per ½ cup)   (or 1 tablespoon Butter
⅓ cup chopped fresh chives or   Buds Sprinkles)
    green onion tops   ⅛ teaspoon ground pepper

♥ Mix all ingredients together. Serve chilled.

Yield: 8 (½-cup) servings

Calories: 80   Total Fat: 0.9 grams (10% fat)
Cholesterol: 4 mg   Sodium: 364 mg

Total Preparation time: 5 minutes or less

Busy People's Low-Fat Cook Book

Menu Ideas: This creamy salad is delicious served with barbecue entrées. Also good as a dip on Baked Tostitos, or spread on a toasted bagel and top with a slice of tomato for an open-faced sandwich.

BROCCOLI AND HAM SALAD

*This is delicious as an entrée by itself or
as a side salad for a cookout.*

½ cup Marzettis' fat-free cole
  slaw dressing
½ cup Hellmans low-fat
  mayonnaise
1 cup shredded fat-free mild
  cheddar cheese

½ pound lean pre-cooked
  ham - chopped
2 pounds frozen broccoli
  cuts - thawed
¼ cup chopped raisins
½ cup chopped red onions

♥ Mix dressing, mayonnaise and cheese together. Let sit for a couple
of minutes. Stir in remaining ingredients.

Yield: 5 (1-cup) entrée servings

Calories: 249
Cholesterol: 36 mg

Total Fat: 4.4 grams (15% fat)
Sodium: 1424 mg

10 (½-cup) side dish servings

Calories: 124
Cholesterol: 18 mg

Total Fat: 2.2 grams (15% fat)
Sodium: 712 mg

Preparation time: 15 minutes or less.

Busy People's Low-Fat Cook Book

*Menu Ideas: As an entree, serve with fresh melon and
tomato slices on the side.*

FRESH BROCCOLI SALAD

⅓ cup Free Miracle Whip
⅓ cup Fat-free Catalina dressing
  (OR Fat-free French dressing)

1 large head fresh broccoli,
  cut into bite-sized pieces

♥ Combine Miracle Whip and dressing. Mix well. Pour dressing over broccoli. Stir until well coated with dressing. Serve chilled.

Yield: 6 servings

Calories: 55
Percent Fat Calories: 0%
Carbohydrate: 12 grams
Protein: 2 grams

Total Fat: 0 grams
Cholesterol: 0 mg
Dietary Fiber: 3 grams
Sodium: 287 mg

Preparation time: 5 minutes.

Down Home Cookin'

RED-WINE VINAIGRETTE CUCUMBER SALAD

A summer must! Great for cookouts!
My children and I like to nibble on these for a snack.

4 cucumbers, peeled
  and sliced into
  ¼-inch slices

16 ounces Seven Seas Fat-
  Free Red-Wine Vinaigrette
  Salad Dressing

♥ Toss cucumber slices in the dressing. Serve chilled.

Yield: 15 Servings

Calories: 13
Percent Fat Calories: 0%
Carbohydrate: 3 grams
Protein: 0 grams

Total Fat: 0 grams
Cholesterol: 0 mg
Dietary Fiber: 1 gram
Sodium: 108 mg

Preparation time: 7 minutes.

Down Home Cookin'

HAM & CHEESE POTATO SALAD

*This hearty, meat and potatoes dish is the answer
to a hungry man's hot summer day!*

2 teaspoons mustard
1 (9-ounce) jar Kraft fat-free tartar sauce
2 teaspoons dried parsley
2 pounds extra lean pre-cooked ham - cut into ¼-inch chunks
1 (8-ounce) package fat-free Healthy Choice shredded cheddar cheese
2 pounds cooked, cooled and cubed potatoes (about 6 medium potatoes)
¾ cup chopped red onion

♥ In a large, bowl mix mustard, tartar sauce and parsley together until well mixed.

♥ Add remaining ingredients. Gently stir until all ingredients are well coated with dressing.

♥ Serve immediately or cover and keep chilled until ready to serve.

Yield: 10 (1-cup) entrée servings

Calories: 254
Cholesterol: 45 mg
Total Fat: 4.6 grams (17% fat)
Sodium: 1662 mg

20 (½-cup) side dish servings

Calories: 127
Cholesterol: 22 mg
Total Fat: 2.3 grams (17% fat)
Sodium: 831 mg

Total time: 20 minutes or less.

Busy People's Low-Fat Cook Book

Menu Ideas: As an entrée serve with a fresh vegetable tray with fat-free salad dressing.

BACON-LETTUCE AND TOMATO SALAD

If you like B.L.T. sandwiches you'll love this salad!

¾ cup fat-free sour cream
(I used Land-O-Lakes)

¾ cup fat-free mayonnaise
(I used Kraft)

⅓ cup Equal Spoonful
(or ⅓ cup sugar)

1 teaspoon liquid smoke
(found in barbecue sauce
section of grocery store)

1 (3.25-ounce) container of
Bac-O's bacon flavor chips

1 quart cherry tomatoes -
halved

2 medium heads Romaine
lettuce - cut into bite-size
pieces (or 2 (1-pound)
packages prepared lettuce)

♥ To make dressing, mix first 5 ingredients together until well blended. Keep chilled until ready to serve.

♥ When ready to serve, gently toss dressing, tomatoes and lettuce together. Serve immediately.

♥ Note: If you want a thinner dressing, add ¼ cup skim milk.

Yield: 10 side dish servings

Calories: 111
Cholesterol: 0 mg

Total Fat: 2.5 grams (20% fat)
Sodium: 312 mg

Total preparation time: 15 minutes or less.

Busy People's Low-Fat Cook Book

Menu Ideas: Good as a side salad with fish,
chicken, beef or pork.

Sour Cream Pasta Salad

1 (16-ounce) carton fat-free sour cream
¾ cup light Miracle Whip
2-3 teaspoons Durkee Salad Seasoning (found in spice section)
1 pound box ziti style pasta - cooked as directed on box (Bow tie pasta or elbow macaroni is fine also)

1 pound Healthy Choice fat-free shredded cheddar cheese
1 cup finely chopped red sweet pepper (1 medium)
1 cup chopped celery (about 3 stalks)
2 tablespoons chopped chives - optional

♥ In a large bowl mix together sour cream, Miracle Whip and Durkee Salad Seasoning until well blended. Stir in remaining ingredients until, well coated with dressing. Serve chilled.

Yield: 12 (1-cup) entrée servings

Calories: 280
Cholesterol: 7 mg

Total Fat: 3.3 grams (11% fat)
Sodium: 484 mg

24 (½-cup) side dish servings

Calories: 140
Cholesterol: 4 mg

Total Fat: 1.6 grams (11% fat)
Sodium: 242 mg

Preparation and cooking time: 23 minutes or less (derived from cooking pasta and chopping vegetables.)

Menu Ideas: Cookouts, Barbecues, luncheons, buffet and potlucks.

Sour Cream Tuna Pasta Salad: *Drain water from 3 (6-ounce) cans of tuna and toss into pasta salad.*

Yield: 12 (1-cup) entrée servings

Calories: 328
Cholesterol: 19 mg

Total Fat: 3.6 grams (10% fat)
Sodium : 624 mg

24 (½-cup) side dish servings

Calories: 164
Cholesterol: 10 mg

Total Fat: 1.8 grams (10% fat)
Sodium: 312 mg

(Sour Cream Pasta Salad continued on next page)

(Sour Cream Pasta Salad continued)

Sour Cream Chicken Pasta Salad:
Add 2 cups cooked, chopped chicken breast.

Yield: 12 (1-cup) entrée servings

Calories: 321   Total Fat: 4.4 grams (13% fat)
Cholesterol: 27 mg   Sodium: 502 mg

24 (½-cup) side dish servings

Calories: 160   Total Fat: 2.2 grams (13% fat)
Cholesterol: 13 mg   Sodium: 251 mg

Sour Cream Turkey Pasta Salad:
Add 2 cups cooked and chopped turkey breast.

Yield: 12 (1-cup) entrée servings

Calories: 313   Total Fat: 3.6 grams (11% fat)
Cholesterol: 27 mg   Sodium: 497 mg

24 (½-cup) side dish servings

Calories: 157   Total Fat: 1.8 grams (11% fat)
Cholesterol: 14 mg   Sodium: 249 mg

Sour Cream Sausage Pasta Salad:
Add on (14- to 16-ounce) package fat-free smoked sausage (Butter Ball and Healthy Choice brands are good.) Cut into tiny pieces.

Yield: 12 (1-cup) entrée servings

Calories: 315   Total Fat: 3.3 grams (10% fat)
Cholesterol: 21 mg   Sodium: 872 mg

24 (½-cup) side dish servings

Calories: 157   Total Fat: 1.6 grams (10% fat)
Cholesterol: 11 mg   Sodium: 436 mg

Busy People's Low-Fat Cook Book

POPEYE'S FAVORITE SALAD

*Even Olive Oyl couldn't create a more
delicious spinach salad than this one! The grilled onions
on this salad are what make it so special!*

1 large sweet white onion cut into ½-inch slices	6 hard boiled egg whites - chopped
1 pound lean eye of round steaks, fat trimmed away	Your favorite fat-free salad dressing. (I like to use T. Marzettis' fat-free raspberry dressing on this salad or fat-free Western)
1 (10-ounce) bag fresh, washed and ready to eat baby spinach	

♥ Spray onion slices on both sides with non-fat cooking spray. If desired, lightly sprinkle one side of each onion slice with salt.

♥ Over medium heat, grill steaks and onion slices on an outdoor grill. Cook to desired doneness.

♥ Cut cooked steaks into long thin strips. If desired sprinkle lightly with garlic salt.

♥ Cut grilled onion slices into quarters.

♥ Place spinach in a large, pretty salad bowl. Top with chopped egg whites, grilled onions and steak strips.

♥ Serve immediately with salad dressing on the side, or keep chilled for later use. Good with the meat and onions either hot off the grill or chilled .

Yield: 4 entrée servings

Calories: 198   Total Fat: 4.3 grams (20% fat)
Cholesterol: 59 mg   Sodium: 192 mg

8 side dish servings

Calories: 99   Total Fat: 2.2 grams (20% fat)
Cholesterol: 29 mg   Sodium: 96 mg

Preparation time: 5 minutes or less.

Grilling time: 10 minutes or less.

Boiling time: 10 or less (boil eggs while steak is cooking).

Total time: 15 minutes or less.

Busy People's Low-Fat Cook Book

CREAMY CUCUMBERS

3 large cucumbers, peeled
   and thinly sliced
1 medium onion, thinly
   sliced

1 16-ounce bottle fat-free
   ranch salad dressing
   (I use Marzetti's)

♥ Toss all ingredients and chill. Serve chilled.

Yield: 14 Servings

Calories: 26
Percent Fat Calories: 0%
Carbohydrate: 6 grams
Protein: 1 gram

Total Fat: 0 grams
Cholesterol: 0 mg
Dietary Fiber: 1 gram
Sodium: 90 mg

Preparation time: 15 minutes.

Down Home Cookin'

TOMATO ZING SALAD

1 package no-fat Italian
   dressing (I use Seven Seas)
   Rice vinegar
2 large cucumbers, peeled
   and thinly sliced

1 pint cherry tomatoes
1 medium onion, chopped

♥ Mix dressing with rice vinegar, according to package directions.
Toss vegetables in dressing. Serve chilled.

Yield: 12 servings

Calories: 18
Percent Fat Calories: 0%
Carbohydrate: 4 grams
Protein: 1 gram

Total Fat: 0 grams
Cholesterol: 0 mg
Dietary Fiber: 1 gram
Sodium: 52 mg

Preparation time: 10-15 minutes.

Down Home Cookin'

Taco Salad

This is a very hearty, stick-to-your-bones salad!
Eat as a meal or a side dish.

1 pound ground eye of round (beef)
1 envelope taco seasoning mix
¾ cup water
2 large heads of iceberg lettuce, torn into bite-sized pieces
8 ounces fat-free shredded cheddar cheese
4 fresh tomatoes, diced
1 medium onion, chopped
8 ounces fat-free Western salad dressing (Use more if desired)
48 low-fat tortilla chips, crushed

♥ Brown hamburger. Drain any juices. Add taco seasoning mix and water. Bring to a boil. Reduce heat. Simmer for 15 minutes. Remove from heat. Set aside to cool.

♥ In a very large bowl toss lettuce with cheese, tomatoes, and onion. Toss the seasoned taco meat, tortilla chips, salad dressing, and sour cream in salad right before serving. You don't want to put the last four ingredients in salad too soon before eating or lettuce will become wilted and tortilla chips will become soggy.

♥ If desired you can use the seasoned taco meat warmed or cooled. I would encourage you NOT to put the meat in warm, unless you are going to eat the salad immediately.

♥ This is excellent served as a meal!

Yield: 6 servings

Calories: 354
Percent Fat Calories: 12%
Carbohydrate: 48 grams
Protein: 34 grams

Total Fat: 5 grams
Cholesterol: 47 mg
Dietary Fiber: 7 grams
Sodium: 1021 mg

Down Home Cookin'

BAR-B-QUED BEAN SALAD

A tangy and colorful side salad
that's great for picnics.

¾ cup of your favorite
   barbecue sauce
1 tablespoon packed brown
   sugar
2 (16-ounce) cans baked
   beans - drained
1 cup frozen chopped onion
   (or 1 medium chopped)

1 (15.5-ounce) can shoepeg
   corn - drained
1 medium sweet red pepper
   - chopped
1 (3-ounce) jar real bacon
   bits

♥ In microwave, heat barbecue sauce and brown sugar together
for 30 seconds or until brown sugar is completely dissolved.

♥ Put remaining ingredients in a medium serving bowl. Toss well
with barbecue sauce mixture. Eat as is or keep chilled until ready
to serve.

Yield: 10 (½-cup) servings

Calories: 174
Percent Fat Calories: 13%
Carbohydrate: 31 grams
Protein: 9 grams

Total Fat: 3 grams
Cholesterol: 6 mg
Dietary Fiber: 6 grams
Sodium: 878 mg

Total time: 15 minutes or less.

2nd Serving Busy People's Low Fat Cook Book

Menu Ideas: Grilled chicken.

MEXICAN CHICKEN SALAD

The perfect flavor combination for a delicious lunch!

½ cup chunky salsa
⅓ cup Ranch fat-free salad dressing (I used Seven Seas)
⅓ cup Western fat-free salad dressing
⅓ cup Healthy Choice fancy shredded cheddar cheese
½ pound cooked chicken breast (or chicken breast lunchmeat - cut into bite-size pieces

1 large head Iceberg lettuce - shredded (or 2 (1-pound) packages prepared salad mix)
1 fat-free tortilla - cut into ¼-inch strips and the strips cut into 1-inch lengths

♥ Mix salsa, Ranch dressing, Western dressing, cheese and chicken until well mixed. Keep refrigerated until ready to serve.

♥ When ready to serve, toss shredded lettuce with chicken mixture and tortilla strips. Do not toss beforehand or salad will become soggy.

Yield: 4 luncheon entrée salad servings

Calories: 227
Cholesterol: 49 mg

Total Fat: 2.8 grams (11% fat)
Sodium: 782 mg

8 side salad servings

Calories: 113
Cholesterol: 25 mg

Total Fat: 1.4 grams (11% fat)
Sodium: 391 mg

Preparation time: 10 minutes or less.

Busy People's Low-Fat Cook Book

Menu Ideas: Perfect as a main entrée for lunch or a light dinner. As a side salad for any fish, chicken, or Mexican entrée.

HEN AND EGGS TOSSED SALAD

Best served with Bacon Salad Dressing. Delicious!

8 ounces cooked chicken breast - cut into tiny pieces

8 cups or 1 (1-pound) bag of Dole cut-up lettuce (I like romaine and iceberg for this salad)

½ cup Egg Beaters - cooked* (like scrambled eggs but with nothing added) and chilled

½ cup fat-free Parmesan - or garlic-flavored croutons

♥ Toss all ingredients together except croutons.

♥ Add croutons and serve.

*Note: To prepare eggs quickly, cook in microwave for 1 minute 30 seconds. Scramble with a whisk after cooking. Put in freezer for 2 to 3 minutes to chill.

Note: Do not add dressing or croutons until ready to serve or the salad will get soggy!

Yield: 8 (1-cup) side servings

Calories: 65
Percent Fat Calories: 16%
Carbohydrate: 2 grams
Protein: 11 grams

Total Fat: 1 gram
Cholesterol: 24 mg
Dietary Fiber: 1 gram
Sodium: 61 mg

Yield: 4 (2-cup) entrée size servings

Calories: 129
Percent Fat Calories: 16%
Carbohydrate: 4 grams
Protein: 22 grams

Total Fat: 2 grams
Cholesterol: 48 mg
Dietary Fiber: 2 grams
Sodium: 122 mg

Total time: 15 minutes.

2nd Serving Busy People's Low Fat Cook Book

Menu Ideas: Great as a meal in itself for lunch. Also good for buffets and potlucks.

GARLIC CRISP

Pita bread (I use Father Sam's
   large size)
Non-fat cooking spray
Garlic salt
Grated Italian topping or
   grated

Parmesan cheese,
   approximately
1 Tablespoon per pita
Dried basil

♥ Preheat oven to 350 degrees. Cut each pita into 8 equal pieces.
Spray bread pieces with non-fat spray. Sprinkle with garlic salt,
grated Italian topping (or Parmesan cheese) and basil, in that
order. Bake for 10 minutes or until slightly brown on edges. Great
warm or serve later with salad instead of croutons.

Yield: 4 Servings

Calories: 59
Percent Fat Calories: 11%
Carbohydrate: 11 grams
Protein: 2 grams

Total Fat: 1 gram
Cholesterol: 1 mg
Dietary Fiber: 0 grams
Sodium: 131 mg

Preparation time: 20 minutes.

Down Home Cookin'

FESTIVE CRANBERRY PINEAPPLE SALAD

Great for the holidays with turkey or ham.

12 ounces fresh cranberries
½ cup NutraSweet Spoonful
   (OR ½ cup sugar)
1 8-ounce carton Cool
   Whip Free
2 cups miniature
   marshmallows

¼ cup chopped walnuts
   (optional)
1 20-ounce can crushed
   pineapple, drained

♥ Grind cranberries in food processor for 1 minute. Pour into bowl and add remaining ingredients. Keep chilled at least 6 hours. The longer it sits the better I think it tastes.°
   ° With Sugar – Calories: 100 – Total Fat: 0 grams
   Percent Fat Calories: 0% – Cholesterol: 0 mg
   Carbohydrate: 1124 grams – Dietary Fiber:1 gram
   Protein: 0 grams – Sodium: 13 mg

Yield: 14 servings

Calories: 75
Percent Fat Calories: 0%
Carbohydrate: 17 grams
Protein: 0 grams

Total Fat:: 0 grams
Cholesterol: 0 mg
Dietary Fiber: 1 gram
Sodium: 13 mg

Down Home Cookin'

WARM CRANAPPLE SALAD

*This warm cranberry salad is a unique and tasty change
to an old favorite. I like serving this side salad with
pork, ham, chicken or turkey entrées.*

1 (16-ounce) can Whole Berry Cranberry Sauce (Ocean Spray)
1 large apple (about 1 cup peeled and chopped into ¼-inch pieces - I use a Granny Smith Apple)
1 teaspoon cinnamon
1 cup miniature marshmallows
1 tablespoon finely chopped walnuts

♥ Preheat oven to 400 degrees.

♥ Spray a 1-quart casserole dish with non-fat cooking spray.

♥ Mix cranberry sauce, chopped apple and cinnamon together. Pour into prepared casserole dish. Arrange marshmallows evenly on top.

♥ Bake at 400 degrees for 7 to 10 minutes or until tops of marshmallows are toasty golden brown.

♥ Sprinkle chopped walnuts on top. Serve warm.

Yield: 6 servings

Calories: 168
Cholesterol: 0 mg
Total Fat: 1.0 grams (5% fat)
Sodium: 26 mg

Preparation time: 10 minutes or less.

Baking time: 7 - 10 minutes.

Total time: 20 minutes or less.

Busy People's Low-Fat Cook Book

*Menu Ideas: Perfect side dish with pork, ham,
chicken or turkey. Great for the holidays instead of the
traditional Cranberry Salad or Jellied Cranberries.*

CRANBERRY APPLE SALAD

*Tasty on its own or as a topping for
angel food cake or frozen yogurt.*

1 (21-ounce) can apple
  pie filling
1 (16-ounce) can whole
  berry Cranberry Sauce
  (I use Ocean Spray)

1 teaspoon cinnamon

♥ Insert a sharp knife into opened can of pie filling and cut apples
  into small pieces while still in the can.

♥ Mix pie filling, cranberry sauce and cinnamon together.

♥ *Refrigerate for at least 20 minutes before serving.

♥ Serve chilled.

Yield: 8 (½-cup) servings

Calories: 162
Cholesterol: 0 mg

Total Fat: 0 grams (0% fat)
Sodium: 49 mg

Total preparation time: 5 minutes.

Busy People's Low-Fat Cook Book

Menu Ideas: *Good with any holiday dinner.*

*To eliminate this step, store cans of apple pie filling and cranberry
sauce in refrigerator before preparing recipe.*

CREAMY BLUE CHEESE SALAD DRESSING

If you like blue cheese, you'll love this!!

¼ cup skim milk
1 cup fat-free sour cream
(I use Land O Lakes)
1 cup fat-free mayonnaise
(I use Kraft Free)

¼ cup blue cheese
(I use Sargento's, natural crumbled)

♥ Mix and cover. Refrigerate for at least 24 hours before using. The refrigeration time allows for the cheese to flavor the dressing.

Yield: 40 servings

Calories: 15
Percent Fat Calories: 17%
Carbohydrate: 2 grams
Protein: 1 gram

Total Fat: trace
Cholesterol: 1 mg
Dietary Fiber: 0 grams
Sodium: 60 mg

Preparation time: 8 minutes.

Down Home Cookin'

COOL & CREAMY SALSA SALAD DRESSING

16 ounces fat-free sour cream
1 16-ounce jar of your favorite salsa or taco sauce

⅓ cup skim milk
Tabasco sauce to taste
(if desired)

♥ Mix all ingredients well. Serve chilled. Keep unused portions refrigerated.

♥ If you like a thinner-runnier salad dressing, just add more skim milk.

Yield: 34 servings

Calories: 20
Percent Fat Calories: 0%
Carbohydrate: 3 grams
Protein: 1 gram

Total Fat: 0 grams
Cholesterol: 1 mg
Dietary Fiber: 0 grams
Sodium: 74 mg

Preparation time: 4 minutes.

Down Home Cookin'

SWEET AND SOUR BACON SALAD DRESSING

What? Bacon salad dressing that's low-fat?
Hard to believe isn't it? If you like sweet
and sour, you're gonna love this!

½ cup Equal Spoonful
  (or ½ cup sugar)
¼ cup apple cider vinegar
¼ cup skim milk

⅔ cup fat-free sour cream
½ (3-ounce) jar real bacon
  bits (I use Hormel –
  Note: only use ½ of the
  3-ounce jar!!)

♥ With a whisk, briskly stir together all igredients until well blended.

♥ Keep chilled until ready to serve.

Yield: 12 (2-tablespoon) servings

With Equal Spoonful:

Calories: 33
Percent Fat Calories: 21%
Carbohydrate: 3 grams
Protein: 2 grams

Total Fat: 1 gram
Cholesterol: 4 mg
Dietary Fiber: 0 grams
Sodium: 128 mg

With Sugar:

Calories: 62
Percent Fat Calories: 10%
Carbohydrate: 11 grams
Protein: 2 grams

Total Fat: 1 gram
Cholesterol: 4 mg
Dietary Fiber: 0 grams
Sodium: 128 mg

Total time: 5 minutes.

2nd Serving Busy People's Low Fat Cook Book

Menu Ideas: Absolutely delicious on fresh salad greens.
It tastes terrific on any type of lettuce.

GRILLED CHEESE SANDWICH

If you like a "cheesier" sandwich, use 2 slices of cheese.

10 sprays "I Can't Believe It's
Not Butter" spray
2 slices fat-free bread
(I use Aunt Millie)

1 slice fat-free cheese
(Kraft and Kroger brands
are good)

♥ Preheat a griddle or skillet to medium-high heat and spray with non-fat cooking spray.

♥ Spray 5 sprays of "I Can't Believe It's Not Butter" spray on one side of each slice of bread.

♥ Lay buttered side of bread on griddle or skillet.

♥ Lay cheese on top of bread.

♥ Lay second slice of bread on top of cheese with buttered side facing up.

♥ Cook on medium-high heat until bottom is golden brown.

♥ Turn over. Continue cooking until bottom is golden brown.

Yield: 1 serving

Calories: 156
Cholesterol: 0 mg

Total Fat: 0 grams (0% fat)
Sodium: 478 mg

Total preparation and cooking time: 3 minutes or less.

Menu Ideas: A piece of fresh fruit, Baked Lays potato crisps (taste like Pringles potato chips) and fresh vegetable sticks. Or tomato soup, made with skim milk, and fresh vegetable sticks.

*Grilled Ham & Cheese or Grilled Turkey & Cheese:

Cook exactly the same except heat extra lean ham or turkey on griddle just enough to warm. Place on cheese before putting second slice of bread on top of cheese. Continue cooking as directed above.

Yield: 1 serving

Calories: 193
Cholesterol: 13 mg

Total Fat: 1.4 grams (7% fat)
Sodium: 883 mg

Busy People's Low-Fat Cook Book

ZESTY SAUSAGE SANDWICHES

These zesty sandwiches are full of flavor.
They are perfect for anyone who would like to
add a little spice and zip to an old favorite!!

1 (14-ounce) package
  Butterball fat-free smoked
  sausage
8 tablespoons honey Dijon
  barbecue sauce

8 tablespoons Healthy
  Choice fat-free mozzarella
  cheese
8 fat-free hot dog buns

♥ Cut each sausage in half (you should have a total of four sausages),

♥ Cut each sausage lengthwise in half (there should now be a total of eight halves).

♥ Cover and microwave all sausages together in carousel microwave on high for 3 minutes or until completely heated.

♥ Meantime while sausages are cooking spread 1 tablespoon of honey Dijon barbecue sauce on the insides of each bun.

♥ Sprinkle 1 tablespoon of mozzarella cheese on each sandwich over the barbecue sauce.

♥ Remove the warmed sausages from the microwave and place one sausage in each bun with the barbecue sauce and cheese.

♥ Return to microwave and re-heat for about 1 minute or until cheese is melted. (The moisture from the barbecue sauce and the juices from the sausage will prevent the cheese from being rubbery.)

Yield: 8 servings

Calories:183
Cholesterol: 22 mg

Total Fat: 0 grams (0% fat)
Sodium: 1027 mg

Preparation time: 5 minutes or less.

Cooking time: 4 minutes.

Total time for all sandwiches: 10 minutes or less.

Busy People's Low-Fat Cook Book

REUBEN SANDWICHES

*You won't miss the calories or fat in
these delicious Reuben sandwiches! (Don't tell
them it's low-fat and they'll never know!).*

14 slices rye bread
14 teaspoons Promise Ultra
70% less fat margarine
2 (2.5-ounce) packages
thin sliced lean corned
beef (chopped, pressed
and cooked - found next
to chipped beef in
refrigerated section.)

1 (14-ounce) can sauerkraut
- rinse and squeeze dry
with hands
7 slices fat-free Swiss
cheese (I use Kraft)
14 teaspoons fat-free
Thousand Island salad
dressing (I use Wish-Bone)

♥ Preheat griddle to 400 degrees.

♥ Spread one side of each slice of rye bread with one teaspoon Promise margarine.

♥ **For each sandwich:**

Lay buttered side of a slice of bread on hot griddle.

Top with 4 slices of corned beef.

Place one-seventh of sauerkraut on corned beef.

Place one slice of Swiss cheese on sauerkraut.

Place another slice of bread (buttered side facing up) on top of cheese.

♥ Once sandwiches are golden brown, turn over to brown other side of sandwich.

♥ Lift top slice of bread of each sandwich and put 2 teaspoons of Thousand Island dressing on meat.

♥ Replace top slice and continue cooking until golden brown.

♥ Cut sandwiches in half diagonally.

♥ Serve immediately.

(Reuben Sandwiches continued on next page)

(Reuben Sandwiches continued)

Yield: 7 (1-sandwich) servings

Calories: 253
Percent Fat Calories: 21%
Carbohydrate: 38 grams
Protein: 12 grams

Total Fat: 6 grams
Cholesterol: 14 mg
Dietary Fiber: 5 grams
Sodium: 1271 mg

Total time: 15 minutes or less.

2nd Serving Busy People's Low Fat Cook Book

Menu Ideas: Fresh vegetable sticks.

SOUTH OF THE BORDER MAGIC POCKETS

2 egg whites
1 pound ground eye of round (beef)
1 envelope taco seasoning for meat
1 cup corn

2 cups fat-free shredded cheddar cheese
2 Tablespoons sugar
1 cup chunky salsa
6 10-count cans of Pillsbury Buttermilk Biscuit dough

♥ Beat egg whites and set aside. Cook beef as directed on taco seasoning package; add taco seasoning. Mix all remaining ingredients — except for egg whites and dough — together until well blended. Spray four cookie sheets with a non-fat cooking spray.

♥ Preheat oven 375 degrees. With hands, flatten 30 of the biscuits into round flat pieces and place on the cookie sheets. Make sure the edges do not touch each other. Brush each flattened dough piece with egg whites on the edges of the dough. Put one rounded tablespoon of meat concoction into center of each piece of flattened dough. With hands flatten one remaining biscuit for each pocket and cover each pocket, one at a time. Seal dough edges together with fork. Brush tops of each pocket with beaten egg whites. Sprinkle with paprika if desired. Bake for 15 minutes.

Yield: 30 servings

Calories: 147
Percent Fat Calories: 13%
Carbohydrate: 23 grams
Protein: 9 grams

Total Fat: 2 grams
Cholesterol: 10 mg
Dietary Fiber: 1 gram
Sodium: 504 mg

Preparation time: 30 minutes.

Down Home Cookin'

PIZZA MAGIC POCKETS

1 pound ground eye
  of round (beef)
2 egg whites
3 10-count cans Pillsbury
  Buttermilk Biscuits
1 cup fat-free mozzarella
  finely shredded cheese
  (I use Healthy Choice)

½ cup mushrooms or
  green peppers (Use any
  combination you desire)
½ cup of your favorite
  pizza sauce (I like Prego)
Garlic salt (optional)

♥ Brown beef and drain fat. Set aside. Beat egg whites. Set aside.
  Spray two cookie sheets with a non-fat cooking spray. With hands
  flatten each biscuit into a thin, flat piece of round dough. Arrange
  15 individual flattened dough pieces on cookie sheets, making
  sure they do not touch. Brush each dough piece with beaten egg
  whites. Set aside.

♥ Preheat oven to 375 degrees. In a bowl mix cheese, mushrooms,
  green peppers, browned meat, and pizza sauce together until
  well coated with sauce. Put a good size rounded tablespoon of
  meat and cheese concoction in the center of each flattened dough
  piece on cookie sheet. Using remaining flattened dough pieces,
  cover each one. Brush sides with egg whites. Using a fork, seal
  dough edges. Brush top with egg whites. Lightly sprinkle tops
  with garlic salt, if desired. Bake for 15 minutes.

Yield: 15 servings

Calories: 158
Percent Fat Calories: 15%
Carbohydrate: 21 grams
Protein: 12 grams

Total Fat: 3 grams
Cholesterol: 18 mg
Dietary Fiber: 1 gram
Sodium: 439 mg

Preparation time: 25-30 minutes.

Down Home Cookin'

ORIGINAL MAGIC POCKETS

(Fast & Easy)

These tasty delectables are fun for children to help make.
Once I created one, it put me on a roll and
I've created many different flavors. Don't limit yourself
to just the ones I've created. Create some of your own!

HAM & CHEESE
MAGIC POCKETS

2   egg whites
3   10-count cans Pillsbury
    Buttermilk Biscuits
¾   pound turkey ham, chopped
    into ¼-inch pieces
1   cup fat-free cheddar cheese
    (I use Healthy Choice)

½   cup mushrooms, chopped
    (optional)
2   Tablespoons fat-free honey
    Dijon salad dressing

♥ Beat egg whites. Set aside. Spray two cookie sheets with a non-fat cooking spray. With hands, flatten each biscuit into a thin, flat piece of round dough. (That's where I have my children help out. While I'm chopping the ingredients, they flatten out the dough.) Arrange 15 individual flattened dough pieces on two cookie sheets making sure they do not touch. Lay extra dough pieces on wax paper until ready to use. Brush each dough piece with egg whites. (The beaten egg whites are the glue which holds the crust together and seals it shut.)

(Ham & Cheese Magic Pockets continued on next page)

(Ham & Cheese Magic Pockets continued)

♥ Preheat oven to 375 degrees. In a bowl, combine chopped ham, cheese, mushrooms, and honey dijon salad dressing. Mix until all ingredients are well coated with dressing. Put a rounded tablespoon of meat and cheese concoction in the center of each flattened dough piece on cookie sheet. Using remaining flattened dough, cover each one and brush sides with egg whites. Using a fork seal dough edges. Brush top with egg whites. Bake for 15 minutes.

Yield: 15 servings

Calories: 144
Percent Fat Calories: 15%
Carbohydrate: 21 grams
Protein: 10 grams

Total Fat: 2 grams
Cholesterol: 17 mg
Dietary Fiber: 1 gram
Sodium: 699 mg

Preparation time: 25 minutes.

Down Home Cookin'

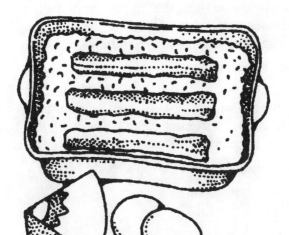

STEAK & ONION PHILLY MAGIC POCKETS

2 egg whites
3 10-count cans Pillsbury
  Buttermilk Biscuits
½ cup onion, finely chopped
¾ pound eye of round (beef),
  sliced into very thin strips,
  ¼ or ½-inch long

¼ cup steak sauce
  (I like Heinz 57)
1 cup fat-free shredded
  mozzarella cheese
  (I use Healthy Choice)

♥ Beat egg whites and set aside. Spray two cookie sheets with a non-fat cooking spray.

♥ With hands, flatten each biscuit into a thin flat piece of round dough. Sauté onion with beef over low heat until thoroughly cooked (4 to 7 minutes). Remove from heat and let cool. Add steak sauce and cheese. Mix until well blended.

♥ Preheat oven to 375 degrees. Arrange 15 pieces of flattened round dough pieces on cookie sheets so that sides do not touch. Brush sides with beaten egg whites. Put a good size tablespoon of meat and cheese concoction in the center of each flattened dough piece on cookie sheet. Using remaining flattened dough pieces, cover each one. With fork seal dough edges together. Brush top with egg whites. Bake for 15 minutes.

Yield: 15 servings

Calories: 150
Percent Fat Calories: 14%
Carbohydrate: 21 grams
Protein: 11 grams

Total Fat: 2 grams
Cholesterol: 14 mg
Dietary Fiber: 1 gram
Sodium: 504 mg

Preparation time: 25-30 minutes.

Down Home Cookin'

PIZZA PASTA

2 7.25-ounce boxes
macaroni and cheese mix
1 envelope Butter Buds, dry
1 cup skim milk

1 14-ounce jar Prego Pizza
Sauce with Ground Sausage
8 ounces fat-free shredded
cheese, if desired

♥ Prepare macaroni and cheese as directed on box, substituting dry Butter Buds for butter and skim milk for ½ cup milk. Once cheese is well mixed in, add pizza sauce. Mix well. Top with fat-free cheese, if desired. Broil at 425 degrees for 3 minutes or until cheese is melted. Serve hot.

♥ This can be made in advance, frozen and baked at 350 degrees for 35-45 minutes when needed.

Yield: 8 servings

Calories: 259
Percent Fat Calories: 15%
Carbohydrate: 46 grams
Protein: 10 grams

Total Fat: 4 grams
Cholesterol: 10 mg
Dietary Fiber: 2 grams
Sodium: 684 mg

Preparation time: 20 minutes.

Down Home Cookin'

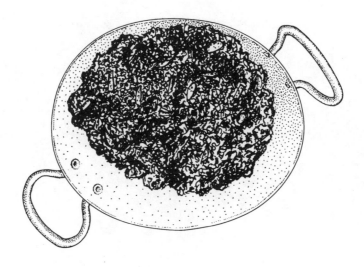

OPEN-FACED
FRESH TOMATO SANDWICHES

2 pieces pocket bread, mini
   size (I use Father Sam's)
8 teaspoons fat-free
   ranch salad dressing
   (I use Seven Seas)

1 medium fresh tomato
   (try to find the deepest
   red-colored one)

♥ Cut pockets in half. Toast each half. Spread 2 teaspoons salad dressing on each half. Cut tomato into 4 slices. Put one slice tomato on each half of toasted pocket bread that has been spread with salad dressing. Eat immediately.

Yield: 4 servings

Calories: 85
Percent Fat Calories: 4%
Carbohydrate: 18 grams
Protein: 3 grams

Total Fat: trace
Cholesterol: 0 mg
Dietary Fiber: 1 gram
Sodium: 233 mg

Preparation time: 10 minutes.

Down Home Cookin'

SWEET PEAS AND PEARL ONIONS

1 (15-ounce) jar pearl onions - drained
2 (15-ounce) cans sweet peas - drained

3 tablespoons reduced-fat vanilla frosting (I use Betty Crocker Sweet Rewards)

♥ Microwave onions and peas together for 2 minutes.

♥ Gently stir in frosting.

♥ Microwave another 2 minutes. Stir.

♥ Serve hot.

Yield: 7 (½-cup) servings

Calories: 109
Percent Fat Calories: 8%
Carbohydrate: 21 grams
Protein: 5 grams

Total Fat: 1 gram
Cholesterol: 0 mg
Dietary Fiber: 4 grams
Sodium: 343 mg

Total time: 5 minutes.

2nd Serving Busy People's Low Fat Cook Book

SPRING ASPARAGUS

1 tablespoon mustard
⅓ cup fat-free sour cream
⅛ teaspoon dried dill weed

2 pounds fresh asparagus - steamed

♥ Mix mustard, sour cream and dill together until well blended. Toss gently with freshly steamed asparagus. Serve immediately. (If needed, this dish can be microwaved for a few minutes to re-warm.)

Yield: 6 servings

Calories: 51
Cholesterol: 0 mg

Total Fat: 0.4 grams (6% fat)
Sodium: 46 mg

Preparation time: 5 minutes or less.

Cooking time: 5 to 7 minutes.

Total time: 12 minutes or less.

Busy People's Low-Fat Cook Book

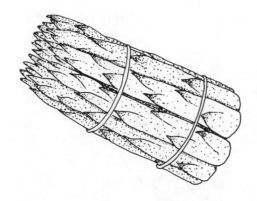

Asparagus and Mushrooms

2 (14.5-ounce) cans
  asparagus - do not drain
1 (4-ounce) can mushroom
  stems and pieces - do
  not drain

½ teaspoon garlic powder
2 tablespoons Promise
  Ultra 70% less fat
  margarine

♥ Mix asparagus and mushrooms together. Cover.

♥ Cook in carousel microwave for 2 to 3 minutes or until fully heated.

♥ Drain juice from vegetables. Gently toss cooked vegetables with garlic powder and Promise Ultra 70% less fat margarine. Serve hot.

Yield: 5 (½-cup) servings

Calories: 48
Percent Fat Calories: 29%
Carbohydrate: 6 grams
Protein: 4 grams

Total Fat: 2 grams
Cholesterol: 0 mg
Dietary Fiber: 2 grams
Sodium: 657 mg

Total time: 5 minutes.

2nd Serving Busy People's Low Fat Cook Book

Menu Ideas: Great served with any lean meat.

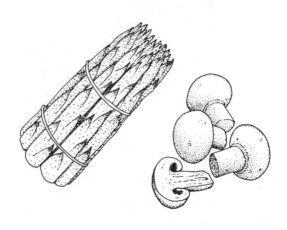

UNFRIED VEGGIES

My arteries and waistline know I can't
eat fried foods. I never miss the fat or the
mess with these crispy unfried veggies!

1 cup instant potato flakes	4 egg whites
⅓ cup Kraft Free non-fat grated topping (made with Parmesan cheese)	4-5 cups bite-sized fresh vegetables (mushrooms, onions and zucchini)
¾ teaspoon garlic salt	Non-fat cooking spray

♥ Preheat oven to 400 degrees.

♥ Spray cookie sheet with non-fat cooking spray. If desired, line cookie sheet with foil for faster clean up.

♥ Mix potato flakes, grated topping and garlic salt together in a small bowl.

♥ In a separate bowl, beat egg whites with a fork for one minute.

♥ Dip vegetables, one at a time, into beaten egg whites. Then dip into dry mixture, coating well.

♥ Place on prepared cookie sheet, making sure vegetables do not touch each other. Spray vegetables lightly with non-fat cooking spray.

♥ Bake at 400 degrees for 10 minutes. Turn over and bake an additional 5 minutes or until crispy and golden brown.

♥ Season with lite salt, if desired.

♥ Serve hot.

Yield: 8 servings

Calories: 46	Total Fat: 0 grams
Percent Fat Calories: 0%	Cholesterol: 0 mg
Carbohydrate: 9 grams	Dietary Fiber: 1 gram
Protein: 3 grams	Sodium: 189 mg

Total time: 30 minutes or less.

2nd Serving Busy People's Low Fat Cook Book

Menu Ideas: Serve with fat-free
Ranch salad dressing for dipping.

CALICO CORN

*This slightly sweet and definitely unique
vegetable dish received it's name because
of its beautiful color combination.*

2   (15¼-ounce} cans whole
    kernel corn - drained
1   tablespoon sugar

¼   cup Western fat-free salad
    dressing
1   cup your favorite chunky
    salsa

♥ In a 2-quart microwavable bowl, mix together all ingredients until well blended.

♥ Heat in microwave on full power for 3 minutes or until completely warmed.

Yield: 7 (½-cup) servings

Calories: 102
Cholesterol: 0 mg

Total Fat: 0.9 grams (7% fat)
Sodium: 436 mg

Preparation time: 3 minutes or less.

Cooking time: 3 minutes.

Total time: 6 minutes or less

Busy People's Low-Fat Cook Book

*Menu Ideas: Compliments any lean meat cooked
on the grill, baked or broiled.*

*Salad topper idea: Sprinkle chilled on top of and toss with
a fresh, crisp, green lettuce salad instead of the
traditional fresh tomatoes or vegetables. Serve salad
dressing of your choice on the side.*

GREEN BEANS ITALIANO'

1-1½ cups thinly sliced onion
(2 medium onions)
¾ cup fat-free Italian salad
dressing (I use Wish Bone)
1 (14½-ounce) can diced
tomatoes - drained
(I use Hunts)

2 (16-ounce) bags frozen
green beans
½ tablespoon lite salt -
optional

♥ In a large non-stick skillet (about 12-inch) sauté onions in salad dressing over medium heat about 2 to 3 minutes or until tender. Add drained diced tomatoes and green beans. Increase heat to medium-high. Stir until well coated. Salt if desired. Cover. Cook for 5 to 7 minutes or until beans are tender.

♥ Serve hot.

Yield: 12 (²/₃-cup) servings

Calories: 39
Cholesterol: 0 mg

Total Fat: 0.2 grams (4% fat)
Sodium: 186 mg

Preparation time: 5 minutes or less.

Cooking time: 10 minutes or less.

Total time: 15 minutes or less.

Busy People's Low-Fat Cook Book

Menu Ideas: They go great with entrées that have a marinara sauce (red sauce) like lasagna or spaghetti.

CARROTS WITH A LIGHT
BUTTERY CARAMEL GLAZE

1 pound mini carrots (peeled - found in produce section)	½ teaspoon lite salt - optional
2 tablespoons Fleischmann's Fat-Free Buttery Spread (found in butter and margarine section of grocery store)	2 tablespoons Smuckers fat-free caramel topping (found in ice cream section of grocery store)

♥ Place carrots in a medium (2-quart) saucepan. Put just enough water in pan to cover carrots. Bring to a boil. Turn off heat and cover. Let sit for 10 to 13 minutes or until carrots are tender when pierced with a fork.

♥ Meantime while carrots are cooking, in a small bowl stir together butter, salt and caramel sauce until well blended.

♥ When cooked, drain carrots and mix with caramel glaze.

♥ Serve hot.

Yield: 5 servings

Calories: 71
Cholesterol: 0 mg

Total Fat: 0.2 grams (2% fat)
Sodium: 84 mg

Preparation time: 3 minutes.

Cooking time: 10-13 minutes.

Total time: 16 minutes or less.

Busy People's Low-Fat Cook Book

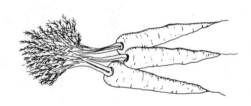

Buttered Collard Greens With Ham

2 15-ounce cans chopped
   collard greens
1 apple, quartered, with
   seeds removed
1 tablespoon Butter Buds

6 ounces deli-thin sliced
   boiled ham, cut into
   bite-sized pieces
   (I use deli-thin Oscar
   Mayer boiled ham)
1 small onion, chopped
   (approximately ⅓ cup)

♥ Drain collard greens. In large saucepan, combine all ingredients, and cook over medium heat. Cover and bring to a boil. Reduce heat to low. Simmer covered for 10 minutes. Remove apple quarters before serving.

Yield: 6 servings

Calories: 60
Percent Fat Calories: 19%
Carbohydrate: 7 grams
Protein: 7 grams

Total Fat: 2 grams
Cholesterol: 14 mg
Dietary Fiber: 3 grams
Sodium: 440 mg

Preparation time: 25 minutes.

Down Home Cookin'

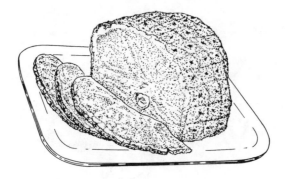

GREEN BEAN DELITE

1 medium onion, chopped
8 ounces mushrooms,
   thinly sliced
½ cup liquid Butter Buds
8 ounces lean ham, diced

3 15.5-ounce cans French-
   style green beans, drained
3 tablespoons honey
1 teaspoon lite salt (optional)

♥ Sauté onions and mushrooms in Butter Buds until tender. Add ham, green beans, and honey. Cook over medium heat until heated thoroughly. Add salt if desired.

Yield: 15 servings

Calories: 54
Percent Fat Calories: 13%
Carbohydrate: 9 grams
Protein: 4 grams

Total Fat: 1 gram
Cholesterol: 6 mg
Dietary Fiber: 2 grams
Sodium: 394 mg

Preparation time: 20 minutes.

Down Home Cookin'

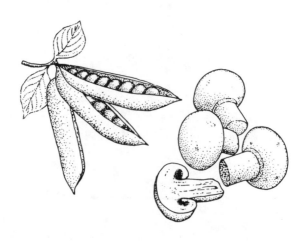

BLACK BEANS AND RICE

*A southern dish made
in a fraction of the original time.*

2 teaspoons minced garlic
(I use the kind in a jar)
1 teaspoon liquid smoke
(found with barbecue
sauce)
4 ounces extra lean cooked
ham - cut into tiny pieces
(lunch meat if fine)

½ cup frozen or fresh
chopped onion
1 (15-ounce) can black
beans - do not drain
(I use Progresso)
1 cup instant long grain
white rice

♥ Bring all ingredients except rice to a full boil in a 4½-quart saucepan over medium-high heat.

♥ Stir in rice. Cover.

♥ Remove from heat. Let sit 5 minutes.

♥ Serve hot.

Yield: 4 (1-cup) entrée servings

Calories: 225
Percent Fat Calories: 14%
Carbohydrate: 34 grams
Protein: 13 grams

Total Fat: 4 grams
Cholesterol: 13 mg
Dietary Fiber: 6 grams
Sodium: 736 mg

Yield: 8 (½-cup) side dish servings

Calories: 112
Percent Fat Calories: 14%
Carbohydrate: 17 grams
Protein: 7 grams

Total Fat: 2 grams
Cholesterol: 7 mg
Dietary Fiber: 3 grams
Sodium: 368 mg

Total time: 25 minutes or less.

2nd Serving Busy People's Low Fat Cook Book

*Menu Ideas: Tastes wonderful with cornbread and
Buttered Collard Greens with Ham.*

GARLIC BEANS

1 (1-pound) bag frozen green beans
4 ounces fresh mushrooms - sliced (for faster preparation, buy them pre-sliced in the produce section)
¼ cup Butter Buds Sprinkles - dry

1 tablespoon minced garlic (I use the kind in a jar)
Light salt - to taste
Black pepper - to taste
½ cup fat-free, reduced - sodium chicken or beef broth (or made from bouillon)

♥ Spray a crockpot with non-fat cooking spray.

♥ Put all ingredients into crockpot. Cover.

♥ Cook on high for 3 hours or on low for 6 hours.

Yield: 8 (½-cup) servings

Calories: 32
Percent Fat Calories: 0%
Carbohydrate: 8 grams
Protein: 2 grams

Total Fat: 0 grams
Cholesterol: 0 mg
Dietary Fiber: 2 grams
Sodium: 187 mg

Preparation time: 5 minutes.

2nd Serving Busy People's Low Fat Cook Book

Menu Ideas: Great side dish for any meal!

8 LAYER CHILI CASSEROLE

If only all vegetarian dishes could be
this satisfying and hearty!

1   medium onion - chopped
1   (16-ounce) can fat-free
    refried beans
1   (15-ounce) can Health Valley
    mild vegetarian fat-free chili
    with black beans

1   (8-ounce) bottle mild taco
    sauce
1   (11-ounce) package 10-inch
    fat-free flour tortillas
    (I used Chi-Chi's)

♥ Spray a 2½-quart, round, covered microwavable casserole dish
with non-fat cooking spray. Set aside.

♥ In a medium bowl, microwave onions, covered, for 2 minutes.

♥ Stir in refried beans, chili and taco sauce until well blended.

♥ Tear 2 of the tortillas into small pieces. (These will be used to fill
in the outer space between the tortilla layer and casserole dish.)

♥ Lay a tortilla flat on bottom of casserole dish. If needed use torn
tortilla to fill in space between casserole dish and edge.

♥ Top with ¾ cup of chili mixture. Top with a tortilla.

♥ Continue layering chili mixture (¾ cup at a time) and tortillas
until all ingredients are used.

♥ Cover and microwave on high for 10 minutes. Let sit for 5 minutes
before serving.

♥ Cut with a sharp knife (a steak knife works well) cutting through
all layers as you would a pie.

Yield: 8 servings

Calories: 219
Cholesterol: 0 mg

Total Fat: 0 grams (0% fat)
Sodium: 852 mg

Preparation time: 10 minutes or less.

Cooking time: 10 minutes. (Plus 5 minutes sitting time)

Total time: 25 minutes or less.

Busy People's Low-Fat Cook Book

HAWAIIAN STYLE BAKED BEANS

A delicious twist to an old time favorite,
which is packed with protein! Great as a meal or side dish!

2 (16-ounce) cans vegetarian baked beans (I use Bush's Best)

¼ cup chopped onion (for faster preparation use frozen chopped onions)

¼ cup Teriyaki Baste and Glaze (I use Kikkoman's) - found in barbecue section of grocery store

4 ounces extra lean cooked ham – cut into bite-size pieces (2 grams of fat per 2 ounces)

1 (8-ounce) can crushed pineapple in unsweetened pineapple juice - drained

♥ Spray container you are going to cook this recipe in with non-fat cooking spray. (For easier clean-up).

♥ Look on chart for desired cooking method and times.

♥ When cooking this dish you have 3 options:

A. 2-quart microwavable container.

B. Crockpot.

C. 2-quart saucepan.

♥ Mix all ingredients in container you are going to cook it in, until well mixed.

♥ Cover and cook:

A. in carousel microwave on high for 3 minutes or until completely heated.

B. in crockpot on low for 4 hours.

C. in a saucepan until sauce is boiling. Turn off heat and let simmer for 3 to 4 minutes.

(Hawaiian Style Baked Beans continued on next page)

(Hawaiian Style Baked Beans continued)

Yield: 11 (½-cup) side dish servings

Calories: 112	Total Fat: 0.9 grams (7% fat)
Cholesterol: 5 mg	Sodium: 622 mg

Yield: 5 (1-cup) entrée size servings

Calories: 245	Total Fat: 2.0 grams (7% fat)
Cholesterol: 11 mg	Sodium: 1369 mg

Preparation time: 5 minutes or less.

Cooking time varies, depending on method you used.

Busy People's Low-Fat Cook Book

"B.B.B." (Best Baked Beans)

My daughters loved these so much that they named the recipe themselves! They are very filling, satisfying and delicious! No one would ever believe they're fat-free! Eat as a meal or side dish. A fun way to serve these when it's the entrée is by using a pie pan as the plate.

*1 (1-pound) package ground meatless all-vegetable burger crumbles (I use Morningstar Farms Brand found in frozen section next to ground turkey) (or 1 pound cooked ground eye of round or 1 pound cooked skinless ground turkey breast)

1 (15-ounce) can butter beans - drained

2 (16-ounce) cans fat-free vegetarian baked beans (I used Bush's Best)

¾ cup Kraft Thick n' Spicy Brown Sugar Flavored barbecue sauce

½ cup chopped onion (for faster preparation use chopped frozen onions)

♥ Spray whatever cooking container you are going to use with non-fat cooking spray. (You have 2 choices, the crockpot or a 2-quart microwavable container.)

♥ Mix all ingredients in the container you are going to cook it in, until well mixed.

♥ Cooking Method:

Carousel microwave: Cover. Cook on high for 5 minutes.
Crockpot: Cover. Cook on low for 4 hours.

♥ *Note: For those of you who don't like vegetarian meat substitute, you'll love this! In regards to the rest of the family . . . don't tell them it's not real beef and they'll never know! (Some things are better left unsaid!)

Yield: 16 (½-cup) side dish servings

("B.B.B." Best Baked Beans continued on next page)

("B.B.B." Best Baked Beans continued)

With Ground Meatless:
Calories: 125   Total Fat: 0.5 grams (4% fat)
Cholesterol: 0 mg   Sodium: 585 mg

With Ground Eye of Round:
Calories: 113   Total Fat: 1.5 grams (12% fat)
Cholesterol: 15 mg   Sodium: 404 mg

With Ground Turkey Breast:
Calories: 109   Total Fat: 0.8 grams (6% fat)
Cholesterol: 19 mg   Sodium: 403 mg

Yield: 8 (1-cup) entrée size servings

With Ground Meatless:
Calories: 249   Total Fat: 1.0 grams (4% fat)
Cholesterol: 29 mg   Sodium: 807 mg

With Ground Eye of Round:
Calories: 225   Total Fat: 3.0 grams (12% fat)
Cholesterol: 29 mg   Sodium: 807 mg

With ground Turkey Breast:
Calories: 217   Total Fat: 1.6 grams (6% fat)
Cholesterol: 39 mg   Sodium: 806 mg

Total preparation time: (Using Ground Meatless) 6 minutes or less.

Cooking time: 5 minutes in microwave on high or 4-5 hours on low in crockpot.

Busy People's Low-Fat Cook Book

Menu Ideas: Great side dish for any cookout or potluck. Also terrific as an entrée, serve with a salad or fresh vegetable sticks with dip, cornbread and strawberries over angel food cake for dessert.

Pizza Burritos

I hit a home run when I created these!
All my fans (family) cheer for more.

1 (16-ounce) can fat-free refried beans

2 (14-ounce) jars of Ragu Pizza Quick Sauce (chunky tomato flavor)

1 (8-ounce) package of fat-free mozzarella cheese (I used Healthy Indulgence)

20 (10-inch) fat-free tortillas

♥ In a medium bowl, combine refried beans, Ragu Pizza Sauce and fat-free cheese. Stir until well mixed.

♥ To soften, put the stack of tortilla shells in the carousel microwave on high for 1 minute.

♥ Take one flour tortilla, put 2 heaping tablespoons of the above mixture, into the center. Roll up the tortilla and place in the carousel microwave for 10 seconds.

♥ If desired, you can make numerous pizza burritos and multiply the number of burritos you have by 10 seconds each to figure out cooking time.

Yield: 20 servings

Calories: 252
Cholesterol: 1 mg

Total Fat: 0 grams (0% fat)
Sodium: 817 mg

Preparation time including cooking: 10-12 minutes.

Busy People's Low-Fat Cook Book

Menu Ideas: This goes good with salsa and fat-free tortilla chips, tossed salad and frozen yogurt topped with fruit.

POTATOES A-LA-LARRY

Chicken broth (from a
  can, preferably)
Instant mashed potatoes
Skim milk
Fat-free margarine
  (I use Fleishmann's)

1 15- to 20-ounce can
    potatoes, drained and
    mashed
¼ cup fresh onion, finely
    chopped (per every
    8 servings)

♥ Substituting chicken broth for water, use exact same measurements needed to prepare instant mashed potatoes, according to package directions. Stir in milk, margarine, mashed potatoes, and onion. Presto!! You're done.

Yield: 4 servings

Calories: 17
Percent Fat Calories: 5%
Carbohydrate: 35 grams
Protein: 5 grams

Total Fat: 1 gram
Cholesterol: 1 mg
Dietary Fiber: 4 grams
Sodium: 672 mg

Preparation time: 20 minutes.

Down Home Cookin'

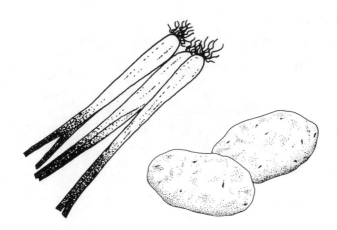

SOUR CREAM AND CHIVES MASHED POTATOES

*No one would believe that these light and fluffy
potatoes aren't made from scratch!*

2²/₃ cups fat-free reduced-
   sodium chicken broth
   (or made from bouillon)
²/₃ cup fat-free half & half
2²/₃ cups instant potatoes
   (I use Betty Crocker
   Potato Buds)

1 (15-ounce) can whole
   potatoes - drained
   (discard liquid)
³/₄ cup fat-free sour cream
¹/₂ cup chopped fresh chives
   (or ¹/₄ cup dried) - divided

♥ In a 2-quart saucepan, bring chicken broth and half & half to a full boil. Turn off heat.

♥ Stir in instant potatoes until moistened. Let sit for 30 seconds or until all liquid is absorbed.

♥ Meantime, mash whole potatoes in a serving bowl into tiny chunks. Microwave potato chunks for up to 2 minutes, or until potato chunks are fully heated.

♥ Stir instant mashed potatoes, warmed potato chunks, sour cream and all but 1 teaspoon chives together in serving bowl until well blended.

♥ Sprinkle reserved 1 teaspoon of chives on top.

Yield: 10 (¹/₂-cup) servings

Calories: 100
Percent Fat Calories: 0%
Carbohydrate: 20 grams
Protein: 5 grams

Total Fat: 0 grams
Cholesterol: 2 mg
Dietary Fiber: 2 grams
Sodium: 255 mg

Total time: 20 minutes.

(Sour Cream and Chives Mashed Potatoes continued on next page)

(Sour Cream and Chives Mashed Potatoes continued)

Twice Baked Mashed Potatoes:

Make the Sour Cream and Chives Mashed Potatoes recipe exactly the same, except stir in ¼ cup real bacon bits. (I use Hormel. It's about ⅓ of a jar.)

Yield: 10 (½-cup) servings

Calories: 110
Percent Fat Calories: 6%
Carbohydrate: 20 grams
Protein: 6 grams

Total Fat: 1 gram
Cholesterol: 4 mg
Dietary Fiber: 2 grams
Sodium: 344 mg

2nd Serving Busy People's Low Fat Cook Book

PARMESAN POTATOES

*Here's a quick and easy
way to perk up your French fries.*

3 tablespoons grated
  fat-free Parmesan cheese
½ teaspoon black pepper
1 teaspoon garlic salt

1 (1-pound) package frozen
  French fries (no more
  than 3 grams of fat per
  100 calories)

♥ Preheat oven to 450 degrees.

♥ Spray a cookie sheet with non-fat cooking spray.

♥ Put Parmesan cheese, pepper and garlic salt in large plastic bag. Shake until well mixed.

♥ Put fries in bag with seasonings. Shake until well coated.

♥ Pour entire contents of bag on prepared cookie sheet. Spray seasoned fries with cooking spray.

♥ Bake at 400 degrees for 20 minutes or until golden brown.

Yield: 4 servings

Calories: 111
Percent Fat Calories: 6%
Carbohydrate: 24 grams
Protein: 3 grams

Total Fat: 1 gram
Cholesterol: 0 mg
Dietary Fiber: 2 grams
Sodium: 562 mg

Total time: 25 minutes.

2nd Serving Busy People's Low Fat Cook Book

*Menu Ideas: Fat-free
hot dogs or lean steak or chicken breast.*

GARLIC RED SKINS

2 pounds red skin
  potatoes - washed
2 tablespoons chopped garlic
  (to save time purchase
  pre-chopped garlic in a jar
  from the produce section)

1 teaspoon lite salt
½ Cup Fleischmann's Recipe
  Fat-Free Buttery Spread
1 teaspoon dried parsley

♥ Cut unpeeled red skins into 1-inch cubes.

♥ Put cubed potatoes into boiling water. Turn heat off. Let set for 15 to 20 minutes or until potatoes are tender when poked with a fork.

♥ In a large 12-inch non-stick skillet, cook garlic over medium heat with salt and butter spread for just a few minutes to heat (and make the home smell yummy!).

♥ Drain water from red skins.

♥ Stir red skins into garlic butter until well coated.

♥ Pour into serving dish. Sprinkle with dried parsley.

♥ Serve immediately.

Yield: 8 servings

Calories: 108
Cholesterol: 0 mg

Total Fat: 0 grams (0% fat)
Sodium: 220 mg

Preparation time: 8 minutes or less.

Cooking time: 15-20 minutes.

Total time: 28 minutes or less.

Busy People's Low-Fat Cook Book

Menu Ideas: Good with meat entrées such as beef tenderloin, chicken, fish or turkey.

SWEET POTATO STICKS

These are a favorite for everyone in our family!
Not crispy like French fries, but they're
definitely delicious!

1   large sweet potato   Lite salt
    Non-fat cooking spray

♥ Preheat oven to 425 degrees.

♥ Spray 2 cookie sheets with non-fat cooking spray.

♥ Scrub sweet potatoes and cut into ¼-inch fries about 3 inches long.

♥ Arrange on prepared cookie sheets. Spray fries with non-fat cooking spray.

♥ Bake at 425 degrees for 10 minutes, or until bottoms are slightly brown. (Baking time will depend on thickness of fries.)

♥ Turn over. Spray again with non-fat cooking spray. Bake an additional 7 to 10 minutes or until potatoes are tender.

♥ Sprinkle lightly with lite salt.

♥ Serve hot.

Yield: 2 servings

Calories: 142   Total Fat: 0 grams
Percent Fat Calories: 0%   Cholesterol: 0 mg
Carbohydrate: 36 grams   Dietary Fiber: 4 grams
Protein: 2 grams   Sodium: 49 mg

Total time: 20 to 25 minutes or less.

Sweet Potato Disks: Bake exactly the same as Sweet Potato Sticks, but cut the potato into very thin slices, like you would potato chips.

2nd Serving Busy People's Low Fat Cook Book

Menu Ideas: Great with sandwiches or
fat-free hot dogs.

Apricot Sweet Potatoes (Yams)

1 (40-ounce) can cut sweet potatoes (yams) in light syrup - drained (discard syrup)

⅓ cup apricot preserves (with no large chunks of apricots)

♥ Spray a microwavable medium serving bowl with non-fat cooking spray.

♥ With mixer mix sweet potatoes (yams) with apricot preserves in prepared bowl until the consistency of thick mashed potatoes, but with large chunks.

♥ Cover lightly with wax paper and microwave for 2 to 3 minutes or until completely heated throughout.

Yield: 8 (½-cup) servings

Calories: 129
Percent Fat Calories: 0%
Carbohydrate: 31 grams
Protein: 2 grams

Total Fat: 0 grams
Cholesterol: 0 mg
Dietary Fiber: 2 grams
Sodium: 62 mg

Total time: 8 minutes or less.

2nd Serving Busy People's Low Fat Cook Book

Menu Ideas: Great for holidays with pork tenderloin, lean ham or turkey.

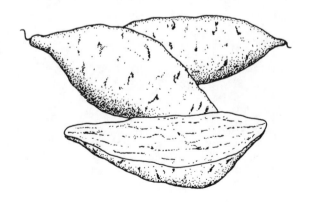

MASHED YAMS WITH AN ORANGE KISS

The orange juice along with the pumpkin pie spice gives this dish an excellent flavor!

2 (40-ounce) cans yams – drained (discard juice)	½ cup fat-free Ultra Promise
½ cup Egg Beaters	¼ cup brown sugar
½ cup orange juice	½ teaspoon pumpkin pie spice

♥ Mash yams in a large microwavable bowl.

♥ Add remaining ingredients and mix well with a mixer for about 1 minute.

♥ Microwave for 7 to 10 minutes or until set, stirring once.

Yield: 14 (½-cup) servings

Calories: 149	Total Fat: 0 grams
Percent Fat Calories: 0%	Cholesterol: 0 mg
Carbohydrate: 33 grams	Dietary Fiber: 2 grams
Protein: 3 grams	Sodium: 158 mg

Total time: 15 minutes

2nd Serving Busy People's Low Fat Cook Book

Menu Ideas: Great as a side dish with lean pork, ham, chicken and of course turkey.

SEASONED RICE

This dish is excellent with the
"Oriental Teriyaki Beef Dinner."

1 cup long grain rice	1 1.4-ounce envelope
2¼ cups water	Knorr vegetable soup mix

♥ Spray medium saucepan with a non-fat cooking spray. Add all ingredients, stir and dissolve soup. Bring to a boil, then reduce heat to simmering. Cover and cook approximately 20 minutes.

Yield: 6 servings

Calories: 133	Total Fat: 0 grams
Percent Fat Calories: 0%	Cholesterol: 0 mg
Carbohydrate: 29 grams	Dietary Fiber: 1 gram
Protein: 3 grams	Sodium: 488 mg

Preparation time: 30 minutes.

Down Home Cookin'

APPLE YAM CASSEROLE

This is a great dish for holidays.

1 20-ounce can apple
  pie filling
½ teaspoon cinnamon
2 tablespoons brown sugar

Dash of salt (optional)
1 24-ounce can yams,
  drained and cut into
  bite-sized pieces

♥ Cut apples in pie filling into bite-sized pieces. In a medium bowl mix apple pie filling, cinnamon, brown sugar, and salt until well blended. Gently stir in cut-up yams. Spray two-quart casserole dish with non-fat cooking spray. Pour in mixture, and microwave until warm about 5 minutes, stirring occasionally. Serve warm.

Yield: 12 servings

Calories: 96
Percent Fat Calories: 0%
Carbohydrate: 23 grams
Protein: 1 gram

Total Fat: 0 grams
Cholesterol: 0 mg
Dietary Fiber
Sodium: 39 mg

Preparation time: 25 minutes.

Down Home Cookin'

ITALIAN RICE

A nice alternative to spaghetti.

1 pound ground beef eye of round (or 1 pound Ground Meatless, or turkey breast)

1 (28-ounce) jar of your favorite fat-free pasta sauce (I use Ragu Light)

1 (8-ounce) can sliced mushrooms

3 cups water

3 cups instant rice

½ cup Kraft Free grated Parmesan cheese topping

♥ In a large, 3-quart nonstick pan, bring ground beef eye of round, pasta sauce, mushrooms and water to a full boil, stirring occasionally.

♥ Stir in rice and cover. Remove from heat. Let sit 5 minutes.

♥ Evenly sprinkle all servings with Kraft Free grated Parmesan cheese topping.

♥ Serve hot.

Yield: 6 (1²/₃ cup) entrée servings

With ground beef eye of round:

Calories: 353

Percent Fat Calories: 9%

Carbohydrate: 54 grams

Protein: 24 grams

Total Fat: 3 grams

Cholesterol: 41 mg

Dietary Fiber: 3 grams

Sodium: 746 mg

With Ground Meatless:

Calories: 336

Percent Fat Calories: 2%

Carbohydrate: 59 grams

Protein: 22 grams

Total Fat: 1 gram

Cholesterol: 0 mg

Dietary Fiber: 6 grams

Sodium: 1064 mg

Total time: 20 minutes.

2nd Serving Busy People's Low Fat Cook Book

KIELBASA AND RICE

Sauerkraut lovers will love this dish.

1 (14-ounce) package
   fat-free Polish kielbasa
   (Butterball) - cut into
   tiny pieces
1 (16-ounce) can sauerkraut
   (rinse and squeeze dry
   with hands)

1 (14.5-ounce) can
   no-salt-added stewed
   tomatoes - cut into
   bite-size pieces
2½ cups low-sodium V8
   vegetable juice
2 cups instant rice

♥ In a large, 3-quart nonstick pan, bring kielbasa, sauerkraut, stewed tomatoes and V8 juice to a full boil, stirring occasionally.

♥ Stir in rice and cover.

♥ Remove from heat and let sit 5 minutes.

Yield: 4 (1¾-cup) servings

Calories: 354
Percent Fat Calories: 0%
Carbohydrate: 66 grams
Protein: 21 grams

Total Fat: 0 grams
Cholesterol: 43 mg
Dietary Fiber: 3 grams
Sodium: 1779 mg

Total time: 20 minutes or less.

2nd Serving Busy People's Low Fat Cook Book

The easiest, quickest way to cut tomatoes is to leave in can. Insert a knife in can and cut.

ZANY ZITI - ONE POT ZITI

*A creamy, zany, ziti dish! I like to take this
dish to new moms. Usually they like it so much they
want the recipe. It's so easy! It becomes a family favorite!*

2¼ cups water
2 (27.5-ounce) jars Ragu
light pasta sauce

1 (16-ounce) package ziti
1 (16-ounce) container
fat-free sour cream
Kraft Free Parmesan cheese
topping - optional

♥ In a 4-quart, nonstick Dutch oven or nonstick soup pot, bring water and pasta sauce to a full boil over medium-high heat.

♥ Add ziti. Stir until well mixed. Return to a full boil over medium-high heat.

♥ Reduce heat to a low boil over medium-low heat and cover.

♥ Cook for 25 minutes, stirring occasionally (every 3 to 4 minutes).

♥ Remove from heat. Stir in sour cream.

♥ Serve immediately with Kraft Free Parmesan cheese on the side, if desired.

Yield: 12 (1-cup) servings

Calories: 225
Percent Fat Calories: 2%
Carbohydrate: 45 grams
Protein: 9 grams

Total Fat: 1 gram
Cholesterol: 3 mg
Dietary Fiber: 3 grams
Sodium: 438 mg

Total time: 30 minutes or less.

2nd Serving Busy People's Low Fat Cook Book

*Menu Ideas: Greek Salad, French bread,
sugar-free Jell-O with Cool Whip Free topping.*

FRENCH FRIES

Childrens' favorite way to eat their vegetables!

4 potatoes - your favorite type of potato   Non-fat cooking spray

♥ Preheat oven to 425 degrees.

♥ Spray cookie sheet with non-fat cooking spray. Set aside.

♥ Cut potatoes into long strips, ¼-inch thickness.

♥ Lay potatoes on cookie sheet. Do not let edges touch.

♥ Spray tops of potatoes with non-fat cooking spray.

♥ Bake at 425 degrees for 20 minutes. Turn fries over. Bake another 15 to 20 minutes. Fries will be crispy and golden when done.

Yield: 4 servings

Calories: 133   Total Fat: 0 grams (0% fat)
Cholesterol: 0 mg   Sodium: 10 mg

Seasoned Fries:
Make the same but sprinkle with Lawry's seasoned salt after you have sprayed the tops with non-fat cooking spray.

Yield: 4 servings

Total preparation time: 40 minutes or less.

Busy People's Low-Fat Cook Book

ALMOST HOMEMADE DRESSING

*The slight crunchiness of the corn mixed with
the turkey, onion, mushrooms, and seasoning makes
this taste homemade — to be honest — just
as good as my homemade!*

3⅓ cups water plus ½ cup
1   medium onion,
    chopped
2   4-ounce cans sliced
    mushrooms
1   package Butter Buds
    - dry - OR 1 tablespoon
    Butter Buds Sprinkles

1   16-ounce can corn
2   boxes chicken stuffing
    (I use Stove Top)
2   cups chopped turkey
    or chicken breast
⅛ teaspoon ground pepper

♥ Put water, chopped onion, mushrooms, Butter Buds, and seasoning packets from stuffing mixes into medium saucepan. Bring to a boil. Reduce heat. Add corn. Simmer 4 minutes. Add bread crumbs from stuffing boxes. Remove from heat. Let sit 5 minutes. Heat turkey in microwave until warm (about 40 seconds). Season turkey with pepper. Stir turkey into stuffing. Serve immediately.

Yield: 15 servings

Calories: 143
Percent Fat Calories: 8%
Carbohydrate: 23 grams
Protein: 10 grams

Total Fat: 1 gram
Cholesterol: 16 mg
Dietary Fiber: 1 gram
Sodium: 498 mg

Preparation time: 20 minutes.

Down Home Cookin'

SAUERKRAUT SPAGHETTI

I know this recipe sounds crazy. To be honest, when I heard it from a friend I thought she was nuts, but my curiosity killed the cat! It's really good!

For however much you want to make, use this formula. This is for one serving.

½ cup low sodium sauerkraut
¾ cup spaghetti sauce
   (I use Prego Extra Chunky
   Garden Combination)

Parmesan cheese (optional)

♥ Drain sauerkraut and rinse. Squeeze dry. Mix spaghetti sauce with sauerkraut. Warm in the microwave. Sprinkle with grated Parmesan cheese, if desired. Serve warm.

Note: Calories can be cut 40 percent by using Healthy Choice Spaghetti Sauce.

Yield: 1 servings

Calories: 149
Percent Fat Calories: 10%
Carbohydrate: 27 grams
Protein: 4 grams

Total Fat: 2 grams
Cholesterol: 0 mg
Dietary Fiber: 6 grams
Sodium: 939 mg

Preparation time: 15 minutes

Down Home Cookin'

HAWAIIAN PUMPKIN CASSEROLE

*A unique and flavorful combination blending
the tropical flavors of the Hawaiian Islands
with "down home" goodness.*

¼ cup shredded coconut
1 (30-ounce) can pumpkin
  pie mix (Libby's)

1 (20-ounce) can crushed
  pineapple - drain and
  discard 1 cup pineapple
  juice

♥ Preheat oven to 500 degrees.

♥ Spray a cookie sheet and a 2-quart microwavable casserole dish with non-fat cooking spray.

♥ Broil coconut on cookie sheet for 45 to 60 seconds or until toasty brown.

♥ Mix pumpkin pie mix, drained crushed pineapple and three-fourths of the toasted coconut together in prepared microwavable bowl. Microwave, covered, for 4 to 5 minutes or until fully heated in a carousel microwave.

♥ Sprinkle remaining toasted coconut on top of casserole.

♥ Serve hot.

Yield: 8 (½-cup) servings

Calories: 126
Percent Fat Calories: 6%
Carbohydrate: 30 grams
Protein: 1 gram

Total Fat: 1 gram
Cholesterol: 0 mg
Dietary Fiber: 3 grams
Sodium: 152 mg

Total time: 10 minutes or less.

2nd Serving Busy People's Low Fat Cook Book

Menu Ideas: Serve with lean ham.

SPICED APPLES

4 Jonathan apples - unpeeled and sliced into ⅛-inch slices
2 tablespoons dry Butter Buds Sprinkles
1 teaspoon ground cinnamon
¼ small cups dark brown sugar

♥ Toss all ingredients together until well mixed.

♥ Put in a microwavable 1-quart casserole dish. Cover with wax paper. Cook on high in carousel microwave for 4 minutes.

Yield: 4 servings

Calories: 144
Cholesterol: 0 mg

Total Fat: 0.5 grams (3% fat)
Sodium: 36 mg

Preparation time: 5 minutes or less.

Cooking time: 4 minutes.

Total time: 9 minutes or less.

Busy People's Low-Fat Cook Book

Menu Idea: Delicious as a side dish, served over frozen fat-free vanilla ice cream or topped with a dab of Cool Whip Free

CHICKEN CAESAR ROLL-UP

1 pound boneless, skinless chicken breast
1 (10-count) package fat-free flour tortillas (I use Buena Vida)
1 (10-ounce) package Dole Special Blends Italian romaine lettuce and radicchio (found in produce section)

¼ cup finely shredded Italian Parmesan cheese (I use Kraft)
¾ cup fat-free Caesar Italian dressing (I use Kraft)

♥ Cut chicken breasts into small bite-size pieces. Cook in a large, nonstick skillet, sprayed with non-fat cooking spray, until no longer pink.

♥ In the meantime, microwave tortillas until warm. (About 1 minute).

♥ After you've cooked chicken, in a bowl toss cooked chicken, salad mix, cheese and dressing together.

♥ Put ½ cup of salad/chicken mixture in center of each warm tortilla. Roll-up and enjoy!

Yield: 10 servings

Calories: 293
Percent Fat Calories: 7%
Carbohydrate: 26 grams
Protein: 15 grams

Total Fat: 1 gram
Cholesterol: 28 mg
Dietary Fiber: 1 gram
Sodium: 657 mg

Total time: 15 minutes.

2nd Serving Busy People's Low Fat Cook Book

Chicken Linguine

1 pound boneless, skinless chicken breasts - cut into small bite-size pieces
1 (16-ounce) package linguine

1 (16-ounce) jar Ragu Cheese Creations Light Parmesan Alfredo
1 (10-ounce) package frozen peas

♥ Cook chicken in a large, nonstick skillet sprayed with non-fat cooking spray until no longer pink.

♥ Meantime, cook linguine according to directions on package. Drain.

♥ Microwave peas just enough to unthaw. (About 1 minute).

♥ Stir cooked chicken, cooked linguine, Alfredo sauce and peas together. Mix well. The heat from the hot chicken and linguine will heat the sauce.

♥ Serve immediately.

Yield: 8 (1¼-cup) servings

Calories: 440
Percent Fat Calories: 21%
Carbohydrate: 60 grams
Protein: 26 grams

Total Fat: 10 grams
Cholesterol: 58 mg
Dietary Fiber: 3 grams
Sodium: 574 mg

Total time: 20 minutes.

2nd Serving Busy People's Low Fat Cook Book

CHICKEN PARMESAN

*It sounds hard to make, but actually
it's quick, easy and impressive.*

4 ounces dry spaghetti or angel hair pasta
1 pound boneless, skinless chicken breast - pound to ¼-inch thick
½ cup Italian breadcrumbs

1 (25.75-ounce) jar pasta sauce (I use Healthy Choice chunky vegetable primavera)
¼ cup shredded fat-free mozzarella cheese

♥ Preheat oven to 450 degrees.

♥ Spray a cookie sheet with non-fat cooking spray.

♥ Cook pasta as directed on package. Drain.

♥ In the meantime, rinse chicken under running water.

♥ Coat moistened chicken with breadcrumbs. Place on prepared cookie sheet. Bake for 10 minutes.

♥ While pasta and chicken are cooking, microwave pasta sauce for 3 minutes in jar. (Remove lid and paper label before microwaving.) Cover top of jar with wax paper before cooking.

♥ Arrange cooked pasta on a serving plate.

♥ Put baked chicken on top of pasta.

♥ Pour pasta sauce over cooked chicken and cooked pasta.

♥ Sprinkle with mozzarella cheese.

♥ If desired, cover for a couple minutes so that the heat from the hot pasta sauce and chicken melts the cheese.

Yield: 4 servings

Calories: 343
Percent Fat Calories: 6%
Carbohydrate: 42 grams
Protein: 36 grams

Total Fat: 2 grams
Cholesterol: 67 mg
Dietary Fiber: 4 grams
Sodium: 862 mg

Total time: 25 minutes.

2nd Serving Busy People's Low Fat Cook Book

CHICKEN SKILLET COBBLER

If you like pot pie, you'll like this.

1 pound boneless, skinless chicken breast - cut into bite-size pieces

1 (1-pound) package frozen mixed vegetables (peas, corn, carrots, green beans and lima beans)

1 cup frozen chopped onion (or 1 medium onion - chopped)

2 (12-ounce) jars fat-free chicken gravy (I use Heinz)

1½ cups dry pancake mix

¾ cup fat-free, reduced-sodium chicken or beef broth

♥ Spray a 12-inch nonstick skillet with non-fat cooking spray.

♥ Over high heat, cook chicken pieces until fully cooked.

♥ Add mixed vegetables, onion and gravy, stirring until well mixed. Bring to a full boil. Let boil for a couple of minutes.

♥ In the meantime, in a separate bowl, stir pancake mix and broth together to make a thick batter.

♥ Spread batter over boiling gravy. You will not have enough batter to cover entire top of gravy. That's okay. Batter spreads as it cooks.

♥ Reduce heat to a low boil. Cover. Cook for 5 to 7 minutes or until batter is fully cooked.

Yield: 4 entrée-size servings

Calories: 439
Percent Fat Calories: 6%
Carbohydrate: 66 grams
Protein: 39 grams

Total Fat: 3 grams
Cholesterol: 80 mg
Dietary Fiber: 5 grams
Sodium: 1775 mg

Total time: 30 minutes or less.

2nd Serving Busy People's Low Fat Cook Book

Menu Ideas: A meal in itself. If desired, a side salad.

TARRAGON CHICKEN AND POTATOES

2 pounds boneless, skinless
   chicken breast
1 teaspoon dried tarragon
1 teaspoon minced garlic

¼ cup Butter Bud Sprinkles
   - dry - divided
5 large red skin potatoes
   Lite salt and ground
   pepper - optional

♥ Sprinkle chicken with dried tarragon, garlic and 2 tablespoons Butter Bud Sprinkles.

♥ Spray a crockpot with non-fat cooking spray.

♥ Place chicken in crockpot.

♥ Place potatoes on top of chicken. Sprinkle potatoes with remaining 2 tablespoons Butter Bud Sprinkles. Cover.

♥ Cook on low for 6½ to 8½ hours or on high for 3 to 4 hours.

♥ Lightly sprinkle chicken with lite salt and ground pepper before serving, if desired.

Yield: 5 servings (5 ounces cooked chicken and 1 potato each)

Calories: 303
Percent Fat Calories: 7%
Carbohydrate: 26 grams
Protein: 44 grams

Total Fat: 2 grams
Cholesterol: 105 mg
Dietary Fiber: 2 grams
Sodium: 413 mg

Preparation time: 10 minutes.

2nd Serving Busy People's Low Fat Cook Book

HONEY MUSTARD CHICKEN

8 (4-ounce) boneless, skinless   2 cups fat-free honey Dijon
   chicken breasts   salad dressing

♥ Marinate chicken in salad dressing overnight or up to 2 days.

♥ Cook chicken in a non-stick skillet or on a grill for 4 to 5 minutes over medium heat. Turn. Continue cooking until chicken is white in center.

♥ In order to use the dressing (you used as a marinate) as a dipping sauce you must bring it to a boil. Boil for 1 minute. Turn off heat. Let cool.

♥ Serve on the side to dip chicken pieces in.

Yield: 8 servings

Calories: 225   Total Fat: 1.4 grams (6% fat)
Cholesterol: 66 mg   Sodium: 743 mg

Total preparation and cooking time: 10 minutes or less.

Busy People's Low-Fat Cook Book

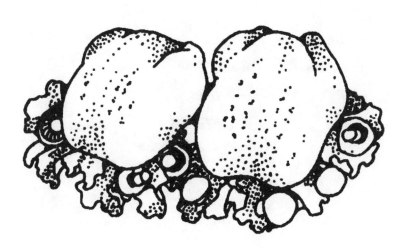

CHICKEN FETTUCCINE

Now this is some good eatin'!

1 (12-ounce) box fettuccine florentine noodles - found in pasta section

1½ pounds boneless, skinless chicken breast - cut into bite-size pieces

1 (26½-ounce) jar Hunts Original spaghetti sauce with mushrooms

Kraft fat-free grated topping (made with Parmesan cheese) - optional

♥ Cook pasta as directed on box.

♥ Over medium heat cook chicken pieces in a non-stick 12-inch skillet until all pieces are fully cooked. (Chicken will be completely white when fully cooked.)

♥ Add spaghetti sauce, Heat for about 4 to 5 minutes or until completely heated.

♥ Serve over hot, drained pasta. If desired sprinkle with Kraft Free non-fat grated topping.

♥ This dish is delicious reheated in the microwave. Simply stir sauce in with pasta and freeze or refrigerate until ready to use.

Yield: 8 (1-cup) servings

Calories: 289

Cholesterol: 49 mg

Total Fat: 2.1 grams (7% fat)

Sodium: 518 mg

Total preparation and cooking time: 15 minutes or less.

Busy People's Low-Fat Cook Book

Menu Idea: Tossed Salad, Green Beans Italiano or Garlic Toast.

Presto Poultry Casserole

A great way to use leftover holiday turkey.

1 (7.25-ounce) box macaroni and cheese (the off brands are fine) - do not make as directed on box
1 cup hot water
1 (15-ounce) can Healthy Choice cream of mushroom soup

1 pound leftover cooked chicken (or turkey breast) - cut into bite-size pieces
1 (15-ounce) can asparagus - drained

♥ Spray a 2-quart covered microwavable casserole dish with non-fat cooking spray.

♥ In prepared casserole dish mix powdered cheese packet (from macaroni and cheese box) with hot water and soup until cheese is completely dissolved.

♥ Stir in chopped chicken (or turkey) and macaroni until well mixed.

♥ Cover. Cook in a *carousel microwave on high for 7 minutes. (Very carefully remove lid, so you do not get a steam burn!)

♥ Stir. Cover and continue cooking in *carousel microwave for an additional 6 minutes.

♥ Stir in drained asparagus. Cover and let sit 2-3 minutes before serving. (If making ahead of time, freeze or refrigerate until needed. Microwave until warm.)

Yield: 5 servings

Calories: 349
Cholesterol: 83 mg

Total Fat: 6.3 grams (17% fat)
Sodium: 731 mg

Preparation time: 5 minutes or less.

Cooking time: 13 minutes.

Total time: 18 minutes or less.

Busy People's Low-Fat Cook Book

CHICKEN CHEESIE PIZZA

*A tasty twist to an old time favorite
of traditional pizza.*

1 (10-ounce) can Pillsbury prepared pizza crust dough
1 boneless, skinless chicken breast (about ½ pound)
⅛-¼ teaspoon ground pepper
¼ cup light Miracle Whip
¼ cup Kraft fat-free grated topping (made with Parmesan cheese and other ingredients)
½ cup fat-free ranch dressing
1 (8-ounce) Healthy Choice fancy shredded mozzarella cheese

♥ Preheat oven to 425 degrees.

♥ Press dough into a jelly roll pan (a cookie sheet with 1-inch sides), that has been sprayed with non-fat cooking spray.

♥ Cook chicken breast in a microwave for about 2 minutes. (Until no pink is visible). Drain juice. Cut cooked chicken breast into tiny ¼-inch pieces. Sprinkle with pepper. Set aside.

♥ Mix Miracle Whip, grated topping and ranch dressing together. Spread mixture over pizza crust.

♥ Sprinkle mozzarella cheese over mixture. Top with peppered chicken pieces.

♥ Bake at 425 degrees for 12 to 15 minutes or until crust is golden brown.

Yield: 4 entrée servings

Calories: 419
Cholesterol: 46 mg
Total Fat: 5.5 grams (12% fat)
Sodium:1378 mg

Preparation time: 10 minutes or less.

Cooking time: 15 minutes or less.

Total time: 25 minutes or less.

Busy People's Low-Fat Cook Book

Menu Idea: Tossed salad and Green Beans Italiano.

Note: Red or green pepper slices, added before baking, would also taste good on top of chicken.

CHICKEN ROLL-UPS

2 cups hot water
1 package Butter Buds - dry
¾ cup chopped mushrooms
1 package stuffing mix
(I use Stove Top)

1 16-ounce package
roasted chicken breast
lunch meat slices

♥ In microwave saucepan, combine hot water, Butter Buds, mushrooms, and seasoning packet from stuffing mix. Microwave on high for 2½ to 3 minutes. Add stuffing. Mix well. Cover tightly and let stand for 5 minutes. Take each chicken breast lunch meat slice and press about 2 tablespoons of stuffing mix in middle of lunch meat slice. Bring sides of slice into middle and secure with toothpick.

♥ Preheat oven to 350 degrees. Lay chicken rolls on jelly roll pan (cookie sheet with edges) that has been sprayed with a non-fat cooking spray. Pour sauce (recipe follows) over tops of each roll, allowing sauce to cover bottom of pan. Cover with foil. Bake for 15 minutes.

Sauce:
½ cup milk
2 tablespoons cornstarch
1 teaspoon garlic salt

½ teaspoon Jambalaya
Cajun Seasoning (optional)
1 can chicken broth

♥ Heat broth. Mix remaining ingredients together and add to broth. Heat until warm.

Yield: 6 servings

Calories: 229
Percent Fat Calories: 11%
Carbohydrate: 30 grams
Protein: 21 grams

Total Fat: 3 grams
Cholesterol: 40 mg
Dietary Fiber: 1 gram
Sodium: 2198 mg

Preparation time: 30 minutes.

Down Home Cookin'

CHICKEN AND POTATO STEW

1 pound boneless, skinless chicken breast - cut into bite-size pieces

1 (15-ounce) can Healthy Choice cream of mushroom soup

2 (16-ounce) packages of frozen vegetables for stew - (potatoes, onions and carrots)

2 tablespoons fat-free Ultra Promise

♥ Layer in crockpot in the following order: chicken, soup, frozen vegetables and Promise.

♥ Cover, Cook on low for 8 to 9 hours. Mix well before serving. If desired, add lite salt and pepper to taste.

Yield: 6 servings

Calories: 199
Cholesterol: 44 mg

Total Fat: 1.2 grams (6% fat)
Sodium: 290 mg

Perparation time: 5 minutes or less.

Cooking time: 8-9 hours on low.

Total time: 9 hours or less.

Busy People's Low-Fat Cook Book

Menu Ideas: Serve with biscuits or sourdough bread for a complete meal.

SOUTHERN STYLE CHICKEN GRAVY OVER BISCUITS

1 cup skim milk
¼ cup cornstarch
1 tablespoon garlic salt (optional)
1 14.5-ounce can chicken broth (I use Campbell's)

Dash of pepper (optional)
3 8-ounce cans of no salt mixed vegetables, drained
1½ pounds skinless chicken breasts, fully cooked and chopped into bite-sized pieces

♥ Put first 5 ingredients into Dutch oven. Mix well before turning on heat, dissolving cornstarch completely. Turn heat on medium. Add drained vegetables and cooked bite-sized pieces of chicken. Stir occasionally and cook for approximately 10 to 12 minutes, until thick and creamy. °

° Serve ½ cup over 2 biscuits (I use Pillsbury Buttermilk Biscuits - 150 calories and 2 grams of fat for 3 biscuits or Kroger Buttermilk Biscuits - 100 calories and 1.5 grams of fat for 2 biscuits) (Analysis doesn't include biscuits.)

Yield: 10 servings

Calories: 126
Percent Fat Calories: 10%
Carbohydrate: 9 grams
Protein: 18 grams

Total Fat: 1 gram
Cholesterol: 40 mg
Dietary Fiber: 2 grams
Sodium: 256 mg

Preparation time: 25 minutes.

Down Home Cookin'

FRIED CHICKEN STRIPS

*Great served plain or with your favorite
fat-free salad dressing as a dip.*

¾ cup toasted bread
  crumbs
¼ cup whole wheat flour
1 teaspoon garlic salt
¼ teaspoon ground black
  pepper
1 tablespoon grated
  Parmesan cheese

4 egg whites
⅓ cup skim milk
1 pound boneless, skinless
  chicken breast, with all
  visible fat removed. Cut
  into long strips ½-inch
  wide.

♥ Preheat oven to 400 degrees. Spray cookie sheet with non-fat cooking spray. Mix together first five ingredients. Set aside. Whip egg whites and milk together with whisk or beater for 1 minute. One at a time, dip chicken strips into egg mixture. Drain off excess, then dip in bread crumb mixture. Repeat this process, dipping each chicken strip a second time into the egg mixture, and then the crumb mixture.

♥ Place prepared chicken strips on cookie sheet and spray chicken strips with non-fat cooking spray. Bake for 8 to 10 minutes. Turn over and bake an additional 7 to 10 minutes. Bottoms will be golden brown when ready to turn.

Yield: 6 servings

Calories: 175
Percent Fat Calories: 11%
Carbohydrate: 15 grams
Protein: 23 grams

Total Fat: 2 grams
Cholesterol: 45 mg
Dietary Fiber: 1 gram
Sodium: 531 mg

Down Home Cookin'

CHICKEN OR TURKEY CASSEROLE

1 cup dry elbow macaroni
1 (10-ounce) can premium chunk chicken in water - drained (Swanson) (or 2 cups cooked turkey breast)
1 (15-ounce) can Healthy Choice cream of mushroom soup

1 cup chicken broth (either from a can or made with bouillon)
½ cup chopped onion (or frozen chopped onion)
1 (4-ounce) can sliced mushrooms - drained

♥ Spray a 2-quart covered casserole dish with non-fat cooking spray.

♥ Combine all ingredients in prepared dish and mix well.

♥ Cook covered in a carousel microwave for 17 to 20 minutes or until pasta is tender.

♥ Let sit for 3 minutes before removing lid. Be very careful when taking off the lid, because the steam is going to be extremely hot!

Yield: 4 servings

With Chicken:
Calories: 206
Cholesterol: 24 mg
Total Fat: 2.0 grams (9% fat)
Sodium: 823 mg

With Turkey:
Calories: 246
Cholesterol: 60 mg
Total Fat: 1.8 grams (7% fat)
Sodium: 642 mg

Preparation time: 5 minutes or less.

Cooking time: 20 minutes.

Total time: 25 minutes or less.

Busy People's Low-Fat Cook Book

Menu Ideas: Green beans along with a tossed salad and fat-free sliced bread on the side. If desired serve sugar-free Jell-O for dessert or Brownie Cookies

SOUTHWESTERN FIESTA

Eat as a main dish or as a dip.
An excellent source of protein!

1 pound ground skinless
  turkey breast
1 (1¼-ounce) package taco
  seasoning mix
2 cups salsa

4 cups tomato sauce
  (or tomato juice)
1 (15-ounce) can black
  beans - drained
2 cups instant rice

♥ Spray a non-stick large soup pan or Dutch oven with non-fat cooking spray. Add turkey and taco seasoning mix and cook over medium heat until fully cooked.

♥ Add salsa, tomato sauce and black beans. Bring to a boil. Add instant rice, making sure rice is covered by liquid. Turn off heat. Stir. Cover. Let sit for 5 minutes.

Yield: 8 (1¼-cup) entrée servings

Calories: 249
Cholesterol: 39 mg

Total Fat: 1.0 grams (4% fat)
Sodium: 1575 mg

26 (about ⅓-cup) dip servings

Calories: 77
Cholesterol: 12 mg

Total Fat: 0.3 grams (4% fat)
Sodium: 485 mg

Total preparation and cooking time: 15 minutes or less.

Busy People's Low-Fat Cook Book

Menu Ideas: As a dip: Serve with Baked Tostitos tortilla chips and fat-free sour cream. Some people like to sprinkle fat-free fancy shredded cheddar cheese (Healthy Choice) on top.

As a entrée: Serve as is or wrapped in a warm, soft flour tortilla. Add a fresh green salad.

TURKEY & DRESSING DINNER

This is so easy that it's almost embarrassing. But don't worry!
This recipe can be made days in advance and refrigerated
until ready to bake. Just cook a little longer to make
sure it's completely warmed.

1 box Stove Top stuffing, chicken or turkey flavor (6-serving size)
2 cups hot water
2 envelopes Butter Buds - dry
12 ounces turkey breast lunch meat (I use Louis Rich smoked turkey breast)

1 15-ounce can green beans, drained
1 12-ounce jar fat-free turkey gravy (I use Heinz Homestyle)
Pepper to taste (optional)

♥ In medium bowl, mix seasoning from stuffing box with bread crumbs, water, and one envelope Butter Buds. Set aside. Preheat oven to 350 degrees. Spray a 9 x 13-inch pan with a non-fat cooking spray. Spread prepared stuffing mixture evenly on bottom of pan. Arrange turkey lunch meat slices on top of stuffing. (Edges of lunch meat should overlap.) Spread gravy evenly over turkey. Evenly arrange green beans on top of gravy. Sprinkle green beans with remaining envelope of Butter Buds and pepper, if desired. Cover pan with foil and bake covered for 30 to 35 minutes, until completely warmed.

Yield: 6 servings

Calories: 203
Percent Fat Calories: 9%
Carbohydrate: 31 grams
Protein: 15 grams

Total Fat: 2 grams
Cholesterol: 22 mg
Dietary Fiber: 2 grams
Sodium: 1596 mg

Preparation time: 45 minutes.

Down Home Cookin'

WORLD'S EASIEST LASAGNA

I converted my Great Aunt Florence Craw's Easy Oven Lasagna to this, which has got to be one of the easiest lasagnas in the world to make! If you love lasagna, but you hate how long it normally takes then this is the answer for you! Now you can say good-bye to cooking the noodles first and it taste terrific!

1½ (26-ounce) jars Healthy Choice Super Chunky Mushroom pasta sauce

1 pound package MorningStar Farms Ground Meatless (found in freezer section of the grocery store next to ground turkey or 1 pound lean ground turkey breast)

1 (8-ounce) package dry lasagna noodles (10 strips)

1 (16-ounce) container fat-free, cottage cheese

2 (8-ounce) packages Healthy Choice fat-free mozzarella, cheese

♥ Preheat oven to 375 degrees.

♥ Line a 9 × 13-inch pan with foil. (For easier clean up). Spray lined pan with non-fat cooking spray.

♥ In a large bowl, mix together pasta sauce and ground meatless (no need to cook ground meatless). (Or if you prefer ground turkey: microwave turkey until fully cooked and add to pasta sauce). Stir until well mixed.

♥ Line bottom of prepared pan with one-third of pasta sauce mixture.

♥ Lay 5 strips of uncooked lasagna noodles on top of pasta sauce mixture.

♥ Spread one cup of cottage cheese over noodles and sprinkle two-thirds of the mozzarella cheese over cottage cheese.

♥ Repeat layers ending with sauce.

♥ Cover with foil and bake at 375 for 1 hour.

(World's Easiest Lasagna continued on next page)

(World's Easiest Lasagna continued)

Yield: 12 servings

With ground meatless:
Calories: 251   Total Fat: 0.3 grams (1% fat)
Cholesterol: 6 mg   Sodium: 1027 mg

With ground turkey breast:
Calories: 230   Total Fat: 0.7 grams (3% fat)
Cholesterol: 32 mg   Sodium: 785 mg

Preparation time: 10 minutes or less.

Cooking time: 1 hour.

Total time: 70 minutes or less.

Busy People's Low-Fat Cook Book

ONE POT SPAGHETTI

*If you like your sauce and pasta mixed
together, you'll like this "whip it up fast" dinner.*

1   pound ground turkey
    breast (or ground beef
    eye of round or Ground
    Meatless)
2   cups water

2   (27.5-ounce) jars Ragu
    light pasta sauce (or your
    favorite fat-free brand -
    I use chunky mushroom
    and garlic)
2   tablespoons grape jelly
1   (16-ounce) package thin
    spaghetti - dry (broken
    into 3-inch pieces)

♥ Spray a nonstick Dutch oven or soup pot with non-fat cooking
spray.

♥ Over high heat, stir turkey breast, water, pasta sauce and jelly
together until it comes to a full boil. You do not need to precook
meat. By the time it comes to a full boil, it will be cooked.

♥ Stir dry spaghetti into sauce, making sure pasta is completely
covered with sauce.

♥ Reduce to medium heat. Cover. Boil for 10 minutes, stirring
frequently.

♥ Turn off heat, cover. Let sit for 7 minutes.

Yield: 8 (1-cup) servings

With turkey breast:
Calories: 368
Percent Fat Calories: 4%
Carbohydrate: 60 grams
Protein: 27 grams

Total Fat: 2 grams
Cholesterol: 49 mg
Dietary Fiber: 4 grams
Sodium: 646 mg

(One Pot Spaghetti continued on next page)

(One Pot Spaghetti continued)

With beef eye of round:
Calories: 363
Percent Fat Calories: 8%
Carbohydrate: 60 grams
Protein: 23 grams

Total Fat: 3 grams
Cholesterol: 31 mg
Dietary Fiber: 4 grams
Sodium: 645 mg

With Ground Meatless:
Calories: 350
Percent Fat Calories: 4%
Carbohydrate: 64 grams
Protein: 21 grams

Total Fat: 1 gram
Cholesterol: 0 mg
Dietary Fiber: 7 grams
Sodium: 884 mg

Total time: 20 minutes or less.

2nd Serving Busy People's Low Fat Cook Book

Menu Ideas: Tossed salad and garlic toast.

MEXICAN CASSEROLE

*This no bake, no boil casserole is the answer
to satisfying hungry tummies – quickly!*

1 (1¼-ounce} packet taco
  seasoning mix
2 cups hot water
1 (7.25-ounce) box macaroni
  and cheese (do not make
  as directed on box.)
1 cup salsa

1 (15-ounce) can whole
  kernel corn - drained
1 pound vegetarian ground
  meatless (or cooked ground
  skinless turkey breast)
¾ cup fat-free sour cream

♥ In a 2-quart microwavable covered casserole dish, mix all ingredients except sour cream, until well mixed and dry cheese mixture (from macaroni and cheese) Is dissolved,

♥ Cover. Cook for 8 minutes on high in carousel microwave.

♥ Carefully remove lid (so you don't get burned from the steam.) Mix well.

♥ Cover. Continue cooking on high in carousel microwave for an additional 6 minutes.

♥ Stir in sour cream. Cover. Let sit 2-3 minutes before serving.

Yield: 6 servings

Calories: 359
Cholesterol: 5 mg

Total Fat: 1.7 grams (4% fat)
Sodium: 1654 mg

Preparation time: 5 minutes or less.

Cooking time: 13 minutes plus 2 minutes sitting time.

Total time: 20 minutes or less.

Busy People's Low-Fat Cook Book

*Menu Ideas: Taco salad, sliced cucumbers
and sliced cantaloupe or melon.*

CHICKEN FRIED STEAK

I don't know why it's called "chicken"
fried steak. It's made of beef. I bake it
until it's crispy. It is so good!

1 pound beef eye of round steaks - cut into 6 (¼-inch thick) steaks	¾ cup seasoned breadcrumbs
⅓ cup all-purpose flour	2 egg whites - beaten
1 teaspoon Lawry's seasoned salt	2 tablespoons skim milk
	1 (12-ounce) jar fat-free chicken gravy (I use Heinz) – optional

♥ Preheat oven to 400 degrees.

♥ Spray a cookie sheet with non-fat cooking spray.

♥ Pound steaks to a ¼-inch to ⅛-inch thickness. Set aside.

♥ In a bowl, stir together flour, seasoned salt and breadcrumbs.

♥ In a separate bowl, beat together egg whites and skim milk.

♥ Coat meat in crumb mixture. Dip the coated meat into egg mixture, then re-dip into crumb mixture.

♥ Place breaded meat on prepared cookie sheet. Spray top of meat with non-fat cooking spray.

♥ Bake at 400 degrees for 10 minutes. Turn over. Spray top of meat with non-fat cooking spray. Bake an additional 10 minutes. Breading will be crispy and slightly golden brown when done.

♥ Microwave gravy for 2 minutes or until fully heated. Pour ¼ cup gravy over each steak before serving.

Yield: 6 servings

Calories: 174	Total Fat: 4 grams
Percent Fat Calories: 19%	Cholesterol: 46 mg
Carbohydrate: 14 grams	Dietary Fiber: 1 gram
Protein: 20 grams	Sodium: 804 mg

Total time: 30 minutes or less.

2nd Serving Busy People's Low Fat Cook Book

CHILI CHEESEBURGER CASSEROLE

1 (7¼-ounce) box macaroni and cheese - do not make as directed on box
1 pound ground beef eye of round (or Ground Meatless or ground turkey breast)
1 (15-ounce) can 99% fat-free Hormel chili
1 cup hot water
½ cup chopped frozen or fresh onion

♥ Spray a large, nonstick skillet with non-fat cooking spray.

♥ Bring all ingredients to a full boil, stirring frequently. (Do NOT precook meat.)

♥ Reduce heat to a low boil. Cover. Cook for 8 minutes, stirring occasionally.

♥ Serve hot.

Yield: 5 (1¼-cup) servings

With ground beef eye of round:
Calories: 335
Percent Fat Calories: 16%
Carbohydrate: 39 grams
Protein: 31 grams
Total Fat: 6 grams
Cholesterol: 58 mg
Dietary Fiber: 3 grams
Sodium: 503 mg

With Ground Meatless:
Calories: 314
Percent Fat Calories: 8%
Carbohydrate: 45 grams
Protein: 28 grams
Total Fat: 3 grams
Cholesterol: 9 mg
Dietary Fiber: 6 grams
Sodium: 885 mg

With ground turkey breast:
Calories: 315
Percent Fat Calories: 8%
Carbohydrate: 39 grams
Protein: 33 grams
Total Fat: 3 grams
Cholesterol: 71 mg
Dietary Fiber: 3 grams
Sodium: 495 mg

Total time: 11 minutes.

2nd Serving Busy People's Low Fat Cook Book

ITALIAN MINI MEATLOAVES

*These tasty little meatloaves are a
cinch to make. They're one of my family's favorites!*

½ teaspoon dried oregano
1 pound ground beef eye
   of round
2 egg whites
¾ cup Italian breadcrumbs
¼ cup chopped fresh or
   frozen onion

1 (14-ounce) jar of your
   favorite light pizza sauce
   (I use Ragu Light)
¼ cup finely shredded
   Parmesan cheese
   (I use Kraft)

♥ Spray a nonstick skillet with non-fat cooking spray.

♥ Combine oregano, ground beef eye of round, egg whites, breadcrumbs and chopped onion until well mixed.

♥ Shape into 6 mini meat loaves with hands and place in skillet over medium heat. Cover.

♥ Cook for 10 minutes or until done, turning meat over once.

♥ Pour pizza sauce over each mini meatloaf. Sprinkle with cheese.

♥ Continue cooking for an additional 5 minutes.

Yield: 6 servings

Calories: 205
Percent Fat Calories: 24%
Carbohydrate: 16 grams
Protein: 23 grams

Total Fat: 5 grams
Cholesterol: 44 mg
Dietary Fiber: 2 grams
Sodium: 557 mg

Total time: 20 minutes.

2nd Serving Busy People's Low Fat Cook Book

Menu Ideas: Tossed salad and Green Beans Italiano'.

Cowboy Grub (Casserole)

For the meat and potato lover and those who love barbecue!
For added extra fun, serve on pie pans instead of plates.

1 pound lean eye of round beef (roast or steaks) - cut into ¼- to ⅓-inch chunks (or pork tenderloin)

1 pound quick cooking shredded hash browns (I use Mr. Deli's)

½ cup chopped onion (or frozen chopped onion for easier use)

½ cup your favorite barbecue sauce (I used Kraft's Thick and Spicy Brown Sugar sauce)

♥ Spray a 12-inch non-stick skillet with non-fat cooking spray.

♥ Turn heat on medium-high. Place meat on bottom of pan. Cover. Cook for 3 to 4 minutes or until brown on bottom. Turn meat over. Top with shredded hash browns and onions. Cover. Cook 3 to 4 minutes or until meat is no longer pink.

♥ Stir entire dish. Cover and cook an additional 3 to 4 minutes, stirring occasionally.

♥ Turn heat down to low. Add barbecue sauce. Gently stir until well mixed. Serve immediately.

Yield: 4 servings

With beef:

Calories: 265

Cholesterol: 59 mg

Total Fat: 5.3 grams (18% fat)

Sodium: 333 mg

With pork:

Calories: 264

Cholesterol: 67 mg

Total Fat: 5.4 grams (19% fat)

Sodium: 328 mg

Preparation time: 3 minutes (derived from cutting meat into chunks).

Cooking time: 12 minutes or less.

Total time: 15 minutes or less.

Busy People's Low-Fat Cook Book

BEEF FAJITAS

1 pound cooked shredded
beef or Healthy Choice
ground beef
½ cup fat-free Italian salad
10 soft flour taco shells
(Buena Vista is fat-free)

1 cup shredded iceberg
lettuce
1 cup chopped tomato
Fat-free taco or cheddar cheese
Fat-free sour cream (optional)
dressing

♥ Marinate beef in dressing. Warm beef in microwave with dressing. Microwave soft taco shell until warm. Put desired amount of marinated beef on soft shell. Top with lettuce, tomato, cheese, and sour cream, if desired.

Yield: 5 servings (2 fajitas per serving)

Calories: 365
Percent Fat Calories: 11%
Carbohydrate: 47 grams
Protein: 32 grams

Total Fat: 4 grams
Cholesterol: 63 mg
Dietary Fiber: 2 grams
Sodium: 903 mg

Preparation time: 30 minutes.

Down Home Cookin'

STUFFED GREEN PEPPERS

Talk about quick to prepare.
It doesn't get any easier than this.

4 large fresh green peppers
1 pound ground beef eye of round (or ground turkey breast)
2 cups dry instant long grain white rice

2 cups V8 juice, mild picante flavor (or regular flavor is fine)
2 (14.5-ounce) cans no-salt-added sliced, stewed tomatoes

♥ Spray a crockpot with non-fat cooking spray. Set aside.

♥ Cut tops off green peppers and discard. Clean out insides of green peppers. Set aside.

♥ In a bowl, mix ground beef eye of round, rice and V8 juice together.

♥ Stuff peppers with meat/rice mixture.

♥ Arrange stuffed peppers in crockpot.

♥ Arrange sliced, stewed tomatoes on top of and around peppers in bottom of crockpot.

♥ Cover. Cook on high for 4 hours or on low for 8 to 9 hours.

♥ When serving, cut each pepper in half vertically. Lay each pepper on a plate on its side with beef and rice mixture facing up.

♥ Spoon stewed tomatoes and the juices in the bottom of the crockpot over each pepper.

Yield: 4 servings

(Stuffed Green Peppers continued on next page)

(Stuffed Green Peppers continued)

With beef eye of round:
Calories: 447
Percent Fat Calories: 11%
Carbohydrate: 63 grams
Protein: 31 grams

Total Fat: 5 grams
Cholesterol: 61 mg
Dietary Fiber: 7 grams
Sodium: 403 mg

With turkey breast:
Calories: 423
Percent Fat Calories: 3%
Carbohydrate: 63 grams
Protein: 34 grams

Total Fat: 1 gram
Cholesterol: 77 mg
Dietary Fiber: 7 grams
Sodium: 394 mg

Preparation time: 10 minutes or less.

2nd Serving Busy People's Low Fat Cook Book

MEXICAN SPAGHETTI

*For fast and easy Mexican Spaghetti Salad,
do the exact same thing but serve chilled.*

1   cup shredded cooked
     beef
2   cups cooked spaghetti

1   16-ounce jar salsa
Fat-free taco or cheddar
     cheese, finely grated
     (optional)

♥ Toss first three ingredients together. Top with cheese if desired. Microwave until warm. Serve warm. Serve extra warmed salsa on the side if desired.

♥ Note: Leftover eye of round roast can be used.

Yield: 4 servings

Calories: 195
Percent Fat Calories: 11%
Carbohydrate: 24 grams
Protein: 14 grams

Total Fat: 2 grams
Cholesterol: 25 mg
Dietary Fiber: 1 gram
Sodium: 552 mg

Preparation time: 20 minutes.

Down Home Cookin'

EASY BEEF STROGANOFF

If they only knew it could be this easy years ago!
Only one pan to clean-up!

1 pound eye of round beef - cut into ½-inch chunks
2 medium onions (as a time saver, use 1 pound of frozen chopped onions)
1 (4-ounce) can mushroom stems and pieces - do not drain
2 teaspoons minced garlic (I use the kind in a jar - already prepared)
3 cups beef broth (or 3 beef bouillon cubes dissolved in 3 cups water)
4 cups medium egg noodles (I use light and Fluffy)
1 cup fat-free sour cream

♥ Spray a large kettle or soup pot with non-fat cooking spray. Over medium heat cook beef, onions, mushrooms and garlic together. Stir occasionally.

♥ Once meat is fully cooked, add beef broth, egg noodles and sour cream. Turn heat to high.

♥ Once boiling, turn heat down to low. (Do not cover.) Cook on low for 5 to 7 minutes until pasta is desired doneness. Stir occasionally.

♥ Remove from heat. Let sit 4 to 5 minutes before serving. (Broth will thicken as it sits.) If desired sprinkle lightly with salt and pepper.

Yield: 7 (1-cup) servings

Calories: 218
Cholesterol: 54 mg
Total Fat: 3.3 grams (14% fat)
Sodium: 491 mg

Preparation time: 5 minutes (mostly derived from cutting meat).

Cooking time: 15 minutes or less.

Total time: 20 minutes or less.

Chicken Stroganoff:
Substitute 1 pound boneless, skinless chicken breast cut into ½-inch chunks instead of beef. Use chicken broth instead of beef broth. Follow directions exactly.

Busy People's Low-Fat Cook Book

BEEF STROGANOFF

*This meal is delicious with warm bread. I like to warm French bread
in the oven. People love to dip their warm French bread into the
juices of the Beef Stroganoff on their plates.*

2 pounds partially frozen eye of round (beef), thinly sliced	1 teaspoon garlic salt
	16 ounces non-fat sour cream
1 large onion, thinly sliced	Pepper to taste
8 ounces fresh mushrooms, thinly sliced	12 ounces "No Yolk" noodles, cooked and drained
½ cup liquid Butter Buds	

♥ Eliminate all visible fat from meat and brown in large pan. Rinse
beef under water. Set aside. Combine onion, mushrooms and
liquid Butter Buds, and sauté until soft. Add cooked beef, garlic
salt, sour cream, and pepper. Stir until well combined. Do *NOT*
boil. Serve hot over warm noodles.

Yield: 8 servings

Calories: 392
Percent Fat Calories: 13%
Carbohydrate: 48 grams
Protein: 35 grams

Total Fat: 6 grams
Cholesterol: 66 mg
Dietary Fiber: 2 grams
Sodium: 410 mg

Preparation time: 40 minutes.

Down Home Cookin'

BEEF AND BROCCOLI SKILLET CASSEROLE

*1 pound beef eye of round (steak or roast) - all visible fat removed - cut into ½-inch chunks
1 (1-pound) bag frozen broccoli florets - cut into 1-inch chunks
3 cups hot water

1 (1-ounce) envelope dry onion soup mix (there are 2 envelopes per box)
3 cups instant rice
¾ cup Western fat-free salad dressing

♥ In a 12-inch non-stick skillet, cook beef on high for 3 to 4 minutes or until bottom is cooked. Turn over.

♥ Pour broccoli, water and dry onion soup mix over beef. Stir until soup mix is dissolved. Cover. Cook on high for 6 minutes.

♥ Add rice. Stir until rice is covered with liquid. Turn off heat. Cover. Let sit 5 minutes.

♥ Stir in Western dressing. Serve immediately. Serve with lite soy sauce on the side if desired.

♥ *Note : Pork tenderloin can be substituted instead of eye of round beef if desired. It tastes equally as good.

Yield: 6 (1-cup) servings

With beef:
Calories: 341
Cholesterol: 39 mg
Total Fat: 3.1 grams (8% fat)
Sodium: 785 mg

With pork:
Calories: 340
Cholesterol: 45 mg
Total Fat: 3.2 grams (8% fat)
Sodium: 782 mg

Preparation time: 3 minutes (derived from cutting beef into chunks).

Cooking time: 15 minutes or less.

Total time: 18 minutes or less.

Busy People's Low-Fat Cook Book

Swiss Steak and Potatoes

1 (14 .5-ounce) can stewed, sliced tomatoes - do not drain
1 (12-ounce) jar fat-free beef gravy
¼ teaspoon dried thyme
1 (1-pound) bag fresh mini carrots (found in produce section)
2 medium onions - quartered
1 pound eye of round steaks - cut into ½-inch thicknesses
4 medium potatoes - washed

♥ Spray crockpot with non-fat cooking spray.

♥ Mix undrained tomatoes, gravy, thyme, carrots and onions together until well mixed.

♥ Place meat into mixture, making sure it is completely covered with sauce.

♥ Place potatoes on top.

♥ Cover. Cook on high for 4 hours or on low for 8 hours. (Completely cooked after documented time, however the meal can remain in the crockpot for up to 1 hour longer without burning.)

Yield: 4 servings

Calories: 359
Cholesterol: 59 mg
Total Fat: 4.6 grams (11% fat)
Sodium: 782 mg

Preparation time: 20 minutes or less.

Cooking time: 4-8 hours (depending on your needs)

Busy People's Low-Fat Cook Book

Menu Ideas: A complete meal in itself.

SMOTHERED STEAK

1   pound whole beef tenderloin
2   large onions - quartered and separated
2   large green peppers - cut into ¾-inch strips
1   (8-ounce) package fresh mushrooms - sliced
¼   cup dry Butter Buds
½   cup water
1   teaspoon celery salt (or garlic salt)

♥ Spray a crockpot with non-fat cooking spray.

♥ Place beef in crockpot and top with onions, peppers, and mushrooms. Mix Butter Buds, water and celery salt together until Butter Buds dissolve. Pour over vegetables. Gently toss vegetables to distribute seasonings.

♥ Cover. Cook on high for 4 to 5 hours or on low for 8 to 9 hours.

♥ Cut beef into 4 (4-ounce) steaks. Arrange on platter.

♥ Toss vegetables in juices. Spoon juice and vegetables over beef. Serve hot.

Yield: 4 servings

Calories: 263
Cholesterol: 72 mg
Total Fat: 8.7 grams (29% fat)
Sodium: 491 mg

Preparation time: 7 minutes or less.

Cooking time: 4-5 hours on high and 8-9 hours on low.

Busy People's Low-Fat Cook Book

Menu Ideas: If there is room in your crockpot, place 12 small red skin potatoes on top. If not, microwave potatoes or serve with Garlic Red Skins.

BEEF-N-NOODLES

1   12-ounce jar of Heinz
    Fat-free Seasoned Pork
    OR Beef Gravy
2   cups pasta, cooked

2   cups eye of round (beef),
    cooked and shredded (OR
    1 pound Healthy Choice
    hamburger, browned)

♥ Mix gravy with cooked pasta and beef. Heat and serve.

♥ Note: Leftover spaghetti noodles will work if you have them. Just soak the cooked spaghetti completely in a bowl of water in the refrigerator until you need them for this recipe.

Yield: 4 servings

Calories: 240
Percent Fat Calories: 15%
Carbohydrate: 24 grams
Protein: 25 grams

Total Fat: 4 grams
Cholesterol: 49 mg
Dietary Fiber: 1 gram
Sodium: 525 mg

Preparation time: 25 minutes.

Down Home Cookin'

HAMBURGER GRAVY OVER BISCUITS

1 pound ground eye
  of round (beef)
1 packet Butter Buds, dry
2 teaspoons garlic salt
  (optional)

Dash of pepper (optional)
3 cups skim milk
½ cup cornstarch

♥ In a large pan or Dutch oven cook ground eye of round, Butter Buds, pepper and garlic salt on medium heat, until meat is fully cooked. Add 2 cups skim milk. Mix cornstarch to remaining 1 cup skim milk, stirring until cornstarch is completely dissolved. Pour into beef, stirring constantly. Cook approximately 5 minutes longer, until thick and creamy.

Yield: 6 servings

Calories: 189
Percent Fat Calories: 17%
Carbohydrate: 18 grams
Protein: 21 grams

Total Fat: 4 grams
Cholesterol: 43 mg
Dietary Fiber: 0 grams
Sodium: 193 mg

Preparation time: 35 minutes.

Down Home Cookin'

HERBED EYE OF ROUND WITH SEASONED POTATOES & BUTTERED MUSHROOMS

Put into a crockpot before a long day away and come home to a mouth-watering aroma that's delicious and ready to eat.

2 pounds beef eye of round - all visible fat removed
1½ teaspoons dried thyme
1½ teaspoons dried basil
1 teaspoon garlic salt

1 (1 pound) bag frozen Bob Evans Seasoned Diced Potatoes
3 tablespoons fat-free Ultra Promise - divided
6 ounces fresh mushrooms - sliced

♥ Spray a crockpot with non-fat cooking spray.

♥ Sprinkle all sides of beef with thyme, basil, and garlic salt.

♥ Place beef in crockpot.

♥ Tear 2 pieces of foil each about 18 inches long. Fold the seams together along the side.

♥ Spray foil with non-fat cooking spray.

♥ Place diced potatoes in center of foil. Spread 2 tablespoons of the Ultra Promise over frozen diced potatoes. Fold the foil (as you would a gifted package) to seal in the flavor of potatoes.

♥ Place potatoes on beef.

♥ Spray another 18-inch piece of foil with non-fat cooking spray. Stack mushrooms in foil. Dab 1 tablespoon of fat-free margarine on top of mushrooms. Sprinkle lightly with garlic salt if desired. Fold foil (as you would a gifted package) to seal in flavor.

♥ Place mushrooms on top of beef and potatoes.

♥ Cover crockpot.

♥ Cook on low for 8 to 10 hours. (Or cook on high for 4 to 5 hours). Serve juices in bottom of crockpot on the side.

(Herbed Eye of Round continued on next page)

(Herbed Eye of Round continued)

Yield: 6 servings

5 ounces serving of beef

1 ounce serving of buttered mushrooms (to top beef)

2½ ounces serving of seasoned potatoes

Calories: 312	Total Fat: 8.6 grams (26% fat)
Cholesterol: 83 mg	Sodium: 456 mg

Preparation time: 10 minutes or less.

Busy People's Low-Fat Cook Book

ORIENTAL TERIYAKI
BEEF DINNER

This meal is a huge hit with our children.

1 20-ounce can pineapple chunks in juice or ½ cup pineapple juice
½ cup lite teriyaki marinade sauce (I use LaChoy)
¼ teaspoon ground ginger
¼ teaspoon garlic powder
1 pound eye of round beef cut into 1⅓-inch cubes (all visible fat removed)

1 medium to small onion cut into eighths (separate layers of onion)
4 cups frozen stir fry vegetables (oriental mixture with pea pods)
2 tablespoons cornstarch

♥ Drain juice from pineapple, retaining juice. In medium bowl, combine teriyaki marinade, pineapple juice, ground ginger, and garlic powder. Mix well until ginger and garlic are completely dissolved. Add beef and onion. Cover tightly and refrigerate, at least 15 minutes. (The longer this marinates, the more flavorful the beef becomes. This can be done days in advance, if desired.)

♥ Drain marinade and set aside. Use either a wok or large pan. Spray pan with a non-fat cooking spray. Cook meat and onions over medium heat for about 5 minutes before adding frozen vegetables. Add 2 tablespoons cornstarch to marinade and mix well until cornstarch is completely dissolved. Pour marinade over meat and vegetables being cooked. Stir and bring to a boil. Cook for about 5 minutes or until vegetables are slightly crisp, yet tender.

Yield: 4 servings

Calories: 379
Percent Fat Calories: 13%
Carbohydrate: 52 grams
Protein: 34 grams

Total Fat: 6 grams
Cholesterol: 61 mg
Dietary Fiber: 7 grams
Sodium: 1677 mg

Down Home Cookin'

"SECONDS PLEASE" MEATLOAF

14 ounces Healthy Choice smoked sausage
1 pound ground eye of round (beef)
¾ cup Italian seasoned bread crumbs

1 medium onion, chopped
1 small green pepper, chopped
½ teaspoon salt, optional
½ teaspoon pepper
2 egg whites, beaten

Topping:
½ cup low-sodium ketchup
1 8-ounce can salt-free tomato sauce

⅓ cup brown sugar
8 packets of Equal (OR ⅓ cup sugar)

♥ Preheat oven to 350 degrees. Grind smoked sausage in food processor or blender. In large bowl, add all ingredients and mix well. For easier cleanup, cover a jelly roll pan (a cookie sheet with edges) with foil. Spray with a non-fat cooking spray. With hands, shape meatloaf mixture into a loaf. Bake for 35-40 minutes.

♥ While meatloaf is baking, mix topping ingredients in medium-sized bowl. Spoon mixture over meatloaf. Return to oven and bake an additional ½ hour. °

° With Sugar – Calories: 283 – Total Fat: 4 grams
Percent Fat Calories: 14% – Cholesterol: 48 mg
Carbohydrate: 38 grams – Dietary Fiber: 1 gram
Protein: 22 grams – Sodium: 642 mg

Yield: 8 servings

Calories: 255
Percent Fat Calories: 16%
Carbohydrate: 30 grams
Protein: 23 grams

Total Fat: 4 grams
Cholesterol: 48 mg
Dietary Fiber: 1 gram
Sodium: 643 mg

Down Home Cookin'

Beefy-Chili Burritos With Cheese

My kids love to roll these up themselves.

1 pound ground eye
   of round (beef)
2 cans Health Valley
   fat-free chili (15-ounce
   spicy vegetarian with
   black beans)

16 ounces fat-free fancy
   shredded cheddar cheese
   (I use Healthy Choice)
10 fat-free flour tortilla
   shells

♥ In medium pan brown ground eye of round. Add chili and 6 ounces of cheddar cheese. Stir over medium low heat until cheese is completely dissolved (about 5 minutes). Put 1/10 of the chili mixture in the middle of a tortilla. Roll up. Sprinkle 1 ounce shredded cheddar cheese on top. Microwave about 10 to 15 seconds to melt cheese. Serve warm.

♥ Note: Garnish with your favorite salsa if desired. With a side tossed salad and fat-free French salad dressing, this is a complete, delicious and nutritious meal! Not included in calorie or fat information.

Yield: 10 servings

Calories: 283
Percent Fat Calories: 6%
Carbohydrate: 35 grams
Protein: 31 grams

Total Fat: 2 grams
Cholesterol: 32 mg
Dietary Fiber: 6 grams
Sodium: 745 mg

Preparation time: 30 minutes.

Down Home Cookin'

SOUTH OF THE BORDER HOT DOGS

A Mexican twist to an all-American food.

1 package 8 fat-free hot dogs (I use Oscar Mayer)
1 package fat-free hot dog buns (I use Aunt Millie's)
8 tablespoons grated fat-free cheddar cheese
8 tablespoons chunky salsa

♥ Put one hot dog in each bun. Top with 1 tablespoon grated cheddar cheese and 1 tablespoon salsa. Microwave each on high for approximately 45 seconds to 1 minute. Enjoy!!

Yield: 8 servings

Calories: 151
Percent Fat Calories: 0%
Carbohydrate: 24 grams
Protein: 12 grams
Total Fat: 0 grams
Cholesterol: 16 mg
Dietary Fiber: 1 gram
Sodium: 839 mg

Preparation time: 5 minutes.

Down Home Cookin'

CHILI MAC

Great with corn bread.

1 pound macaroni
  (I like to use shell shaped)
1 pound ground eye of
  round (beef)

1 15-ounce can Health
  Valley Fat-free Spicy
  Vegetarian Chili With
  Black Beans

♥ Cook macaroni as directed on box. Brown eye of round. Stir together chili, meat, and macaroni. Serve warm!

Yield: 10 servings

Calories: 256
Percent Fat Calories: 9%
Carbohydrate: 39 grams
Protein: 18 grams

Total Fat: 3 grams
Cholesterol: 25 mg
Dietary Fiber: 4 grams
Sodium: 84 mg

Preparation time: 30 minutes.

Down Home Cookin'

STEAK ON A STICK

Substitute chicken for the steak and have chicken sticks!

2 pounds eye of round steak (beef)
1 21-ounce can crushed pineapple in its own juices

Kebob sticks
Garlic salt (optional)

♥ Cut steak into 1½-inch pieces, removing all visible fat. In Ziploc gallon-sized bag marinate steak pieces in crushed pineapple, and juice, for at least 8 hours. (The longer it marinates, the better I think it tastes.)

♥ Arrange about 6 pieces of steak on kebob stick. Sprinkle lightly with garlic salt. Cook on grill, turning once, until the desired doneness is achieved.

Yield: 8 servings

Calories: 154
Percent Fat Calories: 30%
Carbohydrate: 1 gram
Protein: 25 grams

Total Fat: 5 grams
Cholesterol: 61 mg
Dietary Fiber: 0 grams
Sodium: 60 mg

Down Home Cookin'

DOGS IN A BLANKET

Fast, easy and fun for kids to make.

8 Healthy Choice hot dogs

2 cans Pillsbury
Buttermilk Biscuits
(4 biscuits will be left over)

♥ Preheat oven to 350 degrees. Take 2 biscuits and wrap around a hot dog. Pinch biscuit dough with fingers to seal the "blanket." Spray 2 cookie sheets with a non-fat cooking spray. Lay 4 prepared "dogs" on each cookie sheet, making sure they are 2 to 3 inches apart, because the dough will get bigger as they cook. Bake for 10 minutes or until dough is golden brown. Serve with mustard, ketchup or barbeque sauce on the side for dipping.

Yield: 8 servings

Calories: 160
Percent Fat Calories: 16%
Carbohydrate: 25 grams
Protein: 9 grams

Total Fat: 3 grams
Cholesterol: 20 mg
Dietary Fiber: 1 gram
Sodium: 790 mg

Preparation time: 20 minutes.

Down Home Cookin'

CHEESY DOGS IN A BLANKET

4 slices fat-free cheese

♥ Follow "Dogs in a Blanket" recipe exactly, except cut hot dogs ½ way through lengthwise to make just enough room for ½ slice of cheese before wrapping and baking.

Yield: 8 servings

Calories: 168
Percent Fat Calories: 15%
Carbohydrate: 26 grams
Protein: 10 grams

Total Fat: 3 grams
Cholesterol: 20 mg
Dietary Fiber: 1 gram
Sodium: 868 mg

Preparation time: 25 minutes.

Down Home Cookin'

DOGS ON A STICK

Fast, easy and fun for kids to make.

8 Oscar Mayer fat-free
   hot dogs
2 cans Pillsbury Buttermilk
   Biscuits (4 biscuits will
   be left over)

8 popsicle sticks
   Cornmeal (optional)

♥ Preheat oven to 350 degrees. Take 2 biscuits and wrap around hot dog, pinching biscuit dough with fingers to seal the dough around the hot dogs. Place 1 popsicle stick ½ way through each hot dog, leaving ½ of the stick out to later use as a handle. Spray 2 cookie sheets with non-fat cooking spray. Arrange "dogs" on cookie sheets, making sure they are at least 2 to 3 inches apart, because the dough will get bigger as they cook and you don't want them to stick to each other. Sprinkle with cornmeal if desired, before baking. Bake for 10 minutes or until dough is golden brown. Serve with mustard or ketchup.

Yield: 8 servings

Calories: 135
Percent Fat Calories: 9%
Carbohydrate: 21 grams
Protein: 9 grams

Total Fat: 1 gram
Cholesterol: 15 mg
Dietary Fiber: 1 gram
Sodium: 850 mg

Preparation time: 20 minutes.

Down Home Cookin'

PIGS OUT OF THE BLANKET

If you like pigs in the blanket you'll like this! It's just as delicious and a lot less time consuming to prepare.

1 pound ground beef eye of round

2 cups dry instant long grain white rice

1 (16-ounce) jar of your favorite salsa (remember, the spicier your salsa the spicier your dish)

2 cups V8 juice

1 (16-ounce) package cole slaw mix (found in your produce section, it has cabbage and carrots)

2 (14.5-ounce) cans no-salt-added stewed tomatoes

♥ Spray a 4-quart crockpot with non-fat cooking spray.

♥ Mix* all ingredients except stewed tomatoes until well blended in the crockpot. (Remove any large pieces of cabbage and discard.)

♥ Cover. Cook on high for 4 hours.

♥ When ready to serve, microwave stewed tomatoes until fully heated. Evenly pour stewed tomatoes over each serving.

*I find it's easiest to mix with my hands.

Yield: 6 (1-cup) servings

Calories: 313
Percent Fat Calories: 11%
Carbohydrate: 42 grams
Protein: 21 grams

Total Fat: 3 grams
Cholesterol: 41 mg
Dietary Fiber: 4 grams
Sodium: 633 mg

Preparation time: 10 minutes or less.

2nd Serving Busy People's Low Fat Cook Book

Menu Ideas: This is a meal in itself.
Sugar-free Jell-O or a piece of fruit, if desired.

PORK ROAST

An old time favorite made a lot easier!

2 (16-ounce) bags frozen vegetables for stew (I use Freshlike)
1 (14.5-ounce) can no-salt-added stewed tomatoes
1 (10.5-ounce) can Healthy Choice cream of celery soup
1 teaspoon dried thyme (or 2 teaspoons fresh thyme)
1½ pounds pork tenderloin
⅓ cup flour
¼ cup water

♥ Spray a crockpot with non-fat cooking spray.

♥ In a crockpot, mix vegetables, stewed tomatoes, soup and thyme together until well blended.

♥ Push pork to the bottom and the sides of crockpot.

♥ Cover. Cook on low for 8 to 10 hours or on high 4 to 5 hours.

♥ With a slotted spoon, remove vegetables and pork. Leave juice in crockpot and turn crockpot on high.

♥ In a small bowl, mix flour and water together to make a thick paste.

♥ Stir paste into juices in crockpot until well blended.

♥ Cover and cook on high for 5 minutes, or until thick.

♥ If desired, season to taste with garlic salt and black pepper.

♥ Place cooked pork and vegetables on a platter. Serve with the gravy on the side.

Yield: 6 servings

Calories: 298
Percent Fat Calories: 15%
Carbohydrate: 34 grams
Protein: 27 grams
Total Fat: 5 grams
Cholesterol: 76 mg
Dietary Fiber: 4 grams
Sodium: 348 mg

Preparation time: 10 minutes or less.

2nd Serving Busy People's Low Fat Cook Book

HOLIDAY PORK BARBECUE

*The cranberry sauce in this smooth and lightly
sweetened barbecue is a delicious and unique twist
just right for holiday meals!*

1	(16-ounce) can jellied cranberry sauce	2	pounds pork tenderloin (you can substitute chicken breast or extra lean ham)
1	cup honey mustard barbecue sauce (your favorite brand)	8	medium potatoes

♥ Spray a crockpot with non-fat cooking spray.

♥ In crockpot, mix cranberry sauce and barbecue sauce together until well blended.

♥ With a knife, make little cuts about ½-inch deep around the outside of the pork. Place meat in crockpot and cover with sauce.

♥ Place potatoes on top of meat.

♥ Cook on low for 8 to 9 hours or on high for 4 hours.

*Note: If desired, in order for the meat to
absorb more flavor, put your meat and sauce in a
zip lock bag a few days ahead of time.*

Yield: 8 (3-ounces cooked meat and one potato) servings

With pork:

Calories: 361	Total Fat: 4 grams
Percent Fat Calories: 10%	Cholesterol: 74 mg
Carbohydrate: 55 grams	Dietary Fiber: 2 grams
Protein: 26 grams	Sodium: 400 mg

With chicken breast:

Calories: 350	Total Fat: 2 grams
Percent Fat Calories: 4%	Cholesterol: 66 mg
Carbohydrate: 55 grams	Dietary Fiber: 2 grams
Protein: 29 grams	Sodium: 417 mg

Preparation time: 10 minutes or less.

2nd Serving Busy People's Low Fat Cook Book

SAUERKRAUT AND PORK

*Even my children (who do not like sauerkraut) like
this meal. It's not strong or overpowering like a lot
of sauerkraut entrées are.*

1½ pounds pork tenderloin
steaks (or buy a pork
tenderloin roast and cut
into eight 1-inch steaks)
1 (16-ounce) bag fresh
whole baby carrots
½ cup frozen chopped onion

1 (14-ounce) can
sauerkraut - do not drain
2 medium Granny Smith
apples - chopped into tiny
pieces
1 tablespoon packed
brown sugar

♥ Spray a crockpot with non-fat cooking spray.

♥ Lay meat slices on bottom of crockpot, top with carrots. Stir frozen
chopped onion, sauerkraut, apples and brown sugar together.
Spread sauerkraut mixture over pork and carrots. Cover.

♥ Cook on high for 4 to 5 hours or low for 8 to 9 hours.

Yield: 8 servings

Calories: 168
Percent Fat Calories: 18%
Carbohydrate: 16 grams
Protein: 19 grams

Total Fat: 3 grams
Cholesterol: 55 mg
Dietary Fiber: 4 grams
Sodium: 418 mg

Preparation time: 10 minutes.

2nd Serving Busy People's Low Fat Cook Book

Menu Ideas: Serve over mashed potatoes.

PORK STEW

*Another hometown favorite that many
"heart conscious" folks thought they could not eat,
but I'm happy to say, "ENJOY!"*

1½ pounds pork tenderloin –
cut into bite-size pieces
2 tablespoons minced garlic
(I use the kind in a jar)
¾ teaspoon ground sage
1 (14.5-ounce) can no-salt-
added sliced stewed
tomatoes

2 (1-pound) bags vegetables
for stew (I use Freshlike)
2 (12-ounce) jars fat-free
pork gravy (I use Heinz)
¼ teaspoon ground black
pepper

Stovetop Method:

♥ In a 4½-quart nonstick saucepan over high heat, bring all ingredients to a full boil, stirring occasionally to prevent burning.

♥ Once boiling, reduce heat to medium. Continue boiling for 10 to 12 minutes or until vegetables are tender, stirring occasionally.

Crockpot Method:

♥ Put all ingredients in a crockpot. Stir until well mixed.

♥ Cover and cook on low for 8 to 9 hours or on high for 4 to 5 hours.

Yield: 9 (1-cup) servings

Calories: 193
Percent Fat Calories: 13%
Carbohydrate: 22 grams
Protein: 18 grams

Total Fat: 3 grams
Cholesterol: 51 mg
Dietary Fiber: 1 gram
Sodium: 487 mg

Total time: 25 minutes or less.

2nd Serving Busy People's Low Fat Cook Book

Menu Ideas: A meal in itself. If desired, sourdough bread.

DILLED PORK STEAKS

1 cup dill pickle juice
2 pounds pork tenderloin - all visible fat removed and cut into 8 (4-ounce) steaks

dried dill - optional

♥ Marinate overnight in dill pickle juice.

♥ Remove meat from dill juice used to marinate. Discard dill juice.

♥ Cook on a grill or in a non-stick skillet for 4 to 5 minutes. Turn over and continue cooking until center is no longer pink. Sprinkle with dried dill before serving if desired.

Yield: 8 steaks

Calories: 140
Cholesterol: 67 mg

Total Fat: 4.1 grams (28% fat)
Sodium: 110 mg

Preparation time: 5 minutes.

Cooking time: 10 minutes or less.

Total time: 15 minutes or less.

Dilled Chicken Steaks:
Substitute 2 pounds boneless, skinless chicken breast or turkey breast.

Yield: 8 servings

With chicken:
Calories: 125
Cholesterol: 66 mg

Total Fat: 1.4 grams (11% fat)
Sodium: 136 mg

With turkey:
Calories: 125
Cholesterol: 77 mg

Total Fat: 1.1 grams (8% fat)
Sodium: 112 mg

Note: Sodium content of above recipes is an estimate.

Busy People's Low-Fat Cook Book

TROPICAL PORK DINNER

2 pounds pork tenderloin
1 (20-ounce) can crushed pineapple
¼ cup honey
¼ cup apple cider vinegar
¼ cup packed dark brown sugar
4 large yams - washed (or 4 large sweet potatoes)

♥ Spray a crockpot with non-fat cooking spray.

♥ Place pork tenderloin in crockpot.

♥ Mix crushed pineapple, honey, vinegar and brown sugar together until well mixed. Spoon mixture over pork.

♥ Place yams on top of meat mixture. Cover. Cook on high for 3 to 4 hours or on low for 7 to 8 hours.

♥ Cut yams in half before serving. If desired, spoon a little sauce over cut yams and meat.

Yield: 8 servings (3 ounces cooked meat, ½ of a yam and 3 ounces of pineapple mixture)

Calories: 351	Total Fat: 4 grams
Percent Fat Calories: 11%	Cholesterol: 74 mg
Carbohydrate: 53 grams	Dietary Fiber: 5 grams
Protein: 26 grams	Sodium: 72 mg

Menu Ideas: Sassy Slaw and Hawaiian Rolls or cornbread.

Tropical Chicken Dinner: Make recipe exactly the same, but substitute 8 (4-ounce) boneless, skinless chicken breasts for the pork tenderloin.

Yield: 8 servings (3 ounces cooked meat, ½ of a yam and 3 ounces of pineapple mixture)

Calories: 340	Total Fat: 2 grams
Percent Fat Calories: 4%	Cholesterol: 66 mg
Carbohydrate: 53 grams	Dietary Fiber: 5 grams
Protein: 28 grams	Sodium: 89 mg

BREADED PORK TENDERLOINS

Move over old fashioned fried pork tenderloin! This winner is a frequent request that tastes every bit as delicious!

1 pound pork tenderloin roast - cut crosswise into 6 pieces - all visible fat removed
⅓ cup all-purpose flour
1 teaspoon Lawry's seasoned salt
¾ cup Italian bread crumbs (I use Progresso)
2 egg whites - beaten
2 tablespoons skim milk

♥ Preheat oven 400 degrees.

♥ Spray a cookie sheet with non-fat cooking spray. Set aside.

♥ Pound pork to ¼- to ⅛-inch thickness. Set aside.

♥ In a small bowl, stir together flour, seasoned salt and bread crumbs.

♥ In a separate small bowl, beat together egg whites and skim milk. Coat meat in crumb mixture.

♥ Dip the coated meat into egg mixture, then re-dip into crumb mixture.

♥ Place breaded meat on prepared cookie sheet.

♥ Spray top of meat with non-fat cooking spray.

♥ Bake at 400 degrees for 10 minutes.

♥ Turn over. Spray top of meat with non-fat cooking spray. Bake an additional 10 minutes. Breading will be crispy and slightly golden, brown when done.

Yield: 6 servings

Calories: 181
Cholesterol: 45 mg
Total Fat: 3.6 grams (18% fat)
Sodium: 499 mg

Preparation time: 10 minutes or less.

Cooking time: 20 minutes.

Total time: 30 minutes or less.

Busy People's Low-Fat Cook Book

HAM & CABBAGE DINNER

As a child this was one of my favorite meals! It's great to prepare when camping . . . If you're fortunate enough to have electricity when you camp. Some people like to put fresh peeled carrots and chunks of onions in this dish.

2 tablespoons dry Butter Buds Sprinkles

1 (14.5 ounce) can Swanson fat-free, reduced-sodium chicken broth

1 head cabbage - cored and cut into 6 wedges

1½ pounds extra lean ham

¼ cup Fleischmann's Fat-Free Buttery Spread

♥ In a crockpot stir the Butter Buds with the chicken broth until dissolved.

♥ Put cabbage wedges in the bottom of the crockpot. (Don't worry if the broth does not cover the cabbage.)

♥ Place ham on top of cabbage.

♥ Cover. Cook on low for 8 to 10 hours or on high for 4 hours. (Don't worry about overcooking.)

♥ Cut ham into 6 slices.

♥ Stir cooked cabbage wedges in broth before removing from crock pot. With slotted spoon remove cabbage and place in a pretty serving bowl. Toss with Fleischmann's Fat-Free spread. If desired sprinkle lightly with lite salt. Serve immediately. Serve with Fleischmann's Fat-Free spread and salt and pepper on the side.

Yield: 6 servings

Calories: 207
Cholesterol: 53 mg

Total Fat: 6.0 grams (26% fat)
Sodium: 1887 mg

Preparation time: 10 minutes or less.

Cooking time: Varies, depending on temperature.

Busy People's Low-Fat Cook Book

Harvest Ham Steaks

*A lip smackin' and toe tappin' creative way
to use apple butter in a tasty entrée!*

♥ For each 4 ounces extra lean ham steak: spread 1 teaspoon of your favorite apple butter on top of ham steak while cooking it over medium heat on a grill (or skillet) that has been sprayed with non-fat cooking spray.

♥ After turning ham steak over, spread a second teaspoon of apple butter on top.

♥ Once bottom of ham steak is cooked, turn steak over a second time. Cook only for a couple of minutes - just enough to caramelize the apple butter.

♥ Serve right away. Left over steaks taste great as cold ham sandwiches!

♥ Note: If you don't have a terrific apple butter recipe, the one I have published in my "Down Home Cookin' Without the Down Home Fat" cookbook is fabulous!!!

Yield: 1 (4-ounce) steak

Calories: 171   Total Fat: 5.7 grams (30% fat)
Cholesterol: 53 mg   Sodium: 621 mg

Cooking time: 10 minutes of less.

Busy People's Low-Fat Cook Book

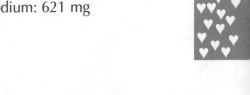

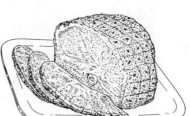

Stir Fried Ham and Cabbage

This is a very easy recipe not to mention delicious, especially for cabbage lovers.

¼ cup Butter Bud Sprinkles - dry

2 (16-ounce) packages pre-cut cole slaw mix - with big pieces of red cabbage removed

12 ounces extra lean ham – cut into tiny pieces

¼ cup hot water

Dash of ground black pepper - optional

♥ In a large, nonstick, covered skillet cook all ingredients over high heat for 8 to 10 minutes, stirring occasionally.

♥ If you desire this dish more tender, cover and continue cooking an additional 5 minutes. Serve hot.

Yield: 6 (¾-cup) servings

Calories: 116
Percent Fat Calories: 21%
Carbohydrate: 12 grams
Protein: 13 grams

Total Fat: 3 grams
Cholesterol: 22 mg
Dietary Fiber: 3 grams
Sodium: 979 mg

2nd Serving Busy People's Low Fat Cook Book

Menu Ideas: Serve with corn muffins.

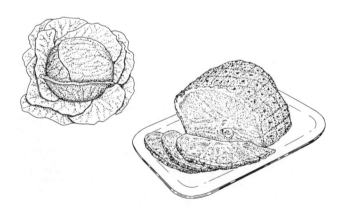

PRESTO HAM CASSEROLE

*Easy is the name of this game and it'll score
high points from your fans for being tasty!*

1 (7.25-ounce) box macaroni and cheese (the off brands are fine) - do not make as directed on box
1 cup hot water
1 (15-ounce) can Healthy Choice cream of mushroom soup

1 pound extra lean ham - cut into 1/3-inch chunks
1 (15-ounce) can sweet peas - drained

♥ Spray a 2-quart covered microwavable casserole dish with non-fat cooking spray.

♥ In prepared casserole dish, mix powdered cheese packet (from macaroni and cheese box) with hot water and soup until cheese is completely dissolved

♥ Stir in chopped ham and the macaroni until well mixed.

♥ Cover. Cook in a *carousel microwave on high for 7 minutes. (Very carefully remove lid, so you do not get a steam burn!)

♥ Stir. Cover and continue cooking in *carousel microwave for an additional 6 minutes.

♥ Stir in drained peas. Cover and let sit 2 to 3 minutes before serving. (If making ahead of time, freeze or refrigerate until needed. Microwave until warm.)

Yield: 5 servings

Calories: 342
Cholesterol: 49 mg

Total Fat: 6.5 grams (17% fat)
Sodium: 1936 mg

Preparation time: 5 minutes or less.

Cooking time: 13 minutes.

Total time: 18 minutes or less.

Busy People's Low-Fat Cook Book

Menu Ideas: Tossed salad and Jell-O with fruit.

AU GRATIN CASSEROLE DINNER

If you like cheesie broccoli, au gratin potatoes and ham you'll like this one dish entrée!

1 (5.5-ounce) box au gratin potatoes - dry
1 (12-ounce) can fat-free evaporated skim milk
1½ cups hot water

12 ounces extra lean ham (or turkey ham) - cut into bite-size pieces
1 (16-ounce) bag frozen broccoli pieces

♥ In a 2-quart microwavable casserole dish, mix dry au gratin potatoes (potatoes and seasoning cheese packet) with evaporated skim milk and water until powdered cheese is completely dissolved.

♥ Stir in ham pieces.

♥ Cover with wax paper. Cook in carousel microwave on high for 5 minutes.

♥ Stir in broccoli pieces. Cover. Continue cooking in carousel microwave on high for an additional 15 minutes, stirring occasionally.

♥ Remove wax paper. Let sit 3 to 5 minutes before serving.

Yield: 4 servings

Calories: 338
Cholesterol: 44 mg

Total Fat: 6.2 grams (15% fat)
Sodium: 2170 mg

Preparation time: 5 minutes or less.

Cooking time: 20 minutes.

Total time: 25 minutes or less.

Busy People's Low-Fat Cook Book

Menu Ideas: A complete meal in itself, however Spiced Apples also taste delicious with this entrée.

CABBAGE ROLLS

Put the cabbage in the freezer until frozen.
(I do this days, even weeks ahead of time.) The leaves
will become soft, once thawed. No need to precook leaves.

1 (14-ounce) package fat-free kielbasa (Butterball) - cut into tiny ¼-inch pieces

1 cup cooked instant rice

¼ cup frozen or fresh chopped onion

2 egg whites

2 (10¾-ounce) cans reduced-sodium condensed tomato soup - do not make as directed on can - divided

8 large cabbage leaves - with stems cut off

♥ Spray a crockpot with non-fat cooking spray.

♥ Mix kielbasa, cooked rice, onion, egg whites and 2 tablespoons condensed soup until well mixed.

♥ Place ⅓ cup of mixture on each cabbage leaf.

♥ Roll up and secure with a toothpick.

♥ Place in crockpot.

♥ Pour remaining condensed soup over the top.

♥ Cover and cook on high for 2½ to 3 hours or on low for 5 to 6 hours or until cabbage is tender.

Yield: 4 servings (2 cabbage rolls each)

Calories: 381
Percent Fat Calories: 8%
Carbohydrate: 65 grams
Protein: 21 grams

Total Fat: 3 grams
Cholesterol: 43 mg
Dietary Fiber: 1 gram
Sodium: 1394 mg

Preparation time: 20 minutes or less.

2nd Serving Busy People's Low Fat Cook Book

Menu Ideas: Tossed salad and warm Vienna bread.

Presto Sausage Casserole

It's hard to believe a casserole so good can be made so quickly.

1 (7.25-ounce) box macaroni and cheese (the off brands are fine) - do not make as directed on box
1 cup hot water
1 (15-ounce) can Healthy Choice Cream of Mushroom Soup

1 pound fat-free Butterball smoked sausage (or 1 pound fat-free Healthy Choice kielbasa) - cut into bite-size pieces
1 (15-ounce) can green beans - drained

♥ Spray a 2-quart covered microwavable casserole dish with non-fat cooking spray.

♥ In prepared casserole dish, mix powdered cheese packet (from macaroni and cheese box) with hot water and soup until cheese is completely dissolved.

♥ Stir in chopped sausage and macaroni until well mixed.

♥ Cover. Cook in a *carousel microwave on high for 7 minutes. (Very carefully remove lid, so you do not get a steam burn!)

♥ Stir. Cover and continue cooking in *carousel microwave for an additional 6 minutes.

♥ Stir in drained beans. Cover and let sit 2 to 3 minutes before serving. (If making ahead of time, freeze or refrigerate until needed. Microwave until warm.)

Yield: 5 servings

Calories: 286
Cholesterol: 45 mg

Total Fat: 1.9 grams (6% fat)
Sodium: 1702 mg

Preparation time: 5 minutes or less.

Cooking time: 13 minutes.

Total time: 18 minutes or less.

Busy People's Low-Fat Cook Book

PIGS ON A STICK

14 ounces Healthy Choice
smoked sausage
2 cans Pillsbury Buttermilk
Biscuits (4 biscuits will
be left over)

8 popsicle sticks

♥ Preheat oven to 350 degrees. Cut smoked sausage into 8 pieces. It will look like short, fat little hot dogs. Wrap each little sausage with two biscuits. Pinch biscuit dough with fingers to seal the "blanket." Place 1 popsicle stick ½ way through each sausage, leaving ½ of the stick out to later use as a handle. Spray 2 cookie sheets with non-fat cooking spray. Arrange "pigs" on cookie sheets, making sure they are at least 2 to 3 inches apart, because the dough will get bigger as they cook and you don't want them to stick to each other. Bake for 10 minutes or until dough is golden brown. Serve with mustard, ketchup, or barbeque sauce for dipping.

Yield: servings

Carbohydrate: 25 grams
Protein: 9 grams

Cholesterol: 18 mg
Dietary Fiber: 1 gram
Sodium: 785 mg

Preparation time: 25 minutes.

Down Home Cookin'

SCALLOP POTATOES AND SAUSAGE

I love these! They're super creamy!
(Please note, although the potatoes are not cut in the
traditional manner of slices, this recipe is every bit as good...
if not better than the traditional recipe).

1   pint fat-free half & half
    (I use Land O Lakes)
⅓   cup all-purpose flour
1   tablespoon Butter Buds
    Sprinkles - dry
½   cup frozen chopped onion
    (or ½ cup fresh chopped
    onion)

2   (14-ounce) packages
    Butterball fat-free
    smoked sausage - cut
    into ¼-inch bite-size
    pieces
1   (2-pound) bag frozen,
    fat-free shredded
    hash browns

♥ Spray a crockpot with non-fat cooking spray.

♥ With a whisk briskly stir half & half, flour and Butter Buds together
  in a crockpot until flour is completely dissolved.

♥ With large spoon stir in onions, smoked sausage and shredded
  hash browns until well mixed.

♥ Cover. Cook on high for 3½ to 4 hours or on low for 8 to 9 hours.

♥ Pepper to taste if desired.

Yield: 8 (1-cup) servings

Calories: 257
Percent Fat Calories: 0%
Carbohydrate: 44 grams
Protein: 22 grams

Total Fat: 0 grams
Cholesterol: 43 mg
Dietary Fiber: 2 grams
Sodium: 1276 mg

Preparation time: 10 minutes or less.

(Scallop Potatoes and Sausage continued on next page)

(Scallop Potatoes and Sausage continued)

Scallop Potatoes and Ham:

Prepare exactly the same, but substitute 2 pounds extra lean ham cut into bite-size pieces for the smoked sausage.

Yield: 8 (1-cup) servings

Calories: 290	Total Fat: 5 grams
Percent Fat Calories: 16%	Cholesterol: 43 mg
Carbohydrate: 34 grams	Dietary Fiber: 2 grams
Protein: 28 grams	Sodium: 1535 mg

Cheesy Scallop Potatoes and Ham:

After Scallop Potatoes and Ham recipe is completely cooked, stir in 5 slices fat-free American cheese (Kraft or Borden brand). Cut cheese into tiny pieces before stirring into dish.

Yield: 8 (1-cup) servings

Calories: 306	Total Fat: 5 grams
Percent Fat Calories: 15%	Cholesterol: 46 mg
Carbohydrate: 35 grams	Dietary Fiber: 2 grams
Protein: 30 grams	Sodium: 1648 mg

Cheesy Scallop Potatoes and Sausage:

After Scallop Potatoes and Sausage recipe is completely cooked, stir in 5 slices fat-free American Cheese (Kraft or Borden brand). Cut cheese into tiny pieces before stirring into dish.

Yield: 8 (1-cup) servings

Calories: 272	Total Fat: 0 grams
Percent Fat Calories: 0%	Cholesterol: 46 mg
Carbohydrate: 46 grams	Dietary Fiber: 2 grams
Protein: 25 grams	Sodium: 1388 mg

2nd Serving Busy People's Low Fat Cook Book

PIGS IN A BLANKET

Fast, easy and fun for kids to make.

14 ounces Healthy Choice smoked sausage

2 cans Pillsbury Buttermilk Biscuits (4 biscuits will be left over)

♥ Preheat oven to 350 degrees. Cut smoked sausage into 8 pieces. It will look like short, fat little hot dogs. Wrap each little sausage with two biscuits. Pinch biscuit dough with fingers to seal the "blanket." Spray two cookie sheets with a non-fat spray. Arrange "Pigs" on cookie sheets, making sure they are at least 2 to 3 inches apart, because the dough will get bigger as they cook and you don't want them to stick to each other. Bake for 10 minutes or until dough is golden brown. Serve with mustard, ketchup, or barbeque sauce for dipping.

Yield: servings

Carbohydrate: 25 grams
Protein: 9 grams

Total Fat: 3 grams
Cholesterol: 18 mg
Dietary Fiber: 1 gram
Sodium: 785 mg

Preparation time: 20 minutes.

Down Home Cookin'

ORANGE ROUGHY

1 pound orange roughy fillets
1 medium onion - cut into thin strips

1 teaspoon lemon pepper seasoning
1 tablespoon dry Butter Buds
½ cup plain bread crumbs

♥ Spray a skillet with non-fat cooking spray and place orange roughy fillets into skillet over medium heat. Place onion on top of fish in skillet.

♥ Sprinkle lemon pepper seasoning and Butter Buds evenly on top of fish,

♥ Cook for 7 minutes. Turn over and cook for an additional 3 to 5 minutes. During the last 3 to 4 minutes of cooking time, sprinkle with bread crumbs.

♥ Fish will be cooked when completely white throughout and when it flakes when cut with fork.

Yield: 3 servings

Calories: 161
Cholesterol: 30 mg

Total Fat: 1.6 grams (9% fat)
Sodium: 348 mg

Preparation time: 10-15 minutes, depending on thickness of fish.

Busy People's Low-Fat Cook Book

Menu Ideas: Delicious served with Garlic Red Skins.

(Oven) Fried Catfish

Oow! These babies are good!

1 (6.5-ounce) package cornbread mix - dry (I use Gold Medal Smart Size)	½ cup Egg Beaters
	½ cup skim milk
	2 pounds catfish
1 cup flour	Garlic salt - optional

♥ Preheat oven to 450 degrees.

♥ Spray a cookie sheet with non-fat cooking spray.

♥ Mix cornbread mix and flour together. Set aside.

♥ In another bowl, mix Egg Beaters and skim milk together.

♥ Dip catfish into flour mixture, then into egg mixture, then again in flour mixture.

♥ Spray top of fish with non-fat cooking spray.

♥ Place on prepared cookie sheets. Bake until fish flakes easily when tested with a fork. (Allow 5 to 6 minutes for each ½-inch of thickness).

♥ If desired, sprinkle lightly with garlic salt before serving.

Yield: 6 (4-ounce cooked) servings

Calories: 257	Total Fat: 6 grams
Percent Fat Calories: 21%	Cholesterol: 82 mg
Carbohydrate: 24 grams	Dietary Fiber: 2 grams
Protein: 25 grams	Sodium: 289 mg

Total time: 25 minutes or less.

2nd Serving Busy People's Low Fat Cook Book

Menu Ideas: Cornbread and Slaw Salad.

Best of BUSY PEOPLE'S Cookbooks

BY DAWN HALL

SWIFTY SWEETS

Low Fat Recipes from 3 AWARD-WINNING COOKBOOKS

HOT FUDGIE CAKE

Many say it is their favorite of my desserts.

3 cups skim milk
1 (5-ounce) box chocolate cook and serve pudding mix (Jell-O brand) - dry (Do not make as directed on box.)

1 (18.25-ounce) box super moist chocolate fudge cake mix - dry (Betty Crocker brand)
1⅓ cups water
½ cup applesauce
6 egg whites

♥ Spray a 3½-quart crockpot with non-fat cooking spray.

♥ Mix skim milk with dry chocolate pudding mix in crockpot until completely dissolved with whisk.

♥ In a medium bowl, mix dry cake mix, water, applesauce and egg whites using a whisk for 2 minutes or until well blended.

♥ Very gently pour cake batter into uncooked pudding mixture in crockpot. DO NOT STIR!

♥ Cover and cook on high for 2½ hours.

♥ Serve hot with a dab of Cool Whip Free.

♥ If desired, after 2½ hours of cooking, just unplug crockpot. It'll stay warm and delicious for hours. It travels well to potlucks or social gatherings.

Yield: 15 servings

Calories: 204
Percent Fat Calories: 14%
Carbohydrate: 39 grams
Protein: 4 grams

Total Fat: 3 grams
Cholesterol: 1 mg
Dietary Fiber: 1 gram
Sodium: 302 mg

Preparation time: 10 minutes or less.

2nd Serving Busy People's Low Fat Cookbook

PUNCHBOWL CAKE

1 (13.5-ounce) angel food cake
1 (21-ounce) can strawberry or blueberry pie filling
2 medium bananas - sliced then quarter the slices
1 (8-ounce) container Cool Whip Free

♥ Cut cake into 3 layers. Tear 1 of the layers into tiny pieces. Set aside.

♥ Mix pie filling with quartered banana slices and mix with spoon until well blended. Set aside.

♥ Place a layer of angel food cake on the bottom of a punch bowl. Use torn pieces of cake to fill in any gaps.

♥ Spread ½ of the fruit mixture over cake.

♥ Place second layer of cake on top of fruit filling. Use torn pieces to fill in any gaps.

♥ Spread remaining fruit mixture on top of cake.

♥ Frost Cool Whip Free evenly on top.

Yield: 12 servings.

Calories: 188
Cholesterol: 0 mg
Total Fat: 0.3 grams (2% fat)
Sodium: 264 mg

Total preparation time: 5 minutes or less.

Busy People's Low-Fat Cookbook

Menu Ideas: Nice and tasty summer delight!

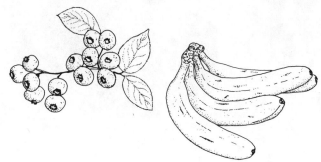

CHERRY PINEAPPLE CAKE

So good! So delicious! So easy!

1 box Betty Crocker Super Moist yellow cake mix with pudding in the mix
1 cup "lite" cherry pie filling

1 20-ounce can crushed pineapple, drained (1 cup of pineapple juice should be drained and discarded)

♥ Preheat oven to 350 degrees. Mix above ingredients all together. Spray a 9 × 13-inch cake pan with a non-fat cooking spray and flour. Pour batter in pan and bake for 30 to 35 minutes or until knife inserted in center comes out clean.

♥ This is excellent served warm with Dream Whip or no-fat frozen yogurt.

♥ Refrigerate unused portions.

Yield: 15 servings

Calories: 174
Percent Fat Calories: 15%
Carbohydrate: 36 grams
Protein: 2 grams

Total Fat: 3 grams
Cholesterol: 0 mg
Dietary Fiber: 0 grams
Sodium: 234 mg

Preparation time: 35 minutes

Down Home Cookin'

BLUEBERRY CAKE

1 cup blueberry pie filling

1 16-ounce box angel food cake mix (I use Pillsbury) - dry

♥ Preheat oven to 350 degrees. Mix pie filling and angel food cake mix together. Spray 9 × 13-inch pan with non-fat cooking spray and pour batter into pan. Bake for 25 to 28 minutes, or until top is deep golden brown and cracks appear on the top. Cool completely. Serve with a little dab of remaining pie filling if desired.

Yield: 20 servings

Calories: 96
Percent Fat Calories: 0%
Carbohydrate: 22 grams
Protein: 2 grams

Total Fat: 0 grams
Cholesterol: 0 mg
Dietary Fiber: 0 grams
Sodium: 204 mg

Preparation time: 30 minutes

Down Home Cookin'

Also great as a snack-cake-type finger food.

Refrigerate unused portions.

Banana Split Cake

1 20-ounce can crushed pineapple in its own juice, no sugar added

1 18.25-ounce box "lite" yellow cake mix (I use Betty Crocker Super Moist) - dry

♥ Preheat oven to 350 degrees. Mix whole can of crushed pineapple along with its juice with cake mix on medium speed for 2 to 3 minutes until well blended. Spray a 9 × 13-inch pan with a non-fat cooking spray and pour batter into pan. Bake for 40 minutes, or until toothpick put into the center of cake comes out clean. Let cool. Once cake is completely cooled, add topping to cake.

Topping:

2 tablespoons NutraSweet Spoonful (OR 2 tablespoons sugar)

1 can "lite" cherry pie filling

2 bananas, thinly sliced

1 8-ounce carton Cool Whip Free

2 Tablespoons Hershey's Chocolate Syrup

♥ In bowl, mix NutraSweet well into pie filling. Spread cherry pie filling over completely cooled cake. Press banana slices lightly into pie filling. Spread Cool Whip over bananas. With spoon drizzle chocolate syrup over Cool Whip. Keep chilled until ready to serve. Refrigerate unused portions.°

° With Sugar – Calories: 245 – Total Fat: 3 grams
Percent Fat Calories: 11% – Cholesterol: 0 mg
Carbohydrate: 54 grams – Dietary Fiber: 2 grams
Protein: 2 grams – Sodium: 258 mg

Yield: 15 servings

Calories: 239
Percent Fat Calories: 11%
Carbohydrate: 52 grams
Protein: 2 grams

Total Fat: 3 grams
Cholesterol: 0 mg
Dietary Fiber: 2 grams
Sodium: 258 mg

Preparation time: 45 minutes.

Down Home Cookin'

CRANBERRY CAKE

Great served warm with a dab of Cool Whip Free or chilled as a snack cake.

1 box super moist yellow cake mix (I use Betty Crocker with pudding in the mix) - dry

1 16-ounce can jellied cranberry sauce (I use Ocean Spray)

♥ Preheat oven to 350 degrees. Spray 9 × 13-inch pan with non-fat cooking spray. Set aside. Set aside ½ cup of the boxed cake mix. With mixer, blend together cranberry sauce and remaining cake mix on low speed. Once well mixed, increase speed to high. Beat on high for 2 minutes. Spread smoothly into prepared pan. Sprinkle with remaining dry cake mix on top. Bake for 30 to 32 minutes or until top is golden brown.

♥ Refrigerate unused portions.

Yield: 15 servings

Calories: 188
Percent Fat Calories: 13%
Carbohydrate: 40 grams
Protein: 1 gram

Total Fat: 3 grams
Cholesterol: 0 mg
Dietary Fiber: 0 grams
Sodium: 241 mg

Preparation time: 35 minutes

Down Home Cookin'

CREAMY FAT-FREE CHOCOLATE FROSTING

¾ cup fat-free margarine
  (I use Ultra Promise)
¾ cup cocoa
1 teaspoon vanilla

4 packets Equal (OR 3 tablespoons more powdered sugar)
3½ cups powdered sugar

♥ Mix margarine, cocoa, vanilla and Equal together with mixer on low speed until well-blended. Slowly add powdered sugar. Beat until creamy smooth.°

° With Sugar – Calories: 81 – Total Fat: 0 grams
Percent Fat Calories: 0% – Cholesterol: 0 mg
Carbohydrate: 20 grams – Dietary Fiber: 1 gram
Protein: 1 gram – Sodium: 46 mg

Yield: 24 servings

Calories: 78
Percent Fat Calories: 0%
Carbohydrate: 19 grams
Protein: 1 gram

Total Fat: 0 grams
Cholesterol: 0 mg
Dietary Fiber: 1 gram
Sodium: 46 mg

Preparation time: 8 minutes

Down Home Cookin'

JELLY ROLL CAKE

1 box Betty Crocker
Super Moist yellow
cake mix with pudding
in the mix - dry

⅓ cup water

6 egg whites (OR ¾ cup
Egg Beaters)

20 ounces fruit preserves
(Use your favorite flavor)

♥ Preheat oven to 350 degrees. Spray two jelly roll pans with non-fat cooking spray. (A jelly roll pan is a cookie sheet with ½-inch sides.) Beat dry cake mix, water, and egg whites in large bowl on low speed for 30 seconds. Beat on medium speed for 2 minutes. Pour ½ cake batter into each pan and spread evenly. Bake for 10 minutes. Cool. Spread each cake with about 7 ounces of preserves.

♥ Roll each cake into a roll, starting from the narrow side. Spread remaining preserves (about 3 ounces each cake) on top.

Yield: 24 servings

Calories: 151
Percent Fat Calories: 7%
Carbohydrate: 34 grams
Protein: 2 grams

Total Fat: 1 gram
Cholesterol: 0 mg
Dietary Fiber: 0 grams
Sodium: 157 mg

Down Home Cookin'

No Bake Eclair Cake

I like this best when prepared 2-3 days before eating.

2 envelopes Dream Whip, prepared as directed
2 3.4 ounce boxes of French vanilla pudding (it has to be French vanilla!) prepared as directed on box
½ jar Smucker's Fat-free Hot Fudge (11.5 ounce size)
Whole graham crackers

♥ Prepare both Dream Whip and pudding as directed. Refrigerate for 5 minutes. Line a 9 × 13-inch pan with whole graham crackers. Seven and a half whole graham crackers (each including 4 sections) will be needed to cover the bottom of the pan.

♥ Mix pudding and Dream Whip together until well blended. Pour ½ of the pudding/Dream Whip mixture on top of graham crackers. Put another layer of 7½ whole graham crackers on top of pudding/ Dream Whip mixture.

♥ Put remaining pudding/Dream Whip mixture on top of graham crackers. Put 7½ whole graham crackers on top of pudding/ Dream Whip mixture.

♥ The cake should be layered in the following order:
7½ graham crackers
½ pudding/Dream Whip mixture
7½ graham crackers
remainder pudding/Dream Whip mixture
7½ graham crackers
hot fudge

♥ Frost top layer of graham crackers with hot fudge that has been microwaved for a few seconds, so that it will spread easier. Refrigerate. Serve chilled. Refrigerate unused portions.

Yield: 15 servings

Calories: 190
Percent Fat Calories: 15%
Carbohydrate: 38 grams
Protein: 2 grams

Total Fat: 3 grams
Cholesterol: 0 mg
Dietary Fiber: 1 gram
Sodium: 334 mg

Down Home Cookin'

Mm! (possibly the world's shortest published recipe title)

This scrumptious crumb cake makes an excellent breakfast cake, coffee cake, snack cake or dessert!

1 (18.25-ounce) box Betty Crocker Reduced Fat Sweet Rewards yellow cake mix, dry (do not make as directed on box) - divided

1 (10-ounce) package frozen strawberries - hawed
1 (8-ounce) package fat-free cream cheese - softened (I used Healthy Choice)

♥ Preheat oven to 350 degrees.

♥ Set aside 1 cup of dry cake mix.

♥ Line a 9 × 13-inch pan with foil. (For easier clean-up). Spray lined pan with non-fat cooking spray.

♥ With mixer on low speed, beat together strawberries and cream cheese for 1 minute.

♥ Add ½ of the remaining cake mix to cream mixture and continue beating until well mixed, then add remaining cake mix. (Do not use the 1 cup reserved!) Beat for 2 minutes on medium speed.

♥ Spread into prepared pan. Sprinkle the 1 cup reserved cake mix on top of batter.

♥ Bake at 350 degrees for 30 minutes or until a knife inserted in center comes out clean.

Yield: 15 servings

Calories: 160
Cholesterol: 1 mg

Total Fat: 1.9 grams (11% fat)
Sodium: 282 mg

Preparation time: 10 minutes or less.

Baking time: 30 minutes.

Total time: 40 minutes or less.

Down Home Cookin'

Menu Ideas: Tea, coffee, skim milk and a piece of fruit.

CAPPUCCINO COOKIES

These babies are excellent!

1 (18.25-ounce) box reduced-fat devil's food cake mix (Betty Crocker Sweet Rewards) - dry - do not make as directed on box

1 tablespoon instant coffee
1 teaspoon ground cinnamon
¾ cup skim milk
2 (4-ounce) containers Egg Beaters (or 8 egg whites)

♥ Preheat oven to 400 degrees.

♥ Spray 4 cookie sheets with non-fat cooking spray. Set aside.

♥ Mix all ingredients together with a spatula until well blended in a medium-sized bowl.

♥ Drop by rounded heaping teaspoonfuls onto prepared cookie sheets.

♥ Bake at 400 degrees for 5 minutes or until centers are set.

Yield: 48 cookies (Nutritional information per cookie)

Calories: 47
Percent Fat Calories: 17%
Carbohydrate: 9 grams
Protein: 1 gram

Total Fat: 1 gram
Cholesterol: 0 mg
Dietary Fiber: 0 grams
Sodium: 93 mg

Preparation time: 10 minutes for 2 dozen - 15 minutes for 4 dozen.

Double Chocolate Cappuccino Cookies:

Make the Cappuccino Cookies recipe exactly the same and stir in 1 cup candy-coated semi-sweet chocolate bits. (Hershey's)

Yield: 48 cookies (Nutritional information per cookie)

Calories: 72
Percent Fat Calories: 27%
Carbohydrate: 12 grams
Protein: 1 gram

Total Fat: 2 grams
Cholesterol: 0 mg
Dietary Fiber: 1 gram
Sodium: 93 mg

(Cappuccino Cookies continued on next page)

(Cappuccino Cookies continued)

Amaretto Cappuccino Cookies:

Make the Cappuccino Cookies recipe exactly the same and stir in 2 teaspoons almond extract.

Yield: 48 cookies (Nutritional information per cookie)

Calories: 48
Percent Fat Calories: 17%
Carbohydrate: 9 grams
Protein: 1 gram

Total Fat: 1 gram
Cholesterol: 0 mg
Dietary Fiber: 0 grams
Sodium: 93 mg

2nd Serving Busy People's Low Fat Cookbook

Menu Ideas: Good for light teas, snacks or lunches.

DELICIOUS DATE COOKIES

⅓ cup plus 1 tablespoon Sunny Delight citrus beverage or orange juice
1 cup reduced-fat Bisquick baking mix
¼ cup packed dark brown sugar

1 teaspoon ground cinnamon
½ cup chopped dates (Dole brand - found in baking section)

♥ Preheat oven to 400 degrees.

♥ Spray 2 cookie sheets with non-fat cooking spray. Set aside.

♥ Mix all ingredients together in a medium bowl with a spoon until well mixed.

♥ Drop by rounded teaspoonfuls onto prepared cookie sheets.

♥ Bake at 400 degrees for 5 minutes or until lightly brown on bottom.

Yield: 24 cookies (Nutritional information per cookie)

Calories: 40
Percent Fat Calories: 7%
Carbohydrate: 9 grams
Protein: 0 grams

Total Fat: trace
Cholesterol: 0 mg
Dietary Fiber: 0 grams
Sodium: 62 mg

Preparation time: 10 minutes or less.

Menu Ideas: Good for breakfast, lunch or snacks.

(Delicious Date Cookies continued on next page)

(Delicious Date Cookies continued)

Incredible Cranberry Cookies:

Follow recipe for Delicious Date Cookies exactly, except omit the chopped dates. Instead use ½ cup sweetened, dried cranberries (Craisins by Ocean Spray).

Yield: 24 cookies (Nutritional information per cookie)

Calories: 38
Percent Fat Calories: 8%
Carbohydrate: 8 grams
Protein: 0 grams

Total Fat: trace
Cholesterol: 0 mg
Dietary Fiber: 0 grams
Sodium: 62 mg

Radical Raisin Cookies:

Follow recipe for Delicious Date Cookies exactly, except omit the chopped dates. Instead use ½ cup raisins.

Yield: 24 cookies (Nutritional information per cookie)

Calories: 40
Percent Fat Calories: 7%
Carbohydrate: 9 grams
Protein: 0 grams

Total Fat: trace
Cholesterol: 0 mg
Dietary Fiber: 0 grams
Sodium: 63 mg

Preparation time: 10 minutes or less.

2nd Serving Busy People's Low Fat Cookbook

CHOCOLATE CHEWY COOKIES

1 (8-ounce) container Cool Whip Free
2 egg whites

1 (18.25-ounce) box reduced-fat chocolate cake mix - dry - do not make as directed on box (Sweet Rewards)
¼ cup powdered sugar

♥ Preheat oven to 350 degrees.

♥ Spray cookie sheets with non-fat cooking spray. Set aside.

♥ Beat Cool Whip Free until smooth, especially if frozen, then combine egg whites with Cool Whip Free in a medium-sized bowl.

♥ Mix dry cake mix into Cool Whip and egg white mixture. Stir until completely mixed.

♥ Dip rounded tablespoonfuls of cookie dough into powdered sugar.

♥ Place each cookie covered with powdered sugar onto prepared cookie sheet. Bake for 10 to 12 minutes until set but not brown.

♥ Cool a few minutes on cookie sheet, then transfer to waxed paper.

Yield: 58 cookies (Nutritional information per cookie)

Calories: 46
Percent Fat Calories: 16%
Carbohydrate: 9 grams
Protein: 0 grams

Total Fat: 1 gram
Cholesterol: 0 mg
Dietary Fiber: 0 grams
Sodium: 59 mg

(Chocolate Chewy Cookies continued on next page)

(Chocolate Chewy Cookies continued)

Lemon Chewy Cookies:

Make exactly the same but substitute lemon cake mix (Super Moist by Betty Crocker).

Yield: 58 cookies (Nutritional information per cookie)

Calories: 45	Total Fat: 1 gram
Percent Fat Calories: 14%	Cholesterol: 0 mg
Carbohydrate: 9 grams	Dietary Fiber: 0 grams
Protein: 0 grams	Sodium: 61 mg

Carrot Chewy Cookies:

Make exactly the same but substitute carrot cake mix. (Super Moist by Betty Crocker).

Yield: 58 cookies (Nutritional information per cookie)

Calories: 46	Total Fat: 1 gram
Percent Fat Calories: 17%	Cholesterol: 0 mg
Carbohydrate: 9 grams	Dietary Fiber: 0 grams
Protein: 0 grams	Sodium: 60 mg

Preparation time: 35 minutes.

2nd Serving Busy People's Low Fat Cookbook

OATMEAL COOKIES

*These crunchy cookies taste to me like a
granola bar even though they are not shaped like one.*

1 cup applesauce	¼ teaspoon nutmeg
1 cup packed brown sugar	4 cups rolled oats
1 teaspoon ground cinnamon	

♥ Preheat oven to 350 degrees.

♥ Spray cookie sheets with non-fat cooking spray. Set aside.

♥ Stir together applesauce, brown sugar, cinnamon and nutmeg until well blended in a medium-sized bowl.

♥ Gradually stir in oats until well blended.

♥ Drop by rounded teaspoonfuls onto prepared cookie sheets.

♥ Bake for 15 minutes or until lightly golden brown.

Yield: 48 cookies (Nutritional information per cookie)

Calories: 46
Percent Fat Calories: 8%
Carbohydrate: 10 grams
Protein: 1 gram

Total Fat: trace
Cholesterol: 0 mg
Dietary Fiber: 1 gram
Sodium: 2 mg

Menu Ideas: Lunches or snacks.

Cranberry Oatmeal Cookies:

Stir in 1 cup chopped, dried cranberries (Ocean Spray) with the oatmeal.

Yield: 60 cookies (Nutritional information per cookie)

Calories: 42
Percent Fat Calories: 8%
Carbohydrate: 9 grams
Protein: 1 gram

Total Fat: trace
Cholesterol: 0 mg
Dietary Fiber: 1 gram
Sodium: 2 mg

(Oatmeal Cookies continued on next page)

(Oatmeal Cookies continued)

Raisin Oatmeal Cookies:

Stir in 1 cup raisins with the oatmeal.

Yield: 60 cookies (Nutritional information per cookie)

Calories: 45
Percent Fat Calories: 7%
Carbohydrate: 10 grams
Protein: 1 gram

Total Fat: trace
Cholesterol: 0 mg
Dietary Fiber: 1 gram
Sodium: 2 mg

Oatmeal Date Cookies:

Stir in 1 cup chopped dates with the oatmeal.

Yield: 60 cookies (Nutritional information per cookie)

Calories: 45
Percent Fat Calories: 7%
Carbohydrate: 10 grams
Protein: 1 gram

Total Fat: trace
Cholesterol: 0 mg
Dietary Fiber: 1 gram
Sodium: 2 mg

Preparation time 20 minutes or less.

2nd Serving Busy People's Low Fat Cookbook

SPICE COOKIES

*Not only does this very versatile cookie satisfy your
sweet tooth, but when they're baking the fragrant aroma
of potpourri fills your home with a warm and cozy feeling.*

2   cups whole wheat flour
1   cup sugar
1   teaspoon baking soda
4   egg whites

½   cup applesauce
½   teaspoon ground cloves
1   teaspoon ground cinnamon

♥ Preheat oven to 350 degrees.

♥ Line cookie sheets with foil. Spray foil with non-fat cooking spray. Set aside.

♥ In a large mixing bowl, mix all ingredients together with a spatula until well mixed.

♥ Drop cookie dough by rounded teaspoonfuls onto prepared cookie sheets.

♥ Bake at 350 degrees for 6 to 7 minutes or until bottoms are lightly browned.

Yield: 6 dozen (Nutritional information per cookie)

Calories: 24
Cholesterol: 0 mg

Total Fat: 0.1 grams (2% fat)
Sodium: 21 mg

Preparation time: 10 minutes or less.

Baking time: 6-7 minutes (for 2 cookie sheets of 1 dozen each).

Total time: 17 minutes or less (for 2 dozen) add an additional 7 minutes for each 2 dozen.

Menu Ideas: Great to eat in the fall and during the holidays.

*Variations using the "Spice Cookies"
recipe above as the base.
Bake as directed in Spice Cookie Recipe.*

(Spice Cookies continued on next page)

(Spice Cookies continued)

Chocolate Chip Spice Cookies:

Press 3 chocolate chips on top of each cookie before baking.

Yield: 6 dozen (Nutritional information per cookie)

Calories: 39   Total Fat: 1.0 grams (22% fat)
Cholesterol: 0 mg   Sodium: 21 mg

Cinnamon Imperial Cookies:

Press 4 cinnamon red hot candies on top of each cookie before baking.

Yield: 6 dozen (Nutritional information per cookie)

Calories: 31   Total Fat: 0.1 grams (2% fat)
Cholesterol: 0 mg   Sodium: 21 mg

Iced Spice Cookies:

Microwave ¼ cup Betty Cracker low-fat vanilla frosting. Lightly drizzle frosting over cooled cookies.

Yield: 6 dozen (Nutritional information per cookie)

Calories: 30   Total Fat: 0.2 grams (6% fat)
Cholesterol: 0 mg   Sodium: 24 mg

Apple Spice Cookies:

Leaving skins on, cut 2 apples into ¼-inch pieces. Stir apple pieces into prepared dough. The best choices of apples to use are Rome Beauty (also known as Red Rome), Golden Delicious, Granny Smith, Jonathan and Macintosh apples. Note: Red Delicious are not good to bake with.

Yield: 6 dozen (Nutritional information per cookie)

Calories: 26   Total Fat: 0.1 grams (3% fat)
Cholesterol: 0 mg   Sodium: 21 mg

(Spice Cookies continued on next page)

(Spice Cookies continued)

Apple-Walnut Cookies:

Leaving skins on cut 2 apples into ¼-inch pieces. Stir apple pieces into prepared dough. (See apple spice cookies for selection of best apple choices to use.) Not using more than ½ cup finely chopped walnuts for the entire recipe, sprinkle walnuts on top of cookies before baking.

Yield: 6 dozen (Nutritional information per cookie)

Calories: 31   Total Fat: 0.6 grams (16% fat)
Cholesterol: 0 mg   Sodium: 21 mg

Iced Apple Walnut Cookies:

Follow Apple Walnut Cookies recipe exactly. Microwave ¼ cup Betty Crocker low-fat vanilla frosting. Lightly drizzle frosting over cooled cookies.

Yield: 6 dozen (Nutritional information per cookie)

Calories: 38   Total Fat: 0.7 grams (17% fat)
Cholesterol: 0 mg   Sodium: 24 mg

Raisin Spice Cookies:

Stir ¾ cup raisins into prepared dough. After baking, sift or sprinkle cooled cookies lightly with ¼ cup powdered sugar.

Yield: 6 dozen (Nutritional information per cookie)

Calories: 31   Total Fat: 0.1 grams (2% fat)
Cholesterol: 0 mg   Sodium: 21 mg

(Spice Cookies continued on next page)

(Spice Cookies continued)

Cranberry Cookies:

Stir ¾ cup chopped, dried cranberries into prepared dough.

Yield: 6 dozen (Nutritional information per cookie)

Calories: 28   Total Fat: 0.1 grams (3% fat)
Cholesterol: 0 mg   Sodium: 21 mg

Cranberry Walnut Cookies:

Stir ¾ cup chopped, dried cranberries into prepared dough. Not using more than ½ cup of finely chopped walnuts for the entire recipe, sprinkle walnuts on top of cookies before baking.

Yield: 6 dozen (Nutritional information per cookie)

Calories: 33   Total Fat: 0.6 grams (15% fat)
Cholesterol: 0 mg   Sodium: 21 mg

Carrot Cookies:

Stir 1½ cups finely grated carrot into prepared cookie dough. After baking, sift or sprinkle cooled cookies lightly with ¼ cup powdered sugar.

Yield: 6 dozen (Nutritional information per cookie)

Calories: 26   Total Fat: 0.1 grams (2% fat)
Cholesterol: 0 mg   Sodium: 22 mg

Busy People's Low-Fat Cookbook

BROWNIE COOKIES

This scrumptious cookie is very versatile. Seven different cookies can be derived from the base, and they're all terrific!

¼ cup brown sugar	2 tablespoons flour
3 tablespoons applesauce	1 (10.25-ounce) Gold Medal
1 egg white	Smart Size brownie mix - dry

♥ Preheat oven to 350 degrees.

♥ Line 2 cookie sheets with foil, spray with non-fat cooking spray. Set aside.

♥ Mix together brown sugar, applesauce and egg white until well blended. Stir in flour and brownie mix until well mixed.

♥ Drop by rounded teaspoonfuls onto prepared cookie sheets. With a damp fork press cookies down into 1½-inch diameter circles.

♥ Bake at 350 degrees for 10 minutes.

Yield: 2 dozen (Nutritional information per cookie)

Calories: 66	Total Fat: 1.6 grams (21% fat)
Cholesterol: 4 mg	Sodium: 39 mg

Preparation time: 5 minutes or less.

Baking time: 10 minutes

Total time: 15 minutes or less

Busy People's Low-Fat Cookbook

The following are cookie recipes using the "Brownie Cookies" recipe as the base.

Double Chocolate Brownie Cookies:

Follow recipe exactly and place 3 Hershey's reduced-fat baking chips on top of each cookie before baking.

Yield: 2 dozen (Nutritional information per cookie)

Calories: 76	Total Fat: 1.9 grams (22% fat)
Cholesterol: 4 mg	Sodium: 39 mg

(Brownie Cookies continued on next page)

(Brownie Cookies continued)

Mint Brownie Cookies:

Follow recipe exactly except add 3 drops mint extract to base before mixing.

Yield: 2 dozen (Nutritional information per cookie)

Calories: 66   Total Fat: 1.6 grams (21% fat)
Cholesterol: 4 mg   Sodium: 39 mg

Double Chocolate Mint Brownie Cookies:

Follow recipe exactly except add 3 drops mint extract before mixing. Place 3 mint flavored baking chips, on top of each cookie before baking.

Yield: 2 dozen (Nutritional information per cookie)

Calories: 82   Total Fat: 2.6 grams (28% fat)
Cholesterol: 4 mg   Sodium: 39 mg

Brownie Sandwich Cookies:

Once cookies are done baking and are cool, spread 2 teaspoons marshmallow creme on bottom of cookie. Place second cookie on top of marshmallow creme and press together.

Yield: 12 cookies (Nutritional information per cookie)

Calories: 170   Total Fat: 3.2 grams (16% fat)
Cholesterol: 8 mg   Sodium: 84 mg

Mint Brownie Sandwich Cookies:

Follow recipe exactly except add 3 drops mint extract before mixing. Once cookies are done baking and are cool, spread 2 teaspoons marshmallow creme on bottom cookie. Place second cookie on top of marshmallow creme and press together.

Yield: 12 cookies (Nutritional information per cookie)

Calories: 170   Total Fat: 3.2 grams (16% fat)
Cholesterol: 8 mg   Sodium: 84 mg

Brownie Nut Cookies:

Follow recipe exactly. Just before baking, lightly sprinkle finely chopped walnuts or pecans over cookies and press in. (No more than ¼ cup for entire recipe.)

Yield: 2 dozen (Nutritional information per cookie)

Calories: 74   Total Fat: 2.4 grams (28% fat)
Cholesterol: 4 mg   Sodium: 39 mg

PERFECT PINEAPPLE COOKIES

*It's hard to eat just one! If you like
pineapple upside down cake you'll love these!*

¼ cup dark brown sugar
1 (20-ounce) can crushed
pineapple in its natural
juices - with one cup juice
drained and discarded
3 egg whites

1 (18.25-ounce) box Betty
Crocker Reduced-Fat
Sweet Rewards yellow
cake mix - dry
½ cup graham crackers crumbs

♥ Preheat oven to 350 degrees.

♥ Line cookie sheets with foil and spray with non-fat cooking spray. Set aside.

♥ With a spatula or spoon, mix together dark brown sugar, drained pineapple, and egg whites until well mixed and sugar is dissolved.

♥ Add cake mix and graham cracker crumbs. Continue stirring until well mixed.

♥ Drop by teaspoonfuls onto prepared cookie sheets. Dip fingers in water and press top of cookie down to 1½-inch diameter circles.

♥ Bake at 350 degrees for 11 to 12 minutes, or until bottoms are golden brown.

Yield: 7 dozen cookies (Nutritional information per cookie)

Calories: 33
Cholesterol: 0 mg

Total Fat: 0.5 grams (14% fat)
Sodium: 50 mg

Preparation time: 5 minutes or less.

Baking time: 11-12 minutes per 2 dozen cookies.

Total time: 17 minutes or less for first 2 dozen. Add an additional 12 minutes baking time for each 2 dozen cookies.

Busy People's Low-Fat Cookbook

*Menu Idea: 3 of these make a great snack - under
100 calories and only 1 ½ grams of fat. Or serve after a
meal to curb your sweet tooth.*

CHOCOLATE CHERRY COOKIES

It doesn't get any easier than this super-soft cookie.

1 box Betty Crocker Super Moist Devil's Food cake mix with pudding in the mix - dry	1½ cups lite cherry pie filling 1 teaspoon almond extract 1¼ cup chocolate chips, if desired

♥ Preheat oven to 350 degrees. Spray cookie sheet with non-fat cooking spray. Mix all ingredients well by hand. Drop by teaspoonfuls onto cookie sheet. Bake for 10 minutes. Remove from cookie sheet and cool. (Frost with creamy fat-free chocolate frosting, if desired.) Do not store in airtight container, which may cause cookies to get too soft.

Yield: 48 servings

Calories: 52
Percent Fat Calories: 19%
Carbohydrate: 10 grams
Protein: 1 gram

Total Fat: 1 gram
Cholesterol: 0 mg
Dietary Fiber: 0 grams
Sodium: 84 mg

Down Home Cookin'

CITY SLICKER S'MORE BALLS

*Fun for kids to make! A neat indoor twist to S'mores
that we make when we are camping.*

2 tablespoons fat-free
   margarine (I use
   Ultra Promise)
2 cups mini marshmallows

60 chocolate chips
3 cups Golden Grahams
   Cereal

♥ Over low heat melt margarine and mix in mini marshmallows, stirring constantly.

♥ When marshmallows have melted down to 1¼ of their original size, remove from heat. Add cereal and mix well. (Don't let marshmallows melt completely.)

♥ Spray your hands with a non-fat cooking spray. Divide mixture into 15 parts. Roll each part with hands and form into balls. Place 4 chocolate chips throughout each ball.

♥ Set each ball on wax paper and let cool completely.

Yield: 15 servings

Calories: 60
Percent Fat Calories: 13%
Carbohydrate: 13 grams
Protein: 1 gram

Total Fat: 1 gram
Cholesterol: 0 mg
Dietary Fiber: 0 grams
Sodium: 87 mg

Preparation time: 20 minutes

Down Home Cookin'

BLUEBERRY DROPS

2 cups blueberry pie filling
(21-ounce can minus
2 tablespoons)

2 16-ounce boxes angel
food cake mixes
(I use Pillsbury)

♥ Preheat oven to 350 degrees. In a large bowl, mix pie filling with cake mixes by slowly adding 1 cup of the cake mix at a time to the filling. Spray a cookie sheet with non-fat cooking spray and drop batter by the teaspoon onto cookie sheet. Bake for 8 to 10 minutes — until bottoms are golden brown. Once cooled, the golden brown bottoms will be crispy.

Yield: 90 servings

Calories: 43
Percent Fat Calories: 0%
Carbohydrate: 10 grams
Protein: 1 gram

Total Fat: 0 grams
Cholesterol: 0 mg
Dietary Fiber: 0 grams
Sodium: 91 mg

Preparation time: 20 minutes

Down Home Cookin'

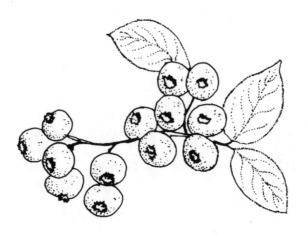

COOKIES AND CREAM BROWNIES

These brownies are super rich!
A little serving goes a long way.

1   (16-ounce) package
     mix brownie - dry - do not
     make as directed on box
3   tablespoons applesauce
5   egg whites - divided
3   tablespoons water

12 reduced-fat Oreo's -
     crushed - divided
1   (8-ounce) package fat-free
     cream cheese - softened
¼   cup sugar

♥ Preheat oven to 350 degrees.

♥ Spray a 9 × 13-inch nonstick pan with non-fat cooking spray. Set aside.

♥ With a fork, mix brownie mix, applesauce, 2 egg whites and water together until well blended in a medium-sized bowl. Stir in three-fourths of the crushed Oreo's.

♥ Spread in prepared pan.

♥ With a mixer, beat 3 egg whites, cream cheese and sugar together until smooth. Spoon cream cheese mixture over batter. Cut through batter with a knife to swirl. Sprinkle with remaining crushed Oreo's.

♥ Bake at 350 degrees for 25 minutes or until a toothpick inserted in center comes out clean.

Yield: 20 servings

Calories: 150	Total Fat: 3 grams
Percent Fat Calories: 19%	Cholesterol: 4 mg
Carbohydrate: 27 grams	Dietary Fiber: 0 grams
Protein: 4 grams	Sodium: 266 mg

Preparation time: 30 minutes or less.

2nd Serving Busy People's Low Fat Cookbook

Menu Ideas: Great for picnics.

PEANUT BUTTER CRUNCH BARS

This homemade version will save you oodles over the small packaged store brand! They're every bit as delicious! The blend of sweet, creamy peanut butter and the crunch make this a real hit for children! Great for school lunches.

8 cups Captain Crunch Peanut Butter Crunch cereal - divided

¼ cup Promise Ultra 70% less fat margarine
1 (10-ounce) bag marshmallows

♥ Spray a 9 × 13-inch pan with non-fat cooking spray. Set aside.

♥ Put 1 cup of the cereal in a zip-lock bag. Make sure the bag is securely closed, squeezing all the air out as you close. Crush the cereal. Set aside.

♥ In a large pan over low heat, melt Promise Ultra with marshmallows.

♥ Stir all of the cereal (crushed and not crushed) into marshmallow mixture.

♥ Spray hands with non-fat cooking spray. Press cereal mixture into prepared pan.

♥ Cool and cut into bars.

Yield: 16 bars

Calories: 137
Percent Fat Calories: 15%
Carbohydrate: 28 grams
Protein: 2 grams

Total Fat: 2 grams
Cholesterol: 0 mg
Dietary Fiber: 1 gram
Sodium: 155 mg

Total time: 15 minutes or less.

2nd Serving Busy People's Low Fat Cookbook

BUTTERFINGER TRIFLE

This is rich!!

4 cups skim milk - divided
2 (1-ounce) boxes instant sugar-free vanilla pudding mix
2 (8-ounce) containers Cool Whip Free - divided
2 (2.1-ounce) Butterfinger candy bars – crushed - divided

1 (12-ounce) fat-free golden dessert cake - cut into ½ - inch pieces (by Tripp Bakers - found at Food Town, or a 12-ounce fat-free pound cake will work)
1 (1.4-ounce) box instant sugar-free chocolate pudding mix
1 (1.4-ounce) box instant sugar-free butterscotch pudding mix

♥ With a whisk, beat 2 cups milk and vanilla pudding together for 1 minute. Stir in 1 container Cool Whip and 1½ crushed candy bars. Gently stir in cake pieces. Set aside.

♥ With whisk, beat 2 cups milk and chocolate and butterscotch puddings together for one minute. Stir in remaining container Cool Whip Free.

♥ In the bottom of a large glass bowl, spread half of the chocolate-butterscotch pudding mixture.

♥ Top with half of the cake mixture.

♥ Smooth on remaining chocolate-butterscotch mixture.

♥ Spread remaining cake mixture on top.

♥ Sprinkle with remaining crushed candy.

♥ Keep chilled until ready to serve.

Yield: 16 servings

Calories: 186
Cholesterol: 1 mg

Total Fat: 1.8 grams (9% fat)
Sodium: 427 mg

Total preparation time: 10 minutes or less.

Busy People's Low-Fat Cookbook

FROZEN CHEESECAKE DESSERT

¾ cup graham cracker crumbs
(for easier use buy the
prepared crumbs)
1 (12-ounce) container Cool
Whip Free

2 (8-ounce) packages fat-free
cream cheese
⅓ cup sugar (or ⅓ cup Equal
Spoonful)
1 (21-ounce) can cherry pie
filling (or blueberry)

♥ Spray a 9 × 13-inch pan with non-fat cooking spray.

♥ Sprinkle graham cracker crumbs in bottom of pan. Set aside.

♥ In a large bowl with a mixer, combine Cool Whip Free, cream
cheese and sugar (or Equal Spoonful) on medium speed for 2
minutes.

♥ Spread into prepared pan.

♥ Top with pie filling. Freeze for 2 hours to set.

♥ Let sit 10 minutes before cutting.

Yield: 15 servings

Calories: 154
Cholesterol: 2 mg

Total Fat: 0.7 grams (4% fat)
Sodium: 199 mg

Preparation time: 10-12 minutes.

Busy People's Low-Fat Cookbook

Menu Ideas: Great on a hot summer day!

OREO MOUSSE

It's hard to believe this thick, rich,
creamy mousse is almost fat-free!

1 (1.5-ounce) sugar free chocolate instant pudding mix - dry	1 (12-ounce) Cool Whip Free 4 reduced-fat Oreos - crushed - divided

♥ Mix pudding and Cool Whip Free together for about 2 minutes by hand (with spatula) until well mixed. Stir in cookie crumbs, reserving about 1 crumbled cookie to sprinkle on top. Put into individual dessert cups. (If you don't have dessert cups, wide mouth wine glasses work great!)

♥ Serve chilled.

Yield: 6 servings

Calories: 147   Total Fat: 0.7 grams (5% fat)
Cholesterol: 0 mg   Sodium: 380 mg

Preparation time: 10 minutes or less.

Total time: 10 minutes or less.

Busy People's Low-Fat Cookbook

CHOCOLATE CHERRY MOUSSE

1 large package sugar-free
   chocolate pudding mix
   (6 serving size)
1 package Dream Whip - dry

1½ cups cold skim milk
1 15-ounce can lite
   cherry pie filling, chilled

♥ Mix together first 3 ingredients and blend until thick, about 3 minutes. Starting with and ending with cherry pie filling, alternate chocolate mousse and pie filling in a pretty glass (wine glasses, dessert cups, etc.). Keep chilled in refrigerator until ready to serve.

♥ Refrigerate unused portions.

Yield: 10 servings

Calories: 82
Percent Fat Calories: 13%
Carbohydrate: 16 grams
Protein: 2 grams

Total Fat: 1 gram
Cholesterol: 1 mg
Dietary Fiber: 0 grams
Sodium: 198 mg

Preparation time: 10 minutes.

Down Home Cookin'

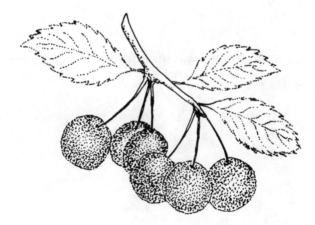

MINT MOUSSE

This rich thick dessert is fabulous!!!

½ teaspoon mint extract
(found next to vanilla)
1 (12-ounce) container Cool
Whip Free

1 (1-ounce) box sugar-free
vanilla instant pudding - dry
(I used Jell-O brand)
6 drops of green food
coloring - optional

♥ Mix all ingredients together.

♥ Keep stirring for 2 minutes.

♥ Spoon into dessert cups. (For a fancier look, spoon into wide mouth wine glasses instead of dessert cups.)

♥ Ready to serve as is or refrigerate until ready to eat.

♥ Garnishing Ideas: Christmas - Place a small candy cane into each dessert - allowing the cane to show or crush 1 candy cane into tiny pieces and sprinkle on top.

♥ St. Patrick's Day - Set a spearmint candy leaf on top of each dessert.

Yield: 5 servings (without garnish)

Calories: 132
Cholesterol: 0 mg

Total Fat: 0 grams (0% fat) 12
Sodium: 272 mg

Preparation time: 5 minutes or less.

Busy People's Low-Fat Cookbook

Menu Ideas: Christmas or St. Patrick's Day celebration meals. Any fancy meal.

CHOCOLATE MOUSSE

1 box sugar-free instant
chocolate pudding mix
(4 serving size)

3 tablespoons fat-free
hot fudge syrup (I use
Smucker's)
1 8-ounce carton Cool
Whip Free

♥ Mix all together until smooth. Serve chilled.

♥ Refrigerate unused portions.

Yield: 6 servings

Calories: 100
Percent Fat Calories: 0%
Carbohydrate: 22 grams
Protein: 1 gram

Total Fat: 0 grams
Cholesterol: 0 mg
Dietary Fiber: 1 gram
Sodium: 240 mg

Preparation time: 10 minutes.

Down Home Cookin'

CREAMY SPICED WHIPPED TOPPING

1 envelope Dream Whip
(A box comes with 2 or 4
envelopes.)

½ cup cold skim milk
½ teaspoon cinnamon
½ teaspoon ground cloves

♥ Combine ingredients and beat with mixer on high for 4 minutes.
Keep refrigerated until ready to eat. If you are planning to frost a
cake, keep refrigerated until time to frost.

Yield: 16 servings

Calories: 17
Percent Fat Calories: 30%
Carbohydrate: 2 grams
Protein: 0 gram

Total Fat: 1 gram
Cholesterol: 0 mg
Dietary Fiber: 0 grams
Sodium: 4 mg

Down Home Cookin'

CHERRY BERRY DESSERT WAFFLES

This is a beautiful dessert to the eyes and a special dessert for any occasion. This is so filling that I eat it as a meal.

1 Special K fat-free waffle

3 ounces sugar-free, fat-free blueberry ribbon frozen dessert (I use Superior Dairy)

½ cup lite cherry pie filling

1 tablespoon Cool Whip Free

1 tablespoon lite blueberry syrup (I use Featherweight)

♥ Pop waffle into the toaster until golden brown. While still warm, put blueberry ribbon dessert on waffle. Top with cherry pie filling and add a dab of Cool Whip on top. Drizzle lite blueberry syrup over dessert, and serve immediately. Refrigerate unused portions.

Yield: 1 serving

Calories: 300
Percent Fat Calories: 0%
Carbohydrate: 71 grams
Protein: 7 grams

Total Fat: 0 grams
Cholesterol: 0 mg
Dietary Fiber: 1 gram
Sodium: 204 mg

Preparation time: 20 minutes.

Down Home Cookin'

SWEET & HEAVENLY TWINKIE DESSERT

2½ cups fresh strawberries, cleaned and cut into bite-sized pieces
1 cup sugar
3 tablespoons cornstarch
2 tablespoons Light Karo Syrup

1 cup water
1 box sugar-free strawberry Jell-O, dry
9 Hostess Light Twinkies, cut in half lengthwise
¼ cup Cool Whip Free

♥ In saucepan over medium low heat, mix sugar, cornstarch, syrup, and water. Bring to a boil. Stirring occasionally, cook until it becomes clear in color. Remove from heat. Let cool a couple of minutes. In the meantime, line a 9 × 13-inch pan with the cut Twinkies, cream side up. Edges will be touching. Stir strawberry sugar-free Jello into clear mixture. Mix well until it is one smooth color of red. Add strawberries. Spread strawberries over Twinkies. Refrigerate for 5 minutes before serving. Top with a dab of Cool Whip and cut it into the top of the dessert with knife to make it look pretty.

♥ Refrigerate unused portions.

Yield: 15 servings

Calories: 156
Percent Fat Calories: 6%
Carbohydrate: 36 grams
Protein: 1 gram

Total Fat: 1 gram
Cholesterol: 6 mg
Dietary Fiber: 1 gram
Sodium: 133 mg

Preparation time: 20-25 minutes.

Down Home Cookin'

WARM FRUIT COCKTAIL DESSERT

Great for cold, snowy days.

1   16-ounce can lite fruit
    cocktail with its juice

1   9-ounce Jiffy Golden
    Yellow Cake mix - dry
    Cool Whip Free

♥ Preheat oven to 350 degrees. Drain juice from fruit cocktail, retaining juice. Beat cake mix and fruit cocktail juice together until well blended. Gently mix fruit with spoon into cake batter until well blended. Spray 8 × 8-inch or a 9 × 9-inch square cake pan with a non-fat cooking spray. Pour cake batter into prepared pan. Bake for 40-45 minutes or until top is golden brown. Serve warm with Cool Whip Free. You need to spoon out this dessert; it will not cut. Refrigerate unused portions.

Yield: 9 servings

Calories: 145
Percent Fat Calories: 18%
Carbohydrate: 29 grams
Protein: 2 grams

Total Fat: 3 grams
Cholesterol: 2 mg
Dietary Fiber: 1 gram
Sodium: 186 mg

Preparation time: 60 minutes.

Down Home Cookin'

BUTTERSCOTCH CAKE SUNDAES

1 4-serving size fat-free
   butterscotch pudding mix
   (or you could substitute
   an already prepared fat-free
   pudding, in the dairy section)
2 cups skim milk

1 12-ounce angel food
   cake (or use 12 ounces
   of larger cake)
1 ounce finely chopped
   pecans
8 teaspoons fat-free hot
   fudge, warmed

♥ Prepare pudding as directed on box, using skim milk. After pudding has thickened, tear the angel food cake up into bite-sized pieces and put into the pudding. Add half of the finely chopped pecans to pudding. Mix pudding, cake, and pecans by hand until cake pieces are well-coated. Spoon equally into 8 individual dessert cups or into a large serving bowl. Microwave hot fudge until easy to drizzle. Drizzle hot fudge over dessert and sprinkle remaining pecans. Keep refrigerated until ready to serve. Serve chilled.

Yield: 8 servings

Calories: 215
Percent Fat Calories: 12%
Carbohydrate: 44 grams
Protein: 5 grams

Total Fat: 3 grams
Cholesterol: 1 mg
Dietary Fiber: 1 gram
Sodium: 551 mg

Preparation time: 25 minutes.

Down Home Cookin'

FLOWER POT PUDDING

Set a gummy worm next to flowers for fun if you'd like.

8 reduced fat SnackWell's
   chocolate cream filled
   cookies, with cream removed
1 4-serving size box sugar-
   free chocolate pudding
2 cups skim milk

4 small flower pots or
   foam coffee cups
4 small bouquets of
   silk flowers
4 Gummy worms
   (optional)

♥ Crush cookies, set aside. Prepare pudding as directed on box, using skim milk. Put ⅛ of cookie crumbs in bottom of each flower pot or coffee cup. Put ¼ of pudding in each cup. Top each with remaining cookie crumbs. Stick small bouquet in each pot. Chill. Serve chilled. Refrigerate unused portions.

Yield: 4 servings

Calories: 144
Percent Fat Calories: 13%
Carbohydrate: 26 grams
Protein: 5 grams

Total Fat: 2 grams
Cholesterol: 2 mg
Dietary Fiber: 1 gram
Sodium: 503 mg

Preparation time: 25 minutes.

Down Home Cookin'

CREAMY RICE PUDDING

This is a terrific way to use leftover white rice.

2 (1-ounce) boxes sugar-free instant vanilla pudding mix - dry - do not make as directed on box (I use Jell-O brand)

3½ cups cold skim milk

½ (8-ounce) container Cool Whip Free - thawed

1 teaspoon almond extract

1 cup raisins

2 cups cooked white rice

♥ With a whisk, in a medium-large bowl, briskly stir together dry pudding mixes and skim milk for 2 minutes.

♥ Stir in Cool Whip Free, almond extract, raisins and rice. Keep stirring until well mixed.

♥ Serve as is or keep chilled until ready to eat.

♥ If desired, sprinkle top very lightly with ground cinnamon before serving.

Yield: 14 (½-cup) servings

Calories: 120
Percent Fat Calories: 0%
Carbohydrate: 26 grams
Protein: 3 grams

Total Fat: 0 grams
Cholesterol: 1 mg
Dietary Fiber: 1 gram
Sodium: 115 mg

Preparation time: 10 minutes or less.

2nd Serving Busy People's Low Fat Cookbook

Menu Ideas: Good anytime, anywhere.

It seems like there is always leftover white rice when ordering Chinese takeout. Use the leftover cooked rice to make this delicious and creamy homestyle recipe without cooking at all!

BLACKBERRY COBBLER

Super easy—Super yummy

2 quarts blackberries	2 cups pancake mix
½ cup sugar and ¼ cup	(I use Staff)
NutraSweet Spoonful	⅓ cup sugar and 2
(or ¾ cup sugar)	tablespoons NutraSweet
1 teaspoon cinnamon	Spoonful (or ½ cup sugar)

♥ Preheat oven to 350 degrees. Gently mix 2 quarts blackberries with ½ cup sugar and ¼ cup NutraSweet Spoonful. Pour into 9 × 13-inch pan. Sprinkle 1 teaspoon cinnamon on top of sugared berries. Combine 2 cups of Staff pancake mix, ⅓ cup sugar, 2 tablespoons NutraSweet Spoonful and stir with enough water to make stiff dough. With fork spread on top of berries. Bake 30-35 minutes or until berries are bubbly and dough golden brown.

Yield: 12 servings

Calories: 187
Percent Fat Calories: 5%
Carbohydrate: 43 grams
Protein: 3 grams

Total Fat: 1 gram
Cholesterol: 0 mg
Dietary Fiber: 6 grams
Sodium: 329 mg

Down Home Cookin'

CHERRY TRIFLE

1 cup powdered sugar	¼ cup chopped pecans or walnuts
1 8-ounce package non-fat cream cheese	5 cups cubed angel food cake
1 8-ounce container fat-free non-dairy whipped topping	1 can lite cherry pie filling

♥ Beat together the powdered sugar and non-fat cream cheese. Add whipped topping and chopped nuts. Stir in angel food cake cubes.

♥ Layer in glass bowl:

½ cake mixture

½ can cherry pie filling

♥ Repeat until all ingredients have been used. Chill for at least 3 hours before serving. Refrigerate unused portions.

Yield: 15 servings

Calories: 162
Percent Fat Calories: 10%
Carbohydrate: 33 grams
Protein: 4 grams

Total Fat: 2 grams
Cholesterol: 1 mg
Dietary Fiber: 1 gram
Sodium: 226 mg

Down Home Cookin'

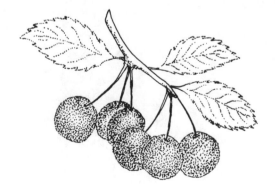

Blueberry Cobbler

⅓ cup sugar
½ teaspoon orange peel
2 cups blueberries
2 cups Hungry Jack
   Pillsbury buttermilk
   pancake/waffle mix, dry

¼ cup NutraSweet Spoonful
   (OR ¼ cup sugar)
⅔ cup water
1 teaspoon almond
   extract

♥ Preheat oven to 350 degrees. Gently stir sugar and orange peel.
  Add blueberries and stir until well coated. Pour into a 9 × 13-
  inch baking pan.

♥ Mix pancake mix, NutraSweet, water, and almond extract. Dough
  will be lumpy. With a fork put dough on top of blueberry mixture.
  Bake approximately 30-35 minutes or until blueberries are bubbly
  and dough golden brown. Refrigerate unused portions.°

° With Sugar – Calories: 72 – Total Fat: 0 grams
Percent Fat Calories: 0% – Cholesterol: 0 mg
Carbohydrate: 18 grams – Dietary Fiber: 0 grams
Protein: 0 grams – Sodium: 6 mg

Yield: 12 servings

Calories: 119
Percent Fat Calories: 6%
Carbohydrate: 26 grams
Protein: 2 grams

Total Fat: 1 gram
Cholesterol: 0 mg
Dietary Fiber: 1 gram
Sodium: 330 mg

Down Home Cookin'

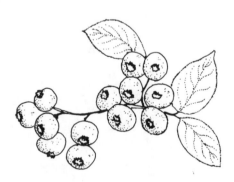

FAT-FREE GRANOLA BARS

This homemade version will save you bundles of money!

1   10.5-ounce bag of mini
    marshmallows
¼ cup fat-free margarine
    (I use Ultra Promise)

3½ cups fat-free granola
     (I use Health Valley,
     12-ounce size)
½   cup raisins
2   cups Rice Krispies

♥ In a large Dutch oven melt margarine and marshmallows over low heat, stirring constantly. Once marshmallows are melted, remove from heat. Add granola, raisins and Rice Krispies. Mix well.

♥ Spray a cookie sheet with edges (approximately 15 × 10-inch with ½-inch edge) with a non-fat cooking spray. Pour onto sheet. Spray palm of hand with non-fat spray. With palm of hand press granola mixture firmly down. Let cool.

♥ Cut into 20 bars. Wrap individual bars with plastic wrap. Keep in a cool, dry place.

♥ For tropical fat-free granola bars: Substitute ¼ cup chopped dried pineapple and ¼ cup chopped dried papaya for the raisins.

♥ Cranberry granola bars: Substitute ½ cup dried cranberries.

Yield: 20 servings

Calories: 128
Percent Fat Calories: 0%
Carbohydrate: 32 grams
Protein: 1 gram

Total Fat: 0 grams
Cholesterol: 0 mg
Dietary Fiber: 2 grams
Sodium: 49 mg

Preparation time: 30 minutes.

Down Home Cookin'

Index

Please send _____ copies of **Best of Busy People's Cookbooks**.

@ $19.95 (U.S.) each $_____

Plus postage and handling @ $3.50 each $_____

Texas residents add sales tax @ $1.45 each $_____

Check or Credit Card (Canada-credit card only) TOTAL $_____

Charge to my: ☐ Master Card or ☐ Visa Card

Account #_____

Expiration Date_____

Signature_____

MAIL, CALL OR EMAIL:
Cookbook Resources
541 Doubletree Drive
Highland Village, Texas 75077
972-317-0245
sheryn@cookbookresources.com

Name_____

Address _____

City _____ State _____ Zip _____

Phone (day) _____ (night) _____

- -

Please send _____ copies of **Best of Busy People's Cookbooks**.

@ $19.95 (U.S.) each $_____

Plus postage and handling @ $3.50 each $_____

Texas residents add sales tax @ $1.45 each $_____

Check or Credit Card (Canada-credit card only) TOTAL $_____

Charge to my: ☐ Master Card or ☐ Visa Card

Account #_____

Expiration Date_____

Signature_____

MAIL, CALL OR EMAIL:
Cookbook Resources
541 Doubletree Drive
Highland Village, Texas 75077
972-317-0245
sheryn@cookbookresources.com

Name_____

Address _____

_____ State _____ Zip _____

Phone (day) _____ (night) _____

For copies of **Down Home Cookin', Busy People's Low Fat Cookbook and 2nd Serving Busy People's Cookbook,** please contact
DAWN HALL, COZY HOMESTEAD PUBLISHING,
5425 S. Fulton-Lucas Road, Swanton, OH 43558 or CALL 888-436-9646.